BREAK A LEG

BREAK A LEG

a memoir by
Peter Sheridan

NEW ISLAND

BREAK A LEG
First published 2012
by New Island
2 Brookside
Dundrum Road
Dublin 14

www.newisland.ie

ISBN PRINT: 978-1-84840-194-5
ISBN EPUB: 978-1-8840-195-2
ISBN MOBI: 978-1-84840-196-9

Internal Design by JM InfoTech India
Cover Design by Sinéad McKenna
Printed by TJ International Ltd, Padstow, Cornwall

New Island received financial assistance from
The Arts Council (An Comhairle Ealaíon), Dublin, Ireland

10 9 8 7 6 5 4 3 2 1

Foreword

I was sitting in the back garden when my grandson Xabi turned and fixed me with the look of a four-year-old in pursuit of serious information.

'Granddad?'

'Yes, Xabi.'

'What did you do in the old days, granddad?'

The old days. That was my father's past, not mine. I didn't belong there.

'Did you have hair in the old days, granddad?'

'Yes I did, I had long hair, down to my shoulders, that was how we rebelled in the old days.'

'Granddad?'

'Yes, Xabi.'

'What does "rebelled" mean?'

That exchange stayed with me for days. I couldn't shake it off. Xabi is a regular at my house. Every time I looked at him I thought about the 'old days.' I felt a great urge to let him know what I had done with my life. So I decided to put something down on paper for him. A record for him to have, something he could dip into. A flavour of the old days that might help him in his own struggle with his present and his future. Something that might make him laugh and cry before he slipped into being part of the 'old days' himself.

I started at the point when the theatre came into my life. It was 1968 and I was sixteen years old. I wanted Xabi to understand that drama for me wasn't an escape but more a way of confronting the world and trying to understand it. There had been the tragedy of my brother Frankie's death in 1967 that almost ripped our family apart. Out of it, my father had started a drama troupe, the Saint Laurence O'Toole's Musical and Dramatic Society, because he had always harboured an ambition to be an actor. I think he realised that life was short and dreams easily went unfulfilled.

The theatre saved our family and became our lives. Through it, my father found his place in the world again. He taught me that the theatre is, at its best, a transformative and healing medium. So, with a few like-minded souls, I tried to put that to the test, seeing the theatre as a social engagement that deepened our understanding of society and its ills. There were many strands of the Irish establishment that were more than happy with how things were – we were a God-fearing island of saints and scholars – and our artistic mission brought us into conflict with the status quo, time and time again.

The theatre was my first love. I threw myself wholeheartedly into the work, to such an extent that my family suffered. In an effort to cope with my shortcomings as a father and husband, I drank too much. I left the rearing of my children to Sheila, who finally told me the truth about myself. With her help, I found the courage to finally stop drinking. I wanted Xabi to know about my struggle, and that it was possible to confront and overcome addiction, especially if you had the support and encouragement of loved ones.

In some ways, through my writing and directing, I tried to fix the world, but I almost lost my own family in the process. I wasn't ashamed of that, and I wanted Xabi to know that failure is an integral part of life. I have also had success, and that is sweet, too. But real success is an inside job. It has taken me all of my life to realise that. I'm bright, but a slow learner.

I started to delve into the past. I took out old scripts and old theatre programmes. I kept Xabi to the forefront of my mind when deciding what would go into this book and what would fall away. The result is, in large measure, an answer to his wonderful question:

'What did you do in the old days, granddad?'

I hope it deepens his understanding of me. I hope it provides him with a good chronology. I hope it makes him want to turn the pages and see what I did next. I hope that when he reflects back on me, long after I've departed this stage, he'll remember someone who cared about the old days and cared about him. And when his own kids enquire about me, I hope he will be able to say:

'A great granddad, he was a great granddad.'

*

In the course of writing this book I have acquired five more grandchildren. So to Ari, Noah, Julen, Luca, Xabi and Daisy, this book is for all of you, my magnificent six.

1

I was hooked on theatre from the get go. I have my father to thank and blame for that.

In April of 1967 our family was torn apart when Frankie, my ten-year-old brother, died of a brain tumour. No one took it harder than Da. He went from being a man who never missed work to a man who never went to work. He started to suffer from severe migraines and spent most of his days in bed with a damp facecloth on his forehead. The shutters were permanently closed and we tiptoed around the house so as not to wake him. He blamed himself for the genetic flaw that had killed Frankie, and he waited for it to take him too. He wanted to die. I know that because I wanted to die also. There had been an incident, I'd told no one about it, when Frankie had banged his head off the road out scutting on the back of a horse and cart with me. I went to sleep every night with the image of his bruised face in my head. I wanted to tell my father that it wasn't genetic, but the decision was taken from me. After several months, he got out of bed, came down to the kitchen and told Ma that the migraine was gone.

'That's great, Da,' she said, 'you'll be going back to work, so.'

'No, I won't be going to work. I'm going to start a drama group. I've always wanted to get up on a stage and act out a part.'

'Do you mean act out a part like Gary Cooper in *High Noon*?'

'Yes, just like Gary Cooper in *High Noon*.'

It was his favourite film. He had brought Ma to see it for one of their wedding anniversaries, and when they came home he acted it out for us in the kitchen, on the stairs and out in the back yard staring in the window, frightening us to death in a nice way. He had other stories, too, like *The Old Man and the Sea,* and one about a time he tried to sell ice-cream off a bike on Dollymount Strand only to discover that his stock had melted. He had sagas about Cuchulainn and Ferdia and another about his father, Grandad Jim, who fought with the IRA in 1916 against the British and ended up escaping from a gaol in Wales after a key was brought in hidden in a Christmas cake. They were good stories, but not as good as *High Noon*. When Da did Gary Cooper you could hear the clock ticking, marking out the tension, making you scared out of your wits. Ma had to keep a straight face, but sometimes you could see the hint of a smile, especially when Da sang *Do Not Forsake Me, O My Darlin'*. I never heard my father tell my mother that he loved her, but when Da acted out being Gary Cooper that was as close as he came.

The drama group saved our family. Da became an actor because the only other option for him was to give up and die. He decided to fulfil his lifelong ambition and he never would have done it if Frankie had lived. It took Frankie's death for him to realise the importance of embracing his dreams. He asked us all to gather in the Oriel Hall for a play reading. I went out of curiosity. I'd never seen a play acted out, apart from a pantomime. We read plays in school and learned speeches off by heart to regurgitate at exam time, a process that made drama about as exciting as a funeral. Now, though, we sat around a table in the Oriel Hall and read plays by Sean O'Casey, W.B. Yeats, John Millington Synge, Hugh Leonard and Brendan Behan.

It was an intimate experience because we shared scripts. Even though Da had been brought back to life, his redemption did nothing for his profligacy – it was four copies between twenty people. We decided on *The Shadow of a Gunman* for our first outing and I was offered the part of Tommy Owens, which I duly accepted. I wrote out my part in a copybook so that I could learn the lines (mercifully he only appears in the first act of the play). It was fascinating to read it back in my own handwriting; somehow it made the character feel more personal. When I started writing my own plays some years later, I kept up the practice of doing it by longhand because it felt more connected, more real, and brought me back to where my journey in theatre began.

Da called the drama group the 'Saint Laurence O'Toole's Musical and Dramatic Society' after the parish where we all lived. There was no discussion regarding the name. Da designed a rubber stamp and sent me to collect it from a shop in Capel Street. We spent one whole rehearsal with the stamp, an ink-pad and squares of cardboard making out tickets for the first performance of *The Shadow of a Gunman*. A space had been left at the bottom for the date, the time and the price of admission which, after much argument, was left at 2/6d. for the evening show and 1/6d. for the Saturday matinee.

I hated the name. It sounded like we were a church group that put on passion plays at Easter, or performed little dramas as part of the mass. It had a craw-thumper feel to it that was starkly at odds with the message of the play. (O'Casey himself had been born a Protestant, but had rejected religion at an early age in favour of socialism. He had lived in a two-storey house at number 18 Abercorn Road – our family had lived in a cottage at number 12 until a growing brood forced the move (in 1956 when I was four) to a bigger house in Seville Place – and it was while he lived there that O'Casey first turned his hand to writing. In 1919, with an inheritance left to him by his mother, he self-published a history of the Irish Citizen Army under the pseudonym P. 'O'Cathasaigh.)

I expressed my reservations on the name to my brother Shea. He hated it too.

'I'll tell Da we don't like it,' Shea said. 'There's no point in bottling it up.'

'No, don't say anything. I'll bring it up with him. There's less chance of a row that way,' I said.

I had a better relationship with him than Shea did. They rubbed each other up the wrong way most of the time. Shea had an uncanny ability to get under his skin. It was a primitive, Oedipal thing. Ma adored Shea, and never hid her adoration. I'm sure Da must have felt displaced in the competition for Ma's affections. Shea, for his part, exulted in and exploited his position at every opportunity.

'Who do you love the most, Ma?' he would say when the Sunday jelly and ice-cream was being doled out. Ma would tut at him through a smile and Shea would glory in the apotheosis that ensured his portion would be larger than everyone else's.

I decided to raise the question with Da on the final Saturday night of the run in the Oriel Hall. The show had gone brilliantly. Six sold-out performances. Da at the top of his game, bringing down the house in his role as the pedlar Seumas Shields. He made an emotional curtain speech, thanking everyone who'd attended and, in a veiled reference to Frankie, he acknowledged those who couldn't be there. He singled out Father Freaney, or to be accurate, the 'Reverend Father,' for gracing the play with his presence. From my position on the stage, I caught Shea throwing his eyes to heaven – he was standing in directorial mode at the back – and while I couldn't mirror his revulsion, I felt it.

Later that night, sitting around the table in Seville Place, we were back to being something like a proper family again. Da was polishing off a bottle of stout, Ma was cutting a loaf to make the supper and I was a little tipsy. I picked my moment and let my words slide across to Da, direct and uninhibited.

'There's going to be trouble over the name of the group,' I said.

There was no immediate reaction. His brow furrowed and he locked on me with concerned eyes.

'You're slurring your words,' he said.

Yes, I was slurring my words, he was right. I was celebrating. Like everyone else in the Saint Laurence O'Toole's Musical and Dramatic Society. We'd come to the end of a successful run – our first outing in front of the public – and I was entitled to be a little drunk. I'd spent three months inside the skin of Tommy Owens, a little twerp of an alcoholic, and just as he was entitled to his opinion on the state of the world, I was entitled to an opinion on the state of our lousy name.

'You shouldn't be drinking,' Ma said, 'you're only sixteen years of age.'

'I'm nearly seventeen,' I said.

'You're drunk, that's what you are,' she said.

'I'm not drunk; I'm tipsy.'

'You should steer clear of alcohol if you can't control it,' Da said. 'It will bite you on the arse before you know it.'

'Alcohol's my friend, that's all I'm going to say.'

It was, too. My dependable, foolproof, one hundred per cent friend. I hadn't known of its power until I was introduced to it at Frankie's wake. Cuz, a man with a purple nose who was related to my father, poured me a whiskey, added a drop of peppermint to it and told me that it would ease the pain. He told me that Jameson was the working man's friend. It burned me on the insides going down, but a few minutes later I was filled with a warm glow. I managed to pour a second Jemmy and pep down my throat. The movie of Frankie falling off the horse and cart disappeared from my brain and I slept that night like a baby. It was a sleep without guilt. I woke up that morning, the day of his funeral, and forgot that he was dead. It was such a shock when I remembered that he was in his coffin.

'You took the pledge at your confirmation, in case you've forgotten,' Ma said.

'I don't forget things,' I said.

'You were supposed to abstain until you were eighteen,' Da said.

'I remember. I know what I promised.'

'You can take it again,' Ma said. 'You can pledge yourself in front of Father Freaney. He'd see you in the sacristy before devotions.'

It was the perfect opportunity to go on the attack. There were lines in *The Shadow of a Gunman* castigating the church for enslaving the people of Ireland. They were more than lines; they were speeches, and Da's character, Seumas Shields, had many of them. I was going to trot them out to Ma and put her in her place. I knew that my mouth, however, could not keep up with my brain. I knew I would start slurring and I couldn't give them that opportunity again. I wanted to stick with the argument in hand. The name of the group was too religious, too Catholic, too subservient. Especially for a group dedicated to O'Casey: a Protestant writer who'd left Ireland and become a communist. Something had to be done and I was determined to carry the fight. I decided to empty my bladder before I went over the top.

I sat on the toilet bowl with my head in my hands and thought about Da. He wasn't an overtly religious man but maybe he had made a pact with God. I once caught him on his hands and knees up on the roof, invoking the holy name.

'Jesus, if you are who you are, come to my aid....'

We were repairing slates and I'd gone down to get some flashing. I came back up and there he was, talking to himself. I said nothing; I just watched. There was a quiver in his voice. I stayed at the top of the ladder, observing him. He became conscious of me and stopped, searching on the ground for nails or something, before he took the flashing off me and started to cut it with a rusty old scissors.

'Never be afraid to get on your knees and ask God for help,' he said. 'It takes a man to do that.'

It was the only advice he ever gave me about religion. I don't know what he was praying for. Maybe he was praying for the third one in a treble to come in. Or, more likely, he'd lost the housekeeping money on a 'good thing' and hadn't yet told Ma. Maybe he was thanking God for having taken away his migraine. Maybe he had made a pact over the name of the drama group and couldn't go back on his word. Everything came back to Frankie, that's how it was in our family. The mere mention of his name was enough to open the wound and make it bleed.

I came back from the bathroom and dived straight into a crusty slice of turnover smothered in bread and jam. I knew they'd been talking about me, the way you do. Da finished off his bottle of stout and Ma buttered more bread. I cracked into the crust and washed it down with perfectly brewed tea. Ma kept the family together. She had that gift of not falling apart. Thanks to her, Da was back in the fold. I was acting on the stage with him, but it hadn't brought us together. It appeared close and connected because of the emotional engagement between the characters on-stage. I could hold his hand (and did) during the final bow, I could put my arm around his shoulder, but off-stage any kind of physical contact seemed impossible. I needed him. I needed his strength and his forgiveness. I needed to tell him about my awful dreams. I needed to tell him and I needed him to make it all right for me, the way he'd always done since I was a child. I couldn't go there with him. He wasn't available to me. The only escape I had was Jameson.

Da finished his bottle of stout and turned to the matter in hand. He wanted to know what faction in the drama group didn't like the name.

'It's not a faction,' I said. 'There are no factions.'

'There are always factions, that's how life works,' he said.

'I'm not in a faction.'

'Maybe you should be. Maybe it would do you good.'

'I'm not into politics, I hate that stuff.'

'If you were in the right faction you might be the next king of the castle.'

'What are you talking about?'

'I don't know. I'm not planning a coup, am I?'

It was Da at his worst, deliberately trying to raise a row. My brain couldn't keep up with him. After a half an hour or so I declared myself a faction and went to bed.

*

Da always strove to unite the community of Saint Laurence O'Toole's, a parish divided along social and economic lines. On one side were the professional classes who lived in the houses around Seville Place, Emerald Street and Oriel Street; on the other were the dockers and manual labourers who lived in the Corporation flats. There were two tribes divided by Sheriff Street, and they didn't mix much, if at all. They drank in different pubs and knelt on opposite sides in the church at Sunday mass. Da never subscribed to this idea and from the time we were small he insisted that we play with the children from the flats in their playground in Sheriff Street. We were the only family from our side to do so.

Tina Molloy was the only member of the drama group from the flats. She was one of eleven children. She left primary school at thirteen and went straight to work in Manning's cake shop on Parnell Street. She was extremely bright and intelligent and the best actor in the company. She played Minnie Powell in *The*

Shadow of a Gunman, her own life of struggle embodying much of the O'Casey heroine. In the course of rehearsing and performing the play, I fell in love with her.

Tina had a very gentle nature. Although her flat in St Brigid's Gardens was a hive of mad, raucous activity, she never raised her voice but was always heard. She had a deep faith and was a member of the Legion of Mary, an organisation I joined because I thought it might impress her. I didn't know at the time that the boys and girls met in separate rooms. Joining the Legion was the first of many wrong moves I was to make where Tina was concerned. I befriended her younger brother Larry, and tried to talk him into joining the Legion of Mary too.

'I might join the French Foreign Legion, go on a real adventure.'

'Your sister's in the Legion of Mary,' I scolded him. 'You trust Tina, don't you?'

'She's a holy Joe, she'll turn into a statue some day.'

I convinced Tina to make up a foursome on a day out to the seaside at Bray. My friend Tommo Hogan and a girl he was chasing, Anna Hederman, were the other couple. We set off one Sunday on an early morning train. On arrival in Bray, we headed straight for the ghost train. Tommo and Anna sat in the front and immediately started kissing. I didn't know what to do. In the darkness that enveloped us, I put my arm around Tina. I turned to kiss her but I missed her face and my mouth ended up in her hair.

After our day out in Bray, I walked Tina home as far as the convent. There was a porchway near to where the Legion of Mary meetings were held. I stopped at it.

'Thanks for a lovely day, Peter,' Tina said.

'I'm glad you enjoyed it.'

I could see that she meant it. She was such a truthful girl. So innocent and wide eyed. Yet, she was a woman. It wasn't an age thing. It had to do with her family and the fact that she supported them. She stood in Manning's cake shop every day, not out of choice but out of necessity.

'Would you like to kiss me?' Tina asked.

I tried to think of something clever but all that came out was one word.

'Yes,' I said.

She turned her head to the side and moved towards me. I stepped in to meet her. Our lips touched. Hers were wet, which was a lovely surprise. I kissed her for as long as I could and then she pulled back. I put my hand to her head and pulled her towards me. I put my lips against hers again. I tried to push my tongue into her mouth but she desisted.

'No tongues,' she said. 'Lips only.'

That porchway became our kissing place. I rehearsed with her in the Oriel Hall and afterwards went for chips with all the others to the Congress Cafe at the Five Lamps. Then I walked with her down Seville Place, and ostensibly escorted her home to the flats, only I never reached there; we stopped off at our porchway and kissed, lips only. I never felt her tongue because that was the rule and I learned to keep it.

*

Tina was inspired casting as Juno Boyle, the heroine of O'Casey's *Juno and the Paycock,* the author's follow up to *The Shadow of a Gunman,* and our second big production. She brought an authority and a maturity way beyond her years to it. My father played the Captain, her no-good husband, and it was fascinating for me to watch her in rehearsal control him, just as she controlled me in my pursuit of her. She had a clear, delineated world-view and she was not going to let any man steer her off course. In the story of the play, she falls for the false promise of the will and the riches it is going to bring, just as the Irish people had fallen for the promises of the newly formed Irish Free State. All we had done, in O'Casey's world-view, was to replace one form of false hope with another. We were still enslaved. Juno becomes the potential for a new order when she rejects the old nationalism and cries out against the murderers of her beloved son Johnny (played by Shea):

Where were you when me darlin' son was riddled with bullets? God, take away our hearts of stone and give us hearts of flesh. Take away this murderin' hate and give us Thine own eternal love.

I was sixteen when my father cast me as Joxer Daly in *Juno,* too young for the part by twenty-five years at least. O'Casey in his stage directions describes Joxer as a 'shoulder-shrugger,' and there were plenty of those to be seen around Sheriff Street. I took Ostler Moore as my prototype, a small man with a connection to horses. He ambled more than walked. It was three steps forward and two back, with a little flick of his coat thrown in every now and then. He wore a permanent smile that was unaffected by the seasons or his mood. He spoke through it and sang through it whether the message was one of catastrophe or joy.

I put his physical quirks into the character and tried them out in rehearsal. People were impressed. But there was still the problem of my age. I sat in front of the mirror, hating myself because I looked sixteen. I thought that if I gave myself a high forehead, it might help me become Joxer. So I started to cut my hair. The more I cut, the better it looked. By the time I finished I had nothing left on top. Ma screamed when she saw me. I was delighted. I looked twenty years older. I didn't look like my father's son; I looked like his buddy.

Tina let me know that Ostler was coming to the play. It was our last night in the Oriel Hall. I had built my character on him and now I was about to parade it in front of him. In some of my quieter moments on-stage, I observed him in the audience. He was sitting in the middle of the second row. It was impossible to tell if he was enjoying himself or in pain. In the play's infamous party scene, I closed my eyes and bawled out my 'shut-eyed' song, *She is Far From the Land*. I could hear his laugh wheezing back at me, and the rest of the audience joining in, not with my antics, but with his.

After the show, he hung out at the back of the hall. In the end, I found myself two feet from him, staring at the smile.

'You were gas, Joxer, I nearly broke me bollix laughing at you.'

'That's great,' I said.

'Your baldy head and all, bleedin' gas. You should come with a warning, do you know that?'

'Yeah, I know.'

'You forgot your words and all, that did it for me. I couldn't stop laughing, did serious damage to me bollix, I'm not joking you.'

'I'm glad you enjoyed it.'

'You remind me of someone. You do, no messin'. Know who you remind me of?'

I shook my head.

'The walk of you and all,' Ostler said. 'The bleedin' shoulders, you were very bleedin' funny, you were now, straight up. You had me in stitches.'

'That's great,' I said, not knowing what to say.

'Know who the funny walk reminded me of?'

'Not really.'

'Larry bleedin' Molloy. Tina's brother. You have him down to a tee. Bleedin' gas, I'm not coddin' you, you had me in stitches, Joxer.'

From that moment on, Ostler only ever called me Joxer. He invited me back to the Ball Alley pub in Sheriff Street because he wanted all his friends to meet me. He wanted to introduce Joxer to the community because he was a gas man, a man who could make people laugh. I was about to decline the invitation when it transpired that all the cast were going back to the Ball Alley for a last night drink. So I ended up playing Joxer and performing some of the lines from the play and singing the shut-eyed song from the party scene.

By the time Ostler started into *Crazy* for the fourth time, shut-eyed to boot, Tina and I left the Ball Alley and headed down Sheriff Street. It was the perfect opportunity to walk her into St Brigid's Gardens and maybe even have a cup of tea in her flat. It was her chance to introduce me to her parents, the way you would if you were comfortable, if you were genuine boyfriend material. As we walked along Sheriff Street towards the flats, Tina turned the corner and headed for our kissing porch.

It was sinful and dark. Our moment was interrupted by approaching voices. They were loud and aggressive, shouting across one another into the night sky. I broke off from the kiss and turned to see who it was. There was Skinnyah Geoghegan slugging from a bottle of whiskey. Then I saw Hardhead Wallace and Dommo Rowe a few steps behind him. I turned back to Tina and put my arms around her neck.

'I think you should go home, Peter,' she whispered in my ear. 'I don't trust them.'

'They're just having a bit of a mess, that's all.'

'They're drunk. Go home now before they catch us.'

Her fear unsettled me. I knew that she wasn't afraid for herself. It was me she was worried for. Why was I in danger? Was there something she wasn't telling me?

'Do you want me to walk you into the flats?' I said.

'No, I want you to go home. Now. Just get out of here. Trust me. They're up to no good.'

We stepped out of the porch, Tina turned right for the flats and I turned left for Seville Place. As she walked away from me, I heard her make conversation with Skinnyah and the others.

'Were you with him?' I heard Skinnyah ask.

'What were you doing with him?' Hardhead wanted to know. 'Did he put a hand on you?'

Tina said something, but I couldn't make out what it was. Then Skinnyah roared out at the top of his voice.

'Stay away from our women, Shero, do you hear me?'

I decided to ignore him. I walked on purposefully, praying that my strategy of non-engagement was the right one.

I heard a bottle smash, followed by the sound of running feet. I broke into a fast walk as I headed around the corner into Seville Place. I put my hand in my pocket to get out the key and realised I hadn't got one. I had no idea who was at home, if anyone, and whether they were having supper or in bed. I'd loaned my key to Shea, I remembered. I'd last seen him in the Ball Alley. I wondered if he was still there. I ran up the steps of our house and knocked on the door. I pressed the bell but didn't know if it rang or not. I knocked again on the door. I looked down the street to see Skinnyah, bottle in hand, coming after me. The front door opened. It was Shea. I fell in the door, just as Skinnyah got to the garden railings behind me. Shea slammed the door and we heard the stump of the bottle hit the wall, smack between the two large windows.

'Leave our women alone!' he roared out before the other two joined in the baying chorus.

*

The following morning, I answered a knock at the front door. Skinnyah stood there;

'I'm sorry, Shero,' Skinnyah said, 'that was the drink talking last night.'

'That's all right, Skinnyah, I understand.'

'Keep your hands off our women and you'll be all right, ok!'

'I don't know what you mean?'

'Dick Elliot asked her out. She's one of us, do you understand?'

'Do you mean she's from the flats and she can't go out with me?'

'That's right. You're posh, so get yourself a posh bird to go out with.'

'I'll go out with Tina if that's what Tina wants.'

'Tina wants Dick. You can ask Larry if you don't believe me.'

Skinnyah turned and waved at Larry, who was sitting on the steps of presbytery, keeping a distant watch he waved back. I knew I'd lost her. Dick and I had been close once. We both boxed for the British Railways club. So did his younger brother

Christy, who was always paired with me. We fought three times in the National Stadium and each time it was a draw. We were only kids and the crowd got a great laugh out of us because we stood in the middle of the ring, closed our eyes and threw punches at a hundred miles an hour. Christy went on to win a European title and fight professionally in America.

When I was twelve, Dick befriended me. He was fifteen at the time. My parents were dead set against it and I could never figure out why. Dick introduced me to the business of 'carrying cases.' We stood at the bottom of the steps at Amiens Street Railway Station and when we spied someone in trouble with their luggage, we pounced. The trick was to get the case into your hand and start walking. Once they felt the relief of not having to lug all that weight, they'd never take the case back. Most of the time they were heading up to the Gresham Hotel in O'Connell Street or a Bed and Breakfast in Gardiner Street. The most we ever got was a pound for carrying two cases to Grooms in Parnell Square. We went down to a sweet shop in Commons Street with the money and bought two hundred and forty penny bars. They were toffee bars, rock hard, wrapped in silver paper that was nearly impossible to get off. I brought the bars home and my parents were disgusted. They thought it was a terrible waste of ten shillings. They couldn't understand why I didn't buy twelve bars and put nine shillings in my post office savings account.

I always thought they took a turn against Dick Elliot over the toffee bars. I now realise that it had nothing to do with that. They were embarrassed, or at least Da was, that Dick and I were working right outside his place of employment. What would his office colleagues say if they saw me? There were porters paid to help people with their luggage and here was his son and a gurrier stealing the work out from under their noses. Any time that Dick called for me at the house, they gave him the cold shoulder, Ma in particular. I once heard her asking him why he couldn't get a friend his own age to play with.

It was time for Dick's revenge. He was working on the docks as a tea boy. He had money and prospects. He could take Tina out of Manning's and make her comfortable. I couldn't fight for Tina because I knew in my heart that she didn't want me. She liked me and I liked her but she had made all these rules because she didn't have the heart to tell me to back off.

Skinnyah was the messenger. He'd come to tell me to stay on my side of the parish. Since I was a child I'd broken that rule. I'd done it with Da's encouragement because that was his philosophy on life. The creation of the Saint Laurence O'Toole's Musical and Dramatic Society was an attempt to build bridges. It was driven by a belief that the theatre was not the preserve of one particular class and that talent was everywhere waiting to be discovered. For that reason, I wanted Tina to stay on in the group, even though I had lost her as a girlfriend.

2

By the end of 1968 I was desperate for a girlfriend, especially as Shea was going steady and, as in most things, I looked up to him and tried to emulate him. There was my older sister Ita too, with whom I had a great relationship. I confided in her about all things dark and secret. It was Ita who consoled me when Tina broke it off.

Ita was the only one in our house who had her own bedroom. It came with being an only girl. At night, I would stop off in her room and pour my heart out to her. When Ita acquired a boyfriend, it made me very jealous. Ken Rafferty was nice, but I resented him – it even crossed my mind that I could do a Skinnyah on him – because Ita became much less available for our chats when he arrived on the scene.

Everyone had someone except me. I had the drama and that was it. No one to walk home and share a bag of chips with after rehearsals. I took to making supper for Shea and his girlfriend Fran. They stayed in the front room and I brought them up their tea and toast. I guarded their privacy. I felt good acting as their protector.

Acting as their gofer brought me close to Fran. I learned a lot about her family. She was very close to her father George, but everyone called him Georgie. He belonged to a famous clan of handballers. Georgie and Larry Roe were multiple all-Ireland champions, the best known handballers in the country; they were an institution. Larry was best man at Georgie's wedding and vice versa. They were joined at the hip and shared everything in life. The Roe brothers. It made me think about Shea and me. The Sheridan brothers. Our shared love of drama. Acting and directing and O'Casey. Shea loved Fran, and maybe I loved her too.

That year, Fran invited me to a new year's eve party in her parents' house. A number of her classmates from teacher training college were there, among them Sheila O'Donoghue, Laura Waldron and Breda O'Shea. Sheila had the most amazing legs I'd ever seen. Most girls had legs that were skinny at the bottom and tree trunks at the top. Sheila's were skinny all the way up to the point where they disappeared beneath her miniskirt. I spent a half an hour inspecting them. Finally, I worked up the courage and approached her.

'Would you like to dance?' I asked.

'No, thank you,' she replied.

'It's New Year's Eve, you can't refuse.'

'I told you, I don't want to dance.'

They were sitting in a row, the four friends. Fran, Laura, Breda and Sheila. I reached out and touched Fran on the shoulder.

'Fran, tell her she has to dance with me.'

'I can't make her dance with you,' Fran said.

'You can't refuse me without a reason,' I said.

Sheila looked me straight in the eyes.

'You're too small,' she said, 'I don't dance with fellows who are smaller than me.'

I made my way to the drinks table and poured a large Jameson. There was no peppermint mixer. I raised the glass and emptied the amber liquid down my throat. It hit my stomach and turned it into a fireball. I put my fist into my mouth and bit down hard on the knuckles. I poured another large whiskey and knocked it back. I headed for the front room. As I did, my legs went funny and my brain slid, like jelly, from one side of my head to the other. I didn't mind. It felt better than rejection.

In the front room of the house, Shea was dancing like a zombie. All the girls were amazed and terrified of him. Jim Morrison was singing about strange days and Shea was making faces to go with the music. It was a performance and he had the floor to himself. Shea put his forehead against mine. The opening bars of *The End* filled the air. A song about the apocalypse. The end of the old order and the start of the new. It was the dying hours of 1968 and the spirit of Aquarius was sweeping the world. Shea put his hands on the side of my face.

'There's someone I want you to meet. He's an actor and he does mime as well. You'll love him. He's mad, like us. Come on and I'll introduce you.'

I asked my legs to move but they refused to obey.

'Are you all right? Shea asked.

'I'm fine,' I said.

'You look a bit drunk, that's all.'

'I'm sober as a judge.'

'What are you drinking?'

'A policeman wouldn't ask me that.'

'I'm not a policeman, I'm your brother.'

He was more of a father to me than a brother, and despite that he still couldn't get me a girlfriend.

'I want you to meet Vincent P. McCabe,' Shea said. 'He's going to teach us all about movement and mime.'

*

Vincent P. McCabe, or Vinnie to his friends, had a guitar across one knee and was tuning it. Sheila O'Donoghue was sitting at his feet, staring up at him. *You're too small.* I wasn't bothered. I'd had enough Jameson not to care.

'Sing us a song,' Sheila said. 'Something by Leonard Cohen.'

'How about *Suzanne*?' Vinnie replied with a smile.

'Perfect,' she smiled back at him. 'That would be perfect.'

Vinnie hit a big chord of E minor that got everyone's attention. He launched into the story of Suzanne, the enigmatic woman who lives by the river and feeds her suitor tea and oranges because she fears rejection; who touches her lover with her mind even though he's after her body; and so on and on to its miserable lack of conclusion. This was marshmallow emotion from the king of slit-your-wrists-music, Leonard wanker Cohen.

'She feeds you tea and toast, tea and toast that comes all the way from the kitchen on a Saturday night, right Shea?' I shouted across the words of Leonard Cohen.

'You'll get your turn in a minute,' Shea said, 'let Vinnie finish, ok?'

I didn't want to sing. I knew that Suzanne was Sheila and Vinnie was Leonard Cohen. There was nothing noble about it. He was after her legs, all the way up to where they merged. The only real lovers in the room were Shea and Fran, and I wasn't going to be fooled by a woman who rejected me because of my height.

30

'Leonard Cohen is a wanker and a liar.'

'Get your brother to shut up!' someone shouted.

Shea came over and put an arm around me. 'Come on, let's go outside for a breath of air.'

We went out into the keyhole cul-de-sac. It was freezing. The year of 1968 was on its last legs and so was I. Shea was about to give out to me but I didn't care. I was too far gone, not on the drink, but emotionally. The thoughts inside my head were running around and I couldn't separate them out. I didn't know if I was thinking something or feeling it. What would happen if I stayed that way? Not able to distinguish a thought from a feeling? What would happen if my mind crashed altogether?

'It's firewater, do you understand that?' Shea said.

I saw his lips moving but I didn't know what he was talking about.

'Whiskey is firewater, it drives you crazy, like the American Indians, that's how they lost all their land, do you understand me?' he said.

It was good to watch his lips. I knew he was giving out to me. I didn't mind. It stopped the black thoughts running around inside my head.

'Come on back inside and behave yourself.'

'I don't mind you giving out to me. Stay out here and give out to me, please.'

'I don't want to give out to you, I love you.'

'If you love me you'll give out to me. Honest.'

Shea put his arms around me. He squeezed me hard. Then he relaxed his grip and smiled.

'It's good to talk,' I said. 'You'll always talk to me, won't you?'

'Of course I will, come on.'

'You won't abandon me, will you?'

'How many times do I have to repeat myself?'
'I don't want to be on my own, that's all, it's too sad.'
'Come on inside, it's freezing.'

*

Vincent P. McCabe, who hailed from Leinster Avenue on the North Strand was the first person to conduct a workshop with the members of the Saint Laurence O'Toole's Musical and Dramatic Society. Up until that night in March 1969 I thought a workshop was a place where tools were stored. I also didn't know that a human being could become a tree; or the sun; or a grain of sand. I wasn't aware that you could mime an object and that you could pass this imaginary object from yourself to the person next to you; I didn't understand the meaning of making a circle; I didn't know what voice work was and I didn't know how to improvise.

Eight of us, including Tina Molloy, turned up for that first workshop in the Oriel Hall, only to discover that the Old Folks had booked it for a committee meeting. Undaunted, Vinnie asked us where else we could find another 'space.' All that the theatre required was a 'space.' I suggested the garage at the back of our house and, while I could see that Da was not entirely enamoured of the idea, he gave his consent. So we pulled the cars out onto the street – Father McCarthy's VW, the Triumph Herald of Eamonn Dooley (the local shopkeeper) and Da's Ford Anglia – and we put up with the kids peeping in at us through cracks in the garage doors while we raised our voices to heaven and relaxed our bodies to the floor.

We stepped through a door that night and caught a glimpse of life as a professional troupe. We played trust games. We held hands and passed messages around the circle. We communicated as a collective. We thought as a team. We stopped operating as a bunch of individuals, interested only in our own part.

'You are players, noble players,' Vinnie informed us as we stood in a circle at the conclusion of the workshop. 'You are the players of Saint Laurence O'Toole.'

'S.L.O.T. players,' Shea said.

'Yes, you are S.L.O.T. players,' Vinnie repeated.

I looked at them and I wondered whether it was rehearsed. The name had been such a bone of contention for Shea. He'd brought Vinnie to the group and between them they'd come up with a new name. Well, a variation on the old one.

'What do you think, Mr Sheridan? Are you happy with the new name?' Tina asked, in that formal way of hers that was so endearing.

'I'm happy if you're all happy,' Da said.

'I think it's nice,' Tina said, 'I really do. S.L.O.T. Players.'

She said it with sincerity, a mother trying to keep the peace and make everyone happy. Only she wasn't a mother, of course. She was a siren, and I envied Dick Elliot who'd stolen her from me.

It wasn't long before we dropped the full stops and became Slot Players. We had a new rubber stamp made, but I think Da missed the old name with its roots in the parish. There was the Saint Laurence O'Toole's Pipe Band, of which Sean O'Casey had been a founding member – it had its headquarters up the street from us at the railway bridge on Seville Place – and the Saint Laurence O'Toole's GAA club – Larriers, as it was known – a key supplier of talent to the Dublin county team, including the famous Sinnott brothers, who now had the newsagents at the top of Sheriff Street where we bought our daily paper. There was history in the name of Saint Laurence O'Toole, certainly, but most of us wanted to get away from that and forge something new.

Vinnie saw the theatre as political, something to destabilise and threaten the status quo. He was drawn to rebellious characters – Brendan Behan, Jean Genet, Bertolt Brecht – and his ultimate hero was Christopher Marlowe. A contemporary of Shakespeare, Marlowe spent his life in trouble with the law. He could have been a child of the sixties, and he wouldn't have been out of place fronting a band like The Rolling Stones or The Doors. Indeed, he was the Jim Morrison of his day. He died from a knife wound to the eye, the result of a pub brawl. He was twenty-nine years old at the time. If Shakespeare was the poet of the Reformation, then Marlowe was its cultural anti-hero. Shakespeare put characters with tormented, individual consciences at the heart of his plays, and Marlowe posited a world that was falling apart. To his way of thinking, we humans were inherently corrupt and debased. In terms of the two great figures of Elizabethan drama, Vinnie put Slot Players firmly on the side of Marlowe.

We read *Doctor Faustus* with Vinnie in the lead role and Da reading Mephistopheles, the messenger sent by the devil to entrap him. Tina and I read Valdes and Cornelius, two students studying for their doctorates under Faustus. There were lots of other parts including the Seven Deadly Sins, the Pope, an Old Man, the Good and Bad Angels, and Helen of Troy. It was too large a cast for our small number, a problem made worse when Da announced that he wouldn't be taking the part of Mephistopheles.

'I think it needs a younger pair of hands,' Da said.

'I think you're wrong,' Vinnie said. 'I think it needs maturity, experience.'

'It needs someone closer in age to play Mephistopheles,' Da said. 'Someone who can argue with Faustus as his friend.'

I knew Da was making excuses. Age wasn't the issue. He had cast me as Joxer Daly when I was twenty-five years too young for the part. I felt that he wanted to play Faustus. He saw himself as the leading man. It was a family thing with him, I believe. He had created the drama for us to strut our stuff and he wasn't interested in others stealing our thunder. Or his. He was expressing his distaste by turning down the role.

'I think you should reconsider,' Vinnie said.

'No, I'm busy with my job in the train station, it's over to you boys now.'

'Maybe you could play the Pope, or the Old Man,' Shea said.

'We'll see,' he said and left the reading.

'Go after your Da and bring him back,' Tina said, 'we can't do the play without him.'

After *Juno and the Paycock*, Tina had become very protective of Da. I could tell that she was upset at developments.

'Let him cool down,' I said, 'he'll be back.'

'Go after him,' she said in a tone that demanded obedience.

He was walking up Oriel Street when I caught sight of him. I was surprised that he wasn't going home. I curbed the instinct to shout after him and just followed. He turned right into Sheriff Street and proceeded along the boundary wall. I studied the walk. It was a Dublin strut, all moving parts bearing an equal strain, the arms moving in tandem with the legs, like a set of pistons. I had often brought his shoes to the menders and they were always the same, the heels worn down on the outside where he put all his weight. It was an O'Casey walk more than a Marlowe walk. How did men amble in the late sixteenth and early seventeenth centuries, I wondered? Had Marlowe seen someone with a Faustus walk before he wrote his play? Was he inspired by an Ostler Moore of his day, or a medicine man, or a university don perhaps?

Marlowe would have loved Sheriff Street. He would have had no difficulty getting into a brawl in Noctor's or the Ball Alley or Bertie Donnelly's. Especially if he had started making eyes at the young men – 'leave our young fellows alone, Marlowe.' He was homosexual and made no bones about it, unlike Shakespeare who, if the sonnets are to be believed, was in the closet over a young man of dark complexion. Shakespeare would have avoided rows and Marlowe would have been at the head of the queue to take people on. The character of Faustus was clearly a version of himself, the descent into debauchery a mirror of his own life. Had Marlowe lived in St Brigid's Gardens, then Tina Molloy would probably have been his Helen of Troy.

Da broke into a little trot and crossed Amiens Street opposite the North Star Hotel. Nobody from Sheriff Street or Seville Place ever used the traffic lights, it was against their religion. I similarly broke the law and followed him across. Maybe he was turning his back on Slot Players to join another drama group. Or perhaps it was just the role of Mephistopheles he was running away from.

He went in the front entrance of Lloyd's Cocktail Lounge. I had no desire to burst in on him if he was meeting someone. I pulled the door slightly ajar. He was standing at the bar counter, ordering a drink. A man came up and stood behind me.

'Are you going in or out?' he said.

I stood aside and let him pass. The doors opened fully and I caught sight of Ma. She saw me. The door swivelled closed but I knew she'd clocked me. I had no choice. I had to go in.

Ma was in flying form.

'You watch that ginger fella,' she said, 'he'll buy and sell the lot of you.'

'Do you mean Vinnie?' I said, knowing full well who she was referring to.

'You mark my words, he's too smart for you, you're only in the ha'penny place with that bucko.'

'I don't think he's as smart as Shea. Or me, for that matter.'

'He'd live in your ear and let the other one out in flats, you mark my words.'

Da came back from the bar with the drinks. He asked me what I was having but I declined. We had another conversation about *Doctor Faustus* and he assured me that he wasn't finished with Slot Players. It was a temporary break. Ma threw her eyes to heaven, and I sensed a difference between them on the subject. I had no desire to exploit it. I told him that we all wanted him back and he was genuinely pleased, but not for turning. Before I left, I made him promise that he would act with me on-stage again. With that secured, I returned to the Oriel Hall and the mad world of Faustus, Wittenberg and Christopher Marlowe.

*

Tina was the second member of the cast to drop out. We were rehearsing the scene where the Seven Deadly Sins appear to Faustus. In the text, each of the Sins makes an appeal to him, like they are competing for his affections. I played Gluttony and Tina played Lust. It felt very long-winded and turgid. Vinnie suggested that I forget the words and mime it. I tried it but I wasn't good enough technically to carry it off. Neither was

Tina. Shea suggested a movement instead. During our pre-rehearsal 'warm-up' (an innovation introduced by Vinnie), we went through some ballet moves – a proper teacher, Anne Sutcliffe, had come in and given us a workshop – so that heel/toe, *pliés* and arabesques formed part of our routine. It wasn't long before we started messing about, introducing our own ballet moves. One of these involved imagining ballet as danced by apes – we christened our movement 'ballitarse,' and when Shea made his suggestion I instinctively reached for it. In the guise of an ape, I tempted Faustus with a tray of culinary delights and it made Tina laugh.

'Don't anybody move,' Shea said, 'I'll be back in a minute.'

In less than five minutes, Shea was back in the Oriel Hall with an LP. Tom Browne, who was the sound engineer for the show, put on the record.

'I think this might work for the Seven Deadly Sins,' Shea said.

We listened to a track from *The Piper at the Gates of Dawn* by Pink Floyd. It was mainly instrumental. The percussion was haunting and exhilarating. It felt like we were about to inject the play with a dose of heroin. Tom Browne walked over and cupped Shea's face in his hands before he kissed him on the top of his head.

'You're a genius,' he said, 'a fucking genius.'

It wasn't long before the scene became a proper orgy. We of the Seven Deadly Sins engulfed our subject, Faustus, and crawled all over him. The idea was that we would eat him, that we would each take a part of his body and consume him, piece by piece. Naturally, there were parts of Vinnie's anatomy that we studiously avoided.

'I can't go to hell if I haven't sinned,' Vinnie said, '"I am wanton and lascivious"'.

It was a line from the play. A line that explained our pre-dicament. It sounded like Marlowe on a Saturday night. Maybe Vinnie was communing with him from beyond the grave.

'What if we danced it in the dark?' I suggested. 'That might help.'

'That's a great idea,' Shea said, and Fran looked at him like she was none too pleased. He'd convinced her to play Envy and, although she was happy to help out and make up the numbers, we were now moving into uncharted territory.

'Are we all happy to give it a go?' Shea asked.

'Yeah,' all the men in the scene immediately replied. That was Vinnie, me, Sean Murphy (who was playing Covetousness), my younger brother Johnny (who was playing Pride) and Pat Darcy (who was Sloth). All of the women, Tina, Fran and Ann Hasson (who was playing Greed) voted with their silence. But there was an unstoppable momentum on the yes side and seconds later the lights were out and we crawled all over our subject in an explo-sion of Dionysian freedom that found me, for my sins, kissing Vinnie's ear. The sounds emanating from Vinnie suggested he was feeling pleasure as demanded.

The door of the hall opened and someone started to shout in at us. It was hard to hear over the music but it was a voice, a lone voice, the voice of a man shouting in through the dark, a voice determined to be heard. I could hear Shea asking who it was and the voice shouting back at him.

'What's going on in here? Do you hear me, what are youse up to in here?'

There was the scratch of the arm coming off the vinyl. A momentary silence and then the angry voice, clear as a bell.

'Is Tina Molloy here?' the voice demanded to know. 'Are you in here, Tina?'

'It's all right, Dick,' Tina said, softly, almost too softly, her voice competing with the dark. 'I'm safe, Dick.'

'No you're not. You're with a bunch of weirdos. Get your coat and come on.'

'They're not a bunch of weirdos, Dick.'

'She's right, Dick,' I said. 'We're not a bunch of weirdos; we're rehearsing a play.'

'What are you doing with the lights off?' Dick asked. 'How can you rehearse in the dark?'

'It's an experiment,' Shea said, 'just a little experiment.'

With that, Shea turned the lights back on and we all felt slightly foolish. Tina scrambled from the stage and grabbed her coat. Dick stood in the centre of the hall like the fighter he was, prepared to take on all comers. It was terribly impressive.

'Tina won't be back. You can find someone else for your play.'

He had come to claim his woman and no one was in any doubt but that she was his. Tina had been a rock as Juno, a woman standing up to her man and standing up to the world. In the silence of the Oriel Hall, I recognised that she was subservient for the first time ever, that in reality she was vulnerable and capable of being bossed about.

'I'm sorry,' Tina said, pulling on her coat and heading for the door. As she exited, she stopped and came back in. 'I want to wish you all the best with the play, I really do.' She paused as if there was more to come, like she had prepared a farewell speech and now found that it was irrelevant, that her action was bigger than her words and made them redundant.

We were down to six Deadly Sins. We had lost Lust, and there was no way that Fran was going to step into that role. It had to be a female and that left Ann Hasson, who was only a wet week with us and still finding her bearings. She was curvaceous and people were talking about her as a possible Helen of Troy. We sat around the hall, individually and in groups, wondering what the consequences were for us of what had transpired.

'You know who that was?' Shea asked.

'That was Dick Elliot from Phil Shanahan House,' I said by way of filling in those from outside the parish. 'I used to play with him as a kid. He taught me how to carry cases.'

'No, that's not who it was,' Shea said.

I looked at my older brother, wondering if he was having a mental seizure or something. How could he not know about Dick and the trouble I got into when I brought home the toffee bars, one hundred and twenty of them? 'I know who that is, I played with him....'

'No, Pedro, think about it, think about the play, think … what are we dealing with here … necromancy … the black arts … think....'

I looked around the room. Everyone seemed bewildered.

'Who was it, Shea?' Vinnie asked.

'Mephistopheles.'

The temperature in the room fell.

'That was Mephistopheles.'

Shea let out a shrill, demonic scream, a scream that seemed to come from hell, a terrifying, possessed scream, a being-burned-alive-at-the-stake scream, a lone scream that became a collective scream, no one knowing at what they were screaming other than the sense that evil was present, or the devil, something malign that was putrid and horrible and made you want your mother's womb or some place where all the crying and screaming could be banished and come to an end.

It took quite a while for any semblance of normality to return. Fran was furious with Shea, and I was furious too. I hadn't seen it coming. People were genuinely upset and Shea apologised, but no one was in a forgiving mood. He had scared the shit out of us. We hugged one another and reassured ourselves that there was nothing sinister going on. We were engaged in the theatre where all was illusion, there were no dark, Satanic forces that could intrude.

'I think there's something in Shea's observation,' Vinnie said.

'What do you mean?' Fran asked him.

'I think the play is haunted. I've felt it before now.'

'Does that mean you're going to go to hell?' I said.

'I don't know, maybe it does.'

'A play can't be haunted,' Sean Murphy chimed in. 'That's all silly superstition. The Scottish play is supposed to be haunted. It's bollox if you ask me.'

'You mean *Macbeth*, don't you?' Vinnie said. 'Why don't you call it by its proper name?'

'Very well then, *Macbeth*,' Sean said.

'"Fair is foul and foul is fair,"' Vinnie said, quoting the witches, '"Hover through the fog and filthy air."'

'You're not supposed to do that,' Pat Darcy said.

'Not supposed to do what?' Vinnie said.

'You're not supposed to quote *Macbeth* inside a theatre,' Pat Darcy said.

'You must go outside, turn around three times, knock on the door and ask our permission to come back in,' Sean said.

'Are you serious?' Vinnie said.

'Yes, I am.'

'I will in my hole.'

*

It was clear by the autumn of 1969 that *Faustus* was doomed, at least in the short term. It was my final year in school and I had exams and university to think about. Da had always insisted that I had the brains to get a degree. No one from our family had made it to university and it was a big thing to be the first. I was determined not to disappoint my parents. Shea and Ita had missed out because third-level scholarships were not available at the time they sat their Leaving Certificates. I was set to carry the flag and to put myself firmly on top of the family pedestal.

Shea, without anyone's knowledge, applied and was accepted for a night-time degree course at University College Dublin (UCD), alma mater of James Joyce.

'Go on, ya boy, ya, you show 'em, Seamus, you show 'em what you can do!' Ma shouted when the acceptance letter arrived at our table.

Shea was working as a clerical officer in CIE, a job that Da had secured for him after he left school. He'd been handing up most of his wages to Ma, a tradition in our house even for summer jobs, and now Ma proudly declared that she was putting that money towards his college fees.

'You'll have to give up the drama for a while, Seamus,' Ma said. 'You'll have to concentrate on your studies now.'

'Yeah,' Shea said, but it was more of a grunt than anything else.

'You'll have to get some new clothes; you can't be going over to Earlsfort Terrace looking like a tramp.'

'I don't need clothes.'

'Mixing with doctors and lawyers and artichecks … you have to look your best.'

Shea looked at me and shook his head.

'It's architects, Ma, not artichecks…' I said.

'You stay out of it, you're too smart for your own boots,' Ma said. 'I'm talking to Seamus. Keep your nose where it's not wanted.'

'I'm doing Arts, Ma, I won't be mixing with that crowd. I'm doing English and History.'

'He'll be hanging out with the hippies and the radicals, Ma,' I said, and she was not one bit pleased with my intervention.

Shea came back from his first night at college with over two dozen books. We only had six books in the house before that, not counting school books. Two of our six were under Da's mattress, *In Praise of Older Women* and *The Tropic of Capricorn* and I'd read them both, in secret, because they were 'dirty.' The other four were on the fireplace in the kitchen, two by Agatha Christie, *Black Beauty* by Anna Sewell and a biography of Matt Talbot, the holy man from Summerhill who'd prayed in our local church.

Shea told us that he was a freshman and that he was in his first semester. They were new words for a new situation and I loved them. At college you went to lectures and attended tutorials. You took on assignments and prepared for your higher diploma in education. In a year I would, hopefully, be able to say the same things. They would apply to me because I would also be an undergraduate. I loved that word, all five syllables of it. An undergraduate at UCD, just like James Joyce, graduating *magna cum laude*, like the great man himself, a mortarboard on my head and a degree scroll in my hand. Books started to accumulate in our house, and Shea had a rare and terrible row with Ma when she covered them with brown paper so that he could pass them down.

Shea wasn't a fortnight in UCD when he discovered Samuel Beckett. He sat up in bed at night and devoured him. I didn't mind because Beckett made Shea laugh in a way I'd never heard him laugh before. I didn't care that it was two o'clock in the morning and that I had to be up for school, Shea's squeals were irrepressible. Every so often I'd ask him what it was and he'd read me a passage.

My mother. I got into communication with her by knocking on her skull. One knock for yes, two for no, three for hello, four for money and five for goodbye. That she should confuse yes, no, hello and goodbye was all the same to me, I confused them myself. That she should confuse the four knocks with anything other than money was something to be avoided at all costs. During the period of indoctrination, therefore, at the same time as I administered the four knocks to her skull, I stuck a banknote under her nose or in her mouth.

Ma ended up banging on the floor of her bedroom above ours to get us to shut up and that, in its Beckettian way, made us ten times worse. Shea read the novels, the short fiction and the plays and then passed them on to me. My obsession grew in tandem with his. Beckett lived in Paris, but his family were from Foxrock on the south side of Dublin. He'd gone to Trinity College and taught there. He'd given tutorials to undergraduates – what a class that must have been – before he headed off to France in the late 1920s. He had worked as a secretary to James Joyce and transcribed passages of *Finnegan's Wake* at the time Joyce was losing his sight. Lucia, Joyce's daughter, had fallen for the shy, young Dublin Protestant but her love went unrequited.

I decided to go to Trinity because of Samuel Beckett. The ban on Catholics was still in force, but flouting that appealed to me. I wanted to walk the same cobblestones Beckett had traversed; I wanted to drink in the Buttery bar and read *The Irish Times* in the student Commons Rooms like he had done. I read his novel, *Murphy*, and when I finished it I started again from page one. *The sun shone, having no alternative, on the nothing new.* He'd written that opening sentence when he was not yet thirty years old. It felt so robust and confident and daring. I wanted to breathe in the Trinity College air in the hope that it might inspire me to write English as brilliant as he. Or should I say brilliantly?

Shea and I decided to make a pilgrimage out to the Beckett family home, Cooldrinagh, in Foxrock. I borrowed a Vespa scooter – a bit feminine in look but reliable in performance – from Ann Hasson, a Derry girl and member of Slot Players—she, later played the dumb girl, Sarah, in the world premiere of Brian Friel's Translations—who'd been given it by her father to help her get to and from her lectures in UCD. She brought it to *Faustus* rehearsals and we used it for the entrance of Valdes and Cornelius, but the smell of burning oil it created was overpowering.

I drove out through Ringsend with Shea tucked in behind me. My destination was Leopardstown Racecourse. I'd been there dozens of times with Da over the years and could have driven it blindfolded. Shea understood the house was on Kerrymount Avenue with a view of the racecourse, because Beckett had alluded to it in his radio play *All That Fall.* I knew that all I had to do was head south and keep the sea on my left and we'd arrive there in due course. Coming out through Blackrock, the lights at the Catholic church went red. I stopped. The lights went green and, as I let out the throttle, the Vespa cut out. I couldn't get it to start again. I tried everything, including pushing it, but to no avail. I dragged it into the church grounds and started to unscrew the spark-plugs to see if the engine had flooded.

As I worked through my limited mechanical repertoire, a Garda car pulled in beside us. They wanted to know what we were doing in the church grounds. They suggested we were casing the church because we were interested in the contents of the poor boxes.

'Which one of you owns the bike?' the taller Garda asked.

'Neither of us,' I said, 'it's borrowed.'

'Stolen, in other words,' the other Garda said.

'No, it belongs to Ann Hasson, a friend of mine, you can check with her if you like.'

They asked us to empty out our pockets. I took out what change I had. Shea held back, reluctant to comply. The taller Garda turned on him and threatened him with a cell in the station. Shea took out some keys, loose change and a box of matches. I thought that was unusual because he didn't smoke, at least not regularly.

'We're students,' Shea said, 'on a college assignment. The bike broke down, that's all.'

'You're quare looking students if you ask me,' the smaller one said.

'Where are you from?' the taller one said.

Shea and I looked at each other. It was an awful dilemma because an address anywhere near Sheriff Street could sink us entirely.

'We're from the East Wall,' I said. 'Abercorn Road.'

The taller one smirked and looked us up and down. Then he looked to his colleague and invited him into the smirk as well.

'I have an aunt that lives in the East Wall,' the taller one said, 'so you better not be lying to me. What number are you on Abercorn Road?'

'Number twelve,' Shea said, 'but we moved to Seville Place.'

'So you are lying.'

'No, we're from Abercorn Road originally,' I said. 'That's where we were born.'

'And you moved, I'd say you moved to Sheriff Street, am I right?'

I wanted to rush in and make a denial but I held my fire. So did Shea.

'What's your name?' he said.

'I'm Peter and he's Shea,' I said.

'Your surname?'

'Sheridan,' we both said at the same time.

He smirked again. 'Your father works on the railway, yeah?'

Shea and I exchanged looks and then a smile. 'Yeah, our Da works in Amiens Street station,' I said, 'in the booking office.'

'There's no tax on this bike and no insurance either. Go home and don't let me catch you on this thing again, do you hear?'

The two Gardaí got into their car. The taller one, who was in the passenger seat, lowered his window. 'I'm Michael Cunningham's son,' he said, 'tell your father that you met me.' Then they sped off down the road.

Shea retrieved the matchbox from his pocket and held it out to me.

'Have a look in that,' he said.

I opened it and there, staring up at me, was a tightly wrapped piece of silver paper. I took it between my fingers. It had the feel of a lump of dope. I unravelled it and it was as I had suspected. The Garda had not seen it. How had he looked inside and not seen it? Could he have decided to ignore it, I wondered? Or perhaps he didn't know what it was. Shea took the lump of silver paper and threw it in bushes nearby, just to be safe.

We pushed the Vespa to the nearest garage, where it turned out we had run out of petrol. It was a huge relief. We abandoned the pilgrimage to Foxrock and headed for home. Beckett could wait. I drove slowly along the coast with the sea now on my right. I made sure to keep within the speed limit; I had no interest in any further engagements with the forces of law and order.

'We were very lucky to meet that Garda today,' I said to Shea.

'Only that wasn't a Garda.'

I thought I'd misheard him so I repeated what I'd said. Again he contradicted me.

'That wasn't a Garda,' Shea said.

'Who was it if it wasn't a Garda?' I said.

'Frankie.'

'Frankie?'

'Yeah, Frankie.'

*

Plays are supernatural things. When you rehearse a play, you feel a presence. Every play has an aura and sometimes it breaks through. As an actor, you feel this weird communion when you stand on a stage and you know that you hold this power in your hands. Your heartbeat is also the heartbeat of the play. You are at the centre of an illusion and you have the power to prolong it or to destroy it. You are inside your life and outside of it at the same time; you are both subject and object. Nowhere else, other than the stage, have I felt this strange, seductive power.

We read Beckett's *Waiting for Godot* in the Oriel Hall and I knew immediately that it was a spooky play. It had famously been described as a play in which nothing happens twice. It is a brilliant observation but it is not true. The tramps, Vladimir and

Estragon, wait for Godot, and he doesn't come. That is how it appears on the surface, but something does happen between the acts, a change takes place and it feels like a redemption, despite the play's nihilistic reputation. The tree, barren in the first half, sports leaves in the second. The character of Pozzo goes blind and Lucky, his slave, goes dumb. Estragon remembers nothing, takes off his boots and goes asleep. Poor Vladimir is then left to wonder what all this means, if anything. In his ruminations, he goes to the heart of the theatre experience itself, he questions whether he is the subject or the object of the story and he wonders if he is flesh or spirit.

> VLADIMIR: Was I sleeping while the others suffered? Am I sleeping now? Tomorrow, when I wake, or think I do, what shall I say of today? That with Estragon, my friend, at this place, until the fall of night, I waited for Godot? That Pozzo passed, with his carrier, and talked to us? Probably. But in all that what truth will there be? (He stares at Estragon who is dozing off.) He'll know nothing. He'll tell me about the blows he received and I'll give him a carrot ... At me too someone is looking, of me too someone is saying, he is sleeping, he knows nothing, let him sleep on. (Pause.) I can't go on! (Pause.) What have I said?

The audience are watching Vladimir, of course, and that is one part of the equation. But there is also posited here the idea of a reality beyond us, a transcendent power that is not indifferent to our struggle and may even be benign. By the end of the play, Vladimir stands at the edge of salvation, unsure whether to embrace it or not.

The play came out of a near-death experience for Beckett. In late 1937, he left a Parisian restaurant and was approached by a pimp who pestered him to go off with one of his girls. He refused, whereupon the pimp produced a knife and stabbed him, the blade just missing his heart and lung by a hair's breadth. He was hospitalised and, though there were fears initially for his life, he survived and recovered well enough to appear in court when the case came up. In the court entranceway he met the pimp, Monsieur Prudent, and asked him why he had done it.

'*Rien ne faire* (nothing to do),' Prudent said, '*je m'excuse* (I'm sorry).'

That infamous answer became the opening line of the play, begun ten years later in 1947 and finished in under six weeks. By that time, Beckett knew of the horrors of the death camps in all their awfulness. He lost many friends in the holocaust, and the world would and could never be the same again for him. It was against this background, and in an attempt to understand it, that Godot emerged.

We abandoned plans to produce *Doctor Faustus* and went head first into staging *Waiting for Godot*. Vinnie played Estragon and I was Vladimir, with Da as Pozzo and my brother Johnny as Lucky. Shea directed, and we ran for three nights in the Oriel Hall before we took it out on the road. Our first stop was in Roundwood, County Wicklow – the self-proclaimed highest village in Ireland – an amateur festival that had never hosted a Beckett play before Slot Players arrived. The audience divided in their response and we faced a few noisy walkouts in the first act. It meant that we had to work harder on-stage to hold what we had and Vinnie, in particular, as was his wont, lost the head a bit. In one sequence he became so animated and emotional that he lost his place in the play and went from the first act into the second. *Godot* is the sort

of play where that is entirely possible. In the middle of this supposed atheistic paean to nihilism, I prayed to the God that lived
in Saint Laurence O'Toole's church – the only one I knew – and
implored Him to save us, and He did.

The adjudicator that night was Colm Ó Briain. He was a
television producer at RTÉ and, more importantly, he'd been
involved in the setting up of the Project Arts Centre in 1966.
(On the fiftieth anniversary of the Easter Rising, Colm Ó Briain
and a number of like-minded souls staged a reading in the Gate
Theatre of some of the banned Irish writers of that time – any
writer worth his or her salt fell foul of the censorship laws – and
the event focused enormous attention on how we treated our
artists on the island of saints and scholars.)

Ó Briain and The Project attracted a number of visual artists,
who formed a collective to exhibit their work – the gallery system back then was not receptive to emerging artists. They had an
exhibition above Tuck's shop in Lower Abbey Street, beside the
Abbey Theatre. Colm Ó Briain invited the Slot Players to think
about a season of plays that might fit with a cutting-edge view
of Irish culture. We didn't know it at the time, but the Project
Arts Centre, and our engagement with it, would change our lives
forever.

3

In the summer of 1970, having completed my Leaving Certificate exam, I made my début as a professional actor. The venue was the Lyric Theatre, Belfast and the play was Sean O'Casey's *The Shadow of a Gunman*. I took on the role of Tommy Owens, just as I had with the Saint Laurence O'Toole's Musical and Dramatic Society a mere two years earlier. It was the start of the Troubles and Belfast was a volatile place. No-warning car bombs were a regular occurrence, and death and destruction lurked around every corner. It was urban guerrilla warfare at its most ugly. I found the experience of being there intoxicating.

A man called Paddy Doherty was the reason I found myself in Belfast. I'd met him earlier that summer in the English city of Peterborough. I'd gone there with my school pal 'Billy Kelly' in search of a pot of gold. The place was crawling with Irish students and, like most of them, we ended up working in Hartley's pea factory. It was tough work, standing in front of a conveyor belt, removing pods from a sea of peas, seven in the evening until seven in the morning, then going back to a grubby flat and getting into a bed vacated by someone on the day shift.

The only subject of conversation in Peterborough was the wages. We had no doubt that we were being exploited. The only solution was for us to form a union. A mass meeting was held at the changeover of shifts. Billy Kelly proposed me to represent the night shift. He said some positive things about me and I shrugged them off, but I was secretly chuffed. I was elected unopposed. Paddy Woodworth, a Trotskyite from Bray, was elected to represent the day shift. We were delegated to meet the factory manager, a Swede named Olaf Berg. On the way in to the meeting, Paddy pulled me aside.

'The first thing is recognition,' he said. 'That's imperative. We have to get Berg to recognise the union.'

It was my first ever lesson in industrial relations. Paddy was a serious politician and a brilliant negotiator. He told Berg that he should be grateful for the presence of so many educated Irish students in his factory.

'This is not my factory,' Berg said. 'I work for Hartley's, just like you men.'

I was glad he called us men. Paddy was singularly unimpressed.

We drew up a list of demands, including an increase in the hourly rate of pay. The only concession the management made was to extend the dinner break by fifteen minutes. We introduced a go-slow in response. The Pakistani workers, who made up the majority, dissociated themselves from us. It proved to be our Achilles heel. The management dropped a bombshell and reduced our hours from seventy-two to forty-eight. The cut in our wages was catastrophic. They diverted peas away from Peterborough to a sister factory, thus making strike action a fruitless exercise. Paddy Doherty, a Belfast schoolteacher whose family had been burned out in the sectarian violence of August

'69, proposed that we work the forty-eight hour week in the hope that good behaviour might lead to increased hours.

'Half a loaf is better than no bread, I'm telling you,' he said. 'I'm thinking about you lads from the south. This is good money; you won't get anything like it back home.'

A heated debate followed. Someone suggested that we add strychnine to the peas and use that as a bargaining tool. I thought it was crazy but it was put to a vote and defeated. A fight broke out. We were divided amongst ourselves. After the meeting ended, Hartley's informed us that they were letting us go. No proposals, no negotiation, no talk. Despite the ultimatum, we managed to get them to pay our boat fare back to Ireland. Or rather, Paddy Woodworth secured the commitment because, in truth, it would never have crossed my mind to ask for it.

I headed to London however, with Billy Kelly and Paddy Doherty, where I became violently ill. It was some kind of virus and it completely floored me. I spent what little money I had on medicine that didn't work. Billy got a job on a building site in Wandsworth and Paddy headed home to Belfast. I was on my own in a cheap hotel in central London. There is nothing that defines loneliness more than a bad fever and no mother to make it better. I missed home so much. The thought of Ma's sugary tea and a slice of toasted batch bread was too much to bear. I dragged myself out onto the Earl's Court Road, found a travel agent and booked a flight to Dublin.

It was my first time in an aeroplane. I didn't care that I'd spent all my money on it; I needed to get home. I vowed that I would never again cross the Irish sea in a cattle boat. I arrived home to altered sleeping arrangements, thanks to the situation in Northern Ireland. After the violence broke out, Ma had taken in refugees. Mrs Dyer and her daughter, "wee" Catherine, were two such. They had been living in Unity Flats – never was a place so gloriously misnamed – when her husband Gerry, 'a wee Protestant,' had his throat slit for crossing over the sectarian divide and marrying a Catholic. He miraculously survived and, from his hospital bed, insisted that his wife and daughter take themselves across the border to the relative safety of Dublin.

Mrs Dyer and her daughter now occupied my old room. Gerard and Paul, the babies of our family, were in the back bedroom. Johnny was in the single bed in Ma and Da's room. That left me with the pull-out bed in the kitchen. Ma realised I was too ill and switched me with Johnny. He moaned about it a great deal. His moans apart, I was too old to be sleeping in a room with my parents. I couldn't live with the guilt and the shame that I might be curtailing their sex lives. I knew I had to move out or go insane.

Paddy Doherty had invited me to call in on him if I was ever in Belfast. It seemed a logical destination. We had a war raging in our country and I was keen to see it at first hand. On my first day in Belfast I visited the Falls Road and got caught up in a riot. Some youngsters were throwing stones when an army vehicle appeared from nowhere, the soldiers jumped out and the youngsters ran. I wanted to run too, but the part of my brain that said I'd done nothing wrong prevailed. Moments later, two soldiers in uniform were asking me to account for my throwing stones. They were aliens in my country, demanding to know my business.

'Whad a ya doing out on the street, mate, are ya throwin' stones?' one of the soldiers barked at me in a thick Geordie accent.

I looked at him and saw that he had a pimple on the corner of his top lip, a place where I was prone to them myself.

'No, I'm not throwing stones,' I said.

'Wha' are ya doin' hangin' round here then?' the other one asked.

I was about to let them have it when Robert Emmet's speech from the dock deserted me. As did Pearse's oration at the grave of O'Donovan Rossa. My only thought was how young they were to be carrying guns. One false move and I'd be history.

'I'm here on holiday. Up from Dublin for the week,' I said.

They asked for identification and I showed them my Irish passport. They handed it back to me without comment and headed off in pursuit of the stone throwers. I'd failed my first test with the British Army. It was one nil to the old enemy.

On my way back to Paddy's house, I went by the Lyric Theatre. On their front-of-house hoarding they had a forth-coming production poster for *The Shadow of a Gunman*. I went in to enquire if they were fully cast. To my astonishment, a woman told me they were seeing people for it the following day. The next morning I stood on the stage of the Lyric in front of Mary O'Malley, the theatre's founder, and her director Pat Brannigan. After I finished my piece, they asked me to wait in the lobby. Half an hour later, Mary O'Malley came out and offered me the role. She asked me who my agent was. I didn't have an agent. I didn't know what an agent did. I was going to say Da, but I didn't know if that might scupper my chances altogether.

'Do you have an agent in Dublin?' she asked me, in a tone that suggested I should have. I was an amateur; no one had told me about agents and I was about to fall at the first hurdle. I was about to lose the job, not because of lack of talent, but because I didn't have an agent. I was marooned. I couldn't even lie. I hated all agents, even though I didn't know one.

'I don't like agents,' I said, only because I didn't know what to say. It made Mary O'Malley laugh, and that surprised me because she didn't look the laughing type. She was running a theatre in the middle of a war zone and she had a face that matched her predicament: angular and serious.

'You want to do the deal yourself, that's fair enough. What did you get in your last job?'

I was surprised that she wanted to know about Hartley's. I was going to tell her when I realised, fortunately, that she was referring to my last acting job.

'I'll offer you fifteen pounds rehearsal and eighteen pounds playing, how does that sound?'

I didn't know what to say. Someone was offering me money to do something I loved. The truth is, I'd have done it for nothing.

'I don't have anywhere to stay,' I said, 'not on a permanent basis. I'll need to find digs.'

'I can't start paying for your accommodation. I'll give you twenty pounds all in, rehearsal and playing. That's a good deal. You start on Monday at ten a.m.' She held out her hand and I shook it.

I was a professional actor. I'd negotiated my own deal. Who needs an agent? I was starting out on my career just as the war was hotting up. I couldn't have been more excited. I dashed home to Paddy, who wasn't quite as enthusiastic. They were limited for space and I was a non-paying guest. I told him I could redress that, I could pay for my keep, but unfortunately they didn't entertain lodgers; it was strictly a family home. I took the hint, thanked him and said goodbye. That evening, I went home to Dublin on the train and broke the news to my parents. Da was genuinely delighted and Ma was genuinely upset. She knew

Belfast and didn't trust it; she'd been betrayed by it and hurt by it. She had spent her teenage years in Cromac Street near the markets, and she'd seen enough of bigotry and pogroms to last her a lifetime.

She asked me about my accommodation and I told her I was staying with Paddy Doherty and his family. She suspected the lie but I brazened it out. That Saturday afternoon, a no-warning IRA car bomb exploded in Belfast city centre, killing five civilians. Ma wasn't convinced that the Lyric Theatre, with its republican ethos, wouldn't be bombed in reprisal.

'The loyalists don't do car bombs' I said, 'they don't have the expertise, Ma.'

'They have the police and the army behind them; they can do whatever they like.'

I returned to Belfast and knocked at doors in the university area looking for digs. My accent elicited a few swift nos. A landlady, Mrs McCabe, who was originally from Monaghan, took me in. I shared a bedroom with a cousin of hers, Aengus, who was attending Queens University, studying Irish. I was surprised they had such a department, but not surprised that Aengus was in the college Sinn Féin society. He was serious on the national question but game for a laugh on everything else. He had a good living allowance thanks to the British Government, and justified taking money from them as a legitimate balancing of the books in favour of republicans.

'Aithníonn ciaróg ciaróg eile,' he would always say as he raised his glass of porter. (It takes one reprobate to know another).

There was Irish in *The Shadow of a Gunman* and I was called on to advise with the southern pronunciation. The northern dialect, or Donegal Irish as it is known, is quite different to the Dublin variety, which comes from the West and is largely Connemara

Peter Sheridan

Irish, with a smattering of west Kerry Irish thrown in for good measure. Louis Rolston, a legend in Belfast theatre circles, was playing Seumas Shields, the role that Da had created in the Oriel Hall. He boasted a Protestant name, but came from west Belfast and was Catholic. I went over the Irish with him and it was a great way to get to know him. He was more serious than Da, and didn't play it for the laughs as much. I watched him in rehearsals, the way the character developed day by day. He never played to the gallery; he always looked for the truth of the situation, what was happening in the moment, and he worked his socks off to be alive to that, to be present in the now.

Having played it before, I was the first off-book – in theatre parlance, I knew my lines – a situation that endeared me to the director but not to my fellow actors. Many actors try to hold on to the script for as long as possible. They use it as a crutch, a way of continuing to explore the character, a defence mechanism against making final decisions about who and what they are. A character has so many lines in a play and he speaks them on the stage. However, that is not the totality of who he/she is. There is the off-stage life of the person, what has been going on in his/her life, the events that have formed who they are, some of which may be spoken about and some inferred. The totality of their existence is more than their time in front of the audience. The rehearsal period is the place for the actors to find all that, the hidden depths that elevate it to something great, hopefully. I came fully formed, as it were, and it took me time with profes-sional actors to see the folly of that. Knowing the lines is a part of the craft but it is not the whole thing. I needed to allow more space between me and them, more room for the unexpected. I was choking the interaction and circumscribing dramatic pos-sibility by finding the character too soon.

One day in rehearsal, the stage manager offered Louis Rolston a line that he seemed to have forgotten. It is an everyday occurrence when actors are trying to get off-book. He didn't pick up the cue, however. He stayed silently looking into space. The stage manager repeated the line and Louis waved it down. He looked across at Pat Brannigan, the director.

'This business about Shields being a teacher,' he said. 'I'm supposed to have taught Irish six nights a week?'

'Yes, that's right,' Pat Brannigan said. 'He tells us that in the first act.'

'I think he's lying. I don't think he taught Irish at all,' Louis said.

There followed a long, intense discussion between actor and director. It was an important insight on Louis' part and he fought with passion to develop the point. The director didn't want to appear like he hadn't seen it so he took an opposing position. It was heading for stalemate when Louis brought me into the discussion. He asked me to read the lines from the text, then he asked me what my opinion was on the standard of Irish employed by the character.

'It's not very good to be honest,' I said. 'You'd expect a teacher of Irish to have a better blas,' I said.

'What's a blas?' the director wanted to know.

I did my best to explain that it was to do with pronunciation and accent. That native speakers sounded different to non-native speakers because they had a blas. Everyone worked to have one but it was very difficult to obtain, you almost had to be born with it.

'He is definitely not a native speaker,' I said, 'that's for sure.'

'That is all I needed to know,' Louis said, 'I know what he's about now.'

It had taken Louis several weeks to figure out that Shields never taught Irish, not at any real level. Once he'd discovered the specific point where the character lied, he'd cracked him. It was a lesson I would take with me because I had always assumed that everyone speaks the truth in a play. Or at least their version of it. Now it opened up to me that characters are more devious than that, and a great and important part of the process is separating truth and untruth, fantasy and reality. In discovering those tipping points, you discover the character.

*

The world of the play and the world of Belfast were proof positive that history repeats itself. The audience were totally clued in to this symbiosis. Certain lines were greeted, every night, with a round of applause.

I don't believe the gunmen are dying for people, rather it's the people who are dying for the gunmen.

I'd die for Ireland. I never got the chance, they never gave me the chance.

Instead of counting their beads now they're countin' bulltets.

It was as though the lines could have been written that afternoon. And, as well as applause, there was laughter from the audience too, the laughter of recognition. I worked hard to exploit the full comic potential of Tommy Owens. One night, as I was about to launch into singing *God Save Ireland*, I tapped my foot off the floor. It was an unselfconscious thing, a moment to mark the beginning of the song, that was all. The audience, to a man, burst out laughing. I couldn't start the song because of their reaction. It was an amazing thing to find, out of nothing. A great moment, a bit of magic. The following night I tapped my foot again and waited for the laugh. It didn't come. Indeed, it never came again. An odd titter but that was all. I was never able to recreate the moment. I didn't have that skill, that ability. Louis Rolston would have elicited a laugh every night because he had it: the ability to appear like he wasn't trying. Essentially it's a gift, timing, you can't teach it; it's something you're born with, just like the blas. I was competent, I knew I was competent and I also knew that I would never be great. Not as an actor. I didn't have that gift.

*

Despite my own perceived lack of talent, I successfully auditioned for the role of Alfred The Boy in the upcoming Lyric production of *Rosencrantz and Guildenstern Are Dead* by Tom Stoppard. It wasn't the biggest part in the world but it was something quite different, a step out of the Dublin working-class milieu into one that was the essence of Englishness itself. It would be a challenge and I couldn't wait to put manners on it. I came off-stage as Tommy Owens the night I found out, determined to celebrate my elevation. I didn't appear in the second act of *Shadow*, so I slipped out to the theatre bar and had two pints of Guinness and two Jameson whiskies. I took my curtain call and headed straight back to the bar and drank some more. I got home to my digs and straight into a row with Aengus on the role of violence in achieving a thirty-two county socialist republic. I took severe umbrage at his continual reference to me as a 'Free Stater.' It ended with the two of us trading insults and Mrs McCabe banging on the floor with her sweeping brush.

When I came down for breakfast on the following morning, Mrs McCabe had a face on her like a peptic ulcer. She put my fry in front of me and poured out the tea.

'I want you out of here by Friday. I won't charge you for the week,' she said.

'Mrs McCabe…' I started in my defence, knowing that this had to do with the events of the previous night, '…I had a few drinks on me, I'm sorry….'

'I have family coming from Monaghan, I need the room. I want you gone by Friday, that's all.'

She reminded me of Ma in one of her moods. Untalkable to. Deaf and dour. I'd been tried and executed before I could offer a full apology. What should I apologise for, exactly? I knew I'd been arguing half the night with Aengus, but I couldn't remember what was said, other than defending myself against being a Free Stater. Now I was homeless and he was safe. It was down to the drink. The demon drink, as Ma called it when Da got out of hand. She'd never put him out over it, never evicted a lodger either.

I vowed never again to celebrate good news by getting drunk. I thought about the Pledge but I didn't know where to go in Belfast to take it. I thought about asking Aengus, but decided against it. He was in large measure to blame for my situation and I didn't want him to think that he'd won the argument, even though I couldn't remember what the argument was about, exactly.

My new digs were to be in a loyalist enclave of north Belfast. Peter Adair, who played Mr Gallogher in *Shadow* and was cast as the Player King in *Rosencrantz*, offered me a room in his house at a modest rent. It was wonderful to be a part of a family again – his wife Terry, and children Kim and Jeremy made me feel totally welcome – and Peter became a father and a mentor to me. The first thing he did was teach me the Belfast accent. It was July and we were in the middle of the marching season, a time when even moderate people become tribal. He didn't want me wandering around the Limestone Road when emotions made it a dangerous place to be, especially for a 'taig' and a Free Stater. I was subsequently glad of his tuition when I was stopped by two men on my way back from the corner shop one afternoon. I knew immediately they were not part of a welcoming committee – one sported a red hand tattoo and the other a crest of Glasgow Rangers football club.

They wanted to know what I was doing in the area. They asked what was in the shopping bag. I showed them. Bread, sugar, milk, some sweets and a newspaper. One of them opened it out. It was the *Belfast Telegraph*.

'You read the *Tele*,' he said.

'Well, I buy it for the crossword, to be honest,' I replied.

It had become part of our routine. Peter and I started it in the bus on our way to the Lyric and we finished it on our way back after the performance.

'Who are the sweets for?' the other one asked.

'They're for the children, Kim and Jeremy.'

'Where's their father, is he at home?' the same one asked.

'No, he's gone to Purdysburn,' I said, delighted that I remembered. 'He's gone to Purdysburn to visit his wife.'

*

Peter was the first person I confided in about Frankie. He asked me had I ever told it in confession and I laughed at him because that wasn't the kind of thing you could tell to a priest.

'I thought that was the great thing about being Catholic,' Peter said. 'You offload it to a priest and walk free.'

'I could do that but it wouldn't stop me feeling lousy. I'd still feel guilty.'

'I wish we Prods had it. We have to live with our sins; we have no easy way out.'

'Why don't you change over then, convert to our side?'

'I might, you know, just for you I might do that.'

He winked over at me and I laughed. He had that ability to turn the most serious conversation into something light. I made him laugh, too, especially in rehearsals when I pursed my lips and tempted him, in dumb show, into my lair, before I poured poison in his ear. I had introduced some 'ballitarse' into my portrayal of Alfred and that cracked him up altogether. The director had a go at me because he said I was making Peter corpse. I was, of course, but I knew that he could stop himself laughing if he wanted to. He was a pro, he'd been at the acting game for years.

'Stop sticking your arse out, it's too much,' Sam McCready, the director, said to me.

'No, please, it's just me,' Peter said, 'leave it in, it helps my motivation.'

It was funny playing as a girl opposite Peter, because in Shakespeare's day, of course, all the female parts were played by boys. It was strange to think of Ophelia with male body parts. Her relationship with Hamlet was so boy/girl, so contemporary in its narcissism, down to his indifference and her rock-star suicide. How weird must that have been for him as a writer? And what went through the collective head of the audience when they heard, for example, Lady Macbeth – a boy – say:

Come to my woman's breasts, and take my milk for gall...
I have given suck, and know how tender 'tis to love the babe that milks me...
Come, you spirits that tend on mortal thoughts, unsex me here...

Alfred, and my experience bringing the character to life, brought home to me how sexually aware and experimental Shakespeare was as a writer. He delighted in playing with identity and gender and knew that he was titillating the prurient desires of all proclivities – hetero, homo and transvestite. He could cater for all tastes without breaking the suspension of disbelief, and he did this while satisfying the vulgar and the poetic at the same time. He was crude and he was sublime in the same breath. He shook his pelvis at the Elizabethan audience and they roared their approval.

I was determined to return to Shakespeare and give him some proper study if I made it to college. Peter was very supportive and wouldn't countenance failure.

'You will write your thesis on The Bard, *when* you're accepted by Trinity College, not *if*,' he said. 'I will pay for it to be bound and on the frontispiece you will put a dedication to me, your patron of the first folio.'

'Only if you become a Catholic,' I said.

'Very well then,' he replied, 'a Catholic, forthwith, I shall be.'

On the final night of *Shadow*, there were drinks in the Lyric bar. Peter couldn't stay because he had a babysitter to relieve. He headed up the street to catch the bus and I ordered a pint of Guinness on the complimentary round from Mary O'Malley. I sat next to Louis Rolston and we chatted, but my mind was with Peter on the bus. I missed the crossword. I loved the competition between us and particularly getting the final clue, when it came down to it.

'That's not fair,' he would say, 'I wanted to get that one.'

It always made me laugh, Peter acting like a baby.

'I'm not doing the crossword with you any more, you're too good.'

It didn't seem right, Peter going home on his own, foregoing the final night party, missing out on all the craic. Not that it was much of a party, to be honest. I remembered a great clue from the night before. Ggse (9,4). A four-letter clue with a thirteen-letter solution. 'Scrambled eggs'. Very clever that was. Right now my brain was scrambled and I decided to leave. I slipped out onto Ridgeway Street and ran all the way to the T-junction at the top. I'd missed the bus. I didn't know if there was another one. I walked to a cab office. The male receptionist asked where to and I said the Limestone Road.

'I don't think we can go up there, son. I think there was trouble there d'night,' he said.

It transpired the 'trouble' had been on the Shankill and so I secured a taxi home. As it turned out, there was rioting on North Queen Street and we were lucky to get through a citizens' roadblock that I assumed was the IRA. Peter was surprised and delighted to see me. He'd finished the crossword and I feigned disgust, but he saw through it. The bottle of Jameson came out and we drank to *Shadow*. We drank to *Rosencrantz* too. We drank to Shakespeare and we drank to Trinity College and I started to get maudlin about Frankie. Peter wouldn't hear of it. He hated maudlin, couldn't tolerate it. He considered maudlin a vice. Life had to be lived without regret.

*

In studying the role of Alfred, it occurred to me that there were many similarities between this play and *Waiting for Godot*. The Player from *Rosencrantz* is an Elizabethan version of Pozzo, just as Alfred is the child of Lucky. Both sets of relationships are based on the master/slave model. Lucky is exploited in the domestic sphere and Alfred in the sexual. Pozzo eats his lunch and tosses Lucky the left-over chicken bones. He treats him worse than if he were a dog. Vladimir is shocked and calls it a scandal. The Player's command to Alfred to put on the skirt is child abuse. It is a mirror of Pozzo's inhumanity. Guildenstern is likewise scandalised and calls the behaviour obscene.

Vladimir and Guildenstern express their indignation, but neither of them effects any change. Pozzo will continue to abuse Lucky, and the Player, Alfred. Alfred was the ghost that slept with me. I had never considered that distinction before playing him, that between experience and naivety, and how the former does not obliterate the latter. Albert has very few words, yet his scenes are the most visceral and poignant in the drama.

GUIL: Do you lose often?
ALFRED: Yes, sir.
GUIL: Then what could you have left to lose?
ALFRED: Nothing, sir.
GUIL: Do you like being … an actor?
ALFRED: No, sir.
GUIL: You and I, Alfred, we could create a dra-
           matic precedent here.
           (Albert starts to cry) Come, come, Albert,
           this is no way to fill the theatres of Europe.

* * *

There was a public phone by the stage door of the Lyric that was taken off the hook before curtain up each night. It was never replaced until after the curtain came down and the house lights went up. One Wednesday night during August, a call came to the phone at about twenty minutes to eight. Peter was standing nearby and answered it. I was in the toilet when I heard him shout out my name. I told him to take a message.

'It's long distance from Dublin,' he said, 'your mother's on the line.'

Ma was very excited. My Leaving Certificate results had come in and I'd won a scholarship. I'd managed honours in English, Irish, Chemistry and Geography. Passes in all the rest, Maths, History and Latin. The four honours did it for me, I had four Grade Cs or better, it was three Cs and a B, in fact, the B coming in Chemistry, to my surprise. I'd have expected it in English. But Ma was over the moon and I was over the moon and so was Da, he was over the moon, too, in fact everyone was over the moon, just like in the nursery rhyme. I came off the phone and Peter asked me how it felt and I just kept saying,

'I'm over the moon, what else can I say?'

Peter got the cast together and made an official announcement, saying how proud he was that I'd made it to Trinity College. That night, I felt Alfred at an altogether deeper level than before.

When we got home that night, Peter asked me how I wanted to mark the occasion and I suggested a stiff glass of Jameson.

'Would you like to say a prayer with me?' he asked. 'We could do that together.'

It was a moment to put the whiskey on hold, a spiritual moment.

'I'd love to do that,' I said.

We knelt down and said the 'Our Father.' Just before the amen, Peter added the words, 'For Thine is the Kingdom, the Power and the Glory, now and forever, Amen.' I looked at him and frowned.

'Oh, yes, that's the Protestant version,' he said, 'we'd better do the Catholic one for balance.'

The two of us started to laugh and it took a while for the giggles to dry up. I thought about fathers. The one in heaven and the one in Dublin. The one in Belfast, too. Peter Sheridan, my father, and Peter Adair. Two Peters. Me, too. Not yet a father. Three Peters. All bound up together, like musketeers. Three actors. All for one, and one for all. I was a scholarship student, about to step across the portal of Trinity College and carry the flag, not just for me but for the whole of the North Wall, and a few more besides.

4

Trinity College turned out to be a major disappointment. It was my own fault to a large extent. I had applied to do Arts, and that meant taking four subjects in my first year. In addition to English, I chose History, Philosophy and Economics. It was only when the lectures started I discovered there was a degree in pure English; with my interest and background in the theatre, it seemed like the perfect course for me. I went to my tutor – he was the Professor of German in the college – and made my case for a switch. He felt my Leaving Certificate grades were not sufficient to warrant entry to the higher, and more demanding, pure English degree course.

I was furious. I took it as a snub against my working-class background. That was how I felt on the Monday. By Tuesday I'd come around to the belief that it was my Catholicism; had I been a Protestant from north of the border, I'd have been facilitated, no problem. On Wednesday, I was sure it was down to my accent. By Thursday, I put it around the college that there was a plot against me. On Friday, I got drunk in the Buttery bar and sang republican songs until I was ejected for disruptive behaviour.

My friend Billy Kelly talked sense into me. We'd come from O'Connell's schools together and we'd gone to Peterborough and worked in the pea factory. He'd stayed on in London when I went to Belfast. I'd had the more stimulating summer but he'd earned more money, a pattern that was to become a graph of my life. He had no interest in acting but had joined Slot Players as a stage manager. I knew that Sheila O'Donoghue was enamoured of him and was hoping to get a date with him.

Billy told me I was being paranoid. I told him that I needed to do the pure English degree because I wanted to be a writer.

'Are you serious about wanting to write?'

'Yeah.'

'Do you see the front gate there, Peter?'

'I do.'

'Get through that gate and run as fast as you can away from this place if you want to write.'

Beckett had turned his back on Trinity and headed to Paris before he established himself as a man of the pen. I knew I would abandon these cobblestones at the earliest opportunity. There was no conspiracy against me. Degree courses were based on points and mine weren't good enough. That was the ugly truth. In addition, I was a lazy bastard who couldn't make it to lectures. Ma was doing her nut over me, claiming that I was sabotaging my university career.

'I don't have a career. They won't let me do the degree I want.'

'Aren't you lucky to have a university to go to?'

'They're a shower of anti-Catholic bastards. I don't want their degree. They'd bring back the Penal Laws if they could get away with it.'

73

'What are you going to do, son? You can't stay in bed all day.'

'I'll go in for the two o'clock lecture. Honest, Ma.'

'Is that a promise?'

'I promise.'

I'd sleep for Ireland if only they'd let me. If I didn't have someone to wake me up, I might never open my eyes again. In her despair, Ma resorted to throwing water over me in the vicinity of my face. Sadly, for her, I could sleep through that, no bother. I ended up missing the two o'clock lectures and then the four o'clock ones – I now believe I was suffering from depression – a condition brought about by my inability to face reality, in this instance my moderate Leaving Certificate results.

Shea, meanwhile, was making great strides at UCD. He won a gold medal in first year for an essay he'd written on Charles Stewart Parnell and the demise of the Irish Parliamentary Party. He'd also established a foothold with Dramsoc, the theatre society of the college. He played the Gravedigger in a production of *Hamlet*, which they staged at Newman House on St Stephen's Green. With his new-found college friends and the remnants of Slot Players, we had a second go at producing *Doctor Faustus*. We got a rehearsal room in Newman House, the important thing being that it was free, and when that was not available we relocated to Muckross College secondary school, another free venue in Donnybrook, Dublin 4. Sister Benvenuta MacCurtain, a Dominican nun who lectured at UCD, had a soft spot for Shea and made it available to us. It wasn't long before Sister Benvenuta was providing us with the props for the show – candle, book and bell – the means by which Doctor John Faustus summoned himself to heaven or to hell.

We rehearsed the play through the end days of 1970 and the opening days of 1971. Indeed, to demonstrate our seriousness to the world, we rehearsed on Christmas Day, outdoors, by the hotel on Claremont Beach at Howth. It took my mind off Trinity and my unhappiness there. I slept through the days and rehearsed through the nights. Neil Jordan had joined us, and with our shared interest in music we became good friends. We played the wandering minstrels in the show, Valdes and Cornelius. Neil composed original music for the mandolin. We put a melody to Marlowe's verse and sang it. In between rehearsals, we taught each other some Buddy Holly and some Everly Brothers' tunes. He introduced me to jazz and Spanish classical and I returned the favour by letting him in on the magic of Oscar Brown Junior and Captain Beefheart.

We opened the show in the Oriel Hall. Vinnie McCabe, as before, played John Faustus. Timmy Dunne, who lived near Vinnie on the North Strand, made his Slot début as Mephistopheles. The production contained music by The Pink Floyd, The Doors, Johann Sebastian Bach, Beethoven, Jethro Tull and Neil Jordan. Gabriel Fallon, who was a contemporary of Sean O'Casey's and had written a number of books about their friendship, came to see the show. The following Saturday, he wrote an extensive account of his *Faustus* experience in the *Evening Press* newspaper – it had little of the style of a review and more the feel of an exultation – and we ended up turning people away from the Oriel Hall. We transferred to the school hall in Muckross, thanks to Benvenuta, and played for three nights there.

We took the show on the festival circuit. Our first port of call was Carnew in south Wicklow. We were all very nervous. Vinnie, in particular, with so many lines and so much responsibility, was feeling the pressure. The first two rows of the auditorium were filled with schoolchildren. At the moment when Faustus sees Helen of Troy – *was this the face that launched a thousand ships and burned the topless towers of Ilium, come Helen make me immortal with a kiss* – the schoolchildren took it as their cue to open, en masse, their packets of Tayto crips. Vinnie took a pregnant pause and continued – *her lips suck forth my soul, see where it flies* – and he followed the journey of his soul out across the heads of the audience. But the next line was not one of Marlowe's – *I cannot continue with this fucking noise! Do you hear me? I cannot fucking continue, someone please get them to stop!* – and Vinnie walked off the stage before the curtain came in and we took an early interval.

It turned into a major diplomatic incident. The Parish Priest demanded that the adjudicator, Louis Lentin, extract a public apology from the actor for his outburst.

'We've never heard language the like of it in Carnew,' the PP repeated over and over again. 'Language like that in front of innocent children, it's not acceptable.' Mention was made of the Tayto crisps and everyone agreed that the noise of the crisp bags was distracting but the language of the actor was an affront, and an apology was the least that was expected. A group of parents were gathered around the PP and we were gathered around Vinnie and there was lots of shuffle diplomacy and Vinnie agreed to apologise on condition that no more crisp bags would be sold or opened during the performance.

So, the second act opened with the words 'I'm sorry' (beautifully underplayed by Vinnie) followed by a round of applause and then Helen of Troy, for the second time that evening, made John Faustus lose his immortal soul. The following day, Vinnie's outburst made the front page of the *Irish Press* newspaper. A local journalist, there to review the show for the south Wicklow Democrat or some such, filed the story to Dublin. Slot Players had arrived on the amateur drama scene. Our next stop was Killarney, where John B. Keane travelled from his home in Listowel to see this Elizabethan version of the Bull McCabe.

'You'll win the Esso Trophy,' he said to us in the bar after the show. 'Mark my words, you'll win it.'

The Esso Trophy was the holy grail of amateur drama. Athlone was the Mecca all pilgrims hoped to visit. Every year, groups selected plays that would propel them to immortality. Or obscurity. The competition was intense and vicious. Inter-group rivalry had competitors attend opposition shows and cough their way through them. Or leave the auditorium at inopportune moments. Or open bags of crisps. Our publicity in Carnew made us hate figures, especially to the rural groups, always keen to put one over on their 'sophisticated metropolitan cousins.'

We were well received in Kerry, one of the few counties in Ireland with a genuine love for the Dubs. That love, of course, is based on the fact that in the matter of Gaelic football they are our masters and enjoy toying with us while they play us off the park. Killarney gave us a good reception and we knew we were in with a chance after John B.'s comments. Our final outing was to New Ross in Wexford, and we knew that we had to do well there if we were to make it to Athlone.

The adjudicator was Alan Simpson, famous for his work in the Pike Theatre, a tiny space in Herbert Lane, off Baggot Street. With his wife Carolyn Swift, he had produced the world premiere of Brendan Behan's *The Quare Fellow*, and the first English language production of *Waiting for Godot*. They'd also caused a huge controversy when they staged Tennessee Williams' *The Rose Tattoo*, during which one of the actors seemingly produced a condom on-stage, an article prohibited for sale or display in the Ireland of 1957. Simpson was arrested, but after a huge public outcry and a farcical court appearance, the case against him was dropped.

I knew of him by reputation and, meeting him in the flesh, he did not disappoint. For a start, he had long hair. He was thinning on top but made up for it on the sides, just like me, hair down to the shoulder. He wore a white suit with a blue stripe, but the stripes were far apart. Around his neck he had a cravat. He looked like the sort of person I'd like to grow up to be. I didn't yet have his courage, however. He was bohemian, eccentric and oblivious to what the world thought of him. He also smoked Gauloises cigarettes, one after the other, and drank gin mixed with tonic, a large bottle of which he carried in his pocket.

The theatre in New Ross was half full on the Wednesday evening we played there. During the sequence featuring the Seven Deadly Sins, I crawled up Vinnie's body and kissed him on the forehead, to help him take his pleasure. There were gasps from the audience and then the gasps turned into something else, outrage mixed with laughter. I looked up. To my right I saw one of our actresses, Rita McCabe (a sister of our leading man), with her breasts exposed. In the exertions of the dance for Faustus and to the strains of the Pink Floyd, Rita's mutton cloth had split down the middle and revealed all. What could she do but carry on to the end of the sequence until the lights came down and she made her exit.

The vibes at half time were good. Word of mouth spread around the town. By the opening of the second act, the theatre was full. They seemed to enjoy the show, even if there was no more nudity on offer. Alan Simpson gave us an adjudication that praised our use of contemporary music and movement. He singled Vinnie out for his performance and Shea for his direction. Neil and I got a mention for our mandolin playing and he awarded Slot Players first place in New Ross. Afterwards, we retired to the local hotel for a private adjudication that turned into an all-night party. Our coach driver got drunk and fell asleep. We all stayed for breakfast to sober up before heading back to Dublin, where I made a ten o'clock lecture for the first time in six months.

A win in Killarney, a second in Carnew and a win in New Ross paved our passage to the all-Ireland finals in Athlone. At Alan Simpson's invitation, we attended a production of *She Stoops to Conquer* that he'd directed for the Abbey Theatre. It had a great scene where everything on the stage went dark, apart from an ultraviolet light. Some of the actors had reflective strips on their costumes and the ultraviolet picked these up and made them look like walking skeletons. It was an astounding effect and Shea decided that we must have it in our production for Athlone. So we went back to Marlowe and found a scene where Faustus visits the Pope in Rome and, at a dinner party, turns him into a donkey. The Abbey loaned us the ultraviolet lights and we hired a pantomime ass from Bourke's Costumiers in Dame Street. I played the front and Neil played the rear. The rest of the cast were the skeletons. We introduced carnival music that gave the scene the feel of a circus.

Shea loved the donkey. For him, it signified decadence, an echo of Berlin in the thirties. So the donkey found himself in lots of scenes. It meant that Neil and I were not available to play Valdes and Cornelius as before, so Shea split the roles. Sometimes we were Valdes and Cornelius, sometimes we were not. Fired up by that, he recast the whole play. Then he thought it would be great if Mephistopheles could transmogrify into the donkey. So the animal became the devil's messenger and got some of the Mephistopheles lines. We brought our new production to Athlone, and five minutes before curtain up the ultraviolet lights blew. They had no replacements in house. We had to go on and play it in full light. It lost its magic and I'm sure it must have looked odd from out front. And the recasting felt strange. It wasn't the same show. I missed playing the Old Man, one of my favourite characters in the show. I missed the scenes with Neil. I missed kissing Vinnie's forehead in the Seven Deadly Sins because now that I was playing Sloth, I'd been redirected to fall asleep on his leg.

Despite the technical cock-up, Shea thought it was a better show. So did Vinnie, interestingly. I wasn't as sure. 'If it's not broken, don't fix it' has always appealed to me as a sound working principle. Shea, on the other hand, always loved anarchy. He loved creating chaos and then being the one to fix it. It can be brilliant but it is dangerous and predicated entirely on his judgement. I am more of a collaborator. I like the group dynamic, creating a team and setting out a vision that everyone can take possession of. In Greek terms, I'm more of an Apollo and Shea more of a Dionysus. Good when the two philosophies fuse, disaster when they don't.

The Athlone results were to be announced on the final Saturday night of the festival. Sheila O'Donoghue threw a May Day party in her house in Clontarf to coincide with it. All of Slot Players gathered in her Hollybrook Road home, apart from Billy Kelly. He went to Athlone to represent us. There was a lot of energy around, which made the party boisterous. It was a rap, essentially, and there was a lot of drinking going on. Her father seemed an affable man but nervous of this crowd who'd taken over his house. I didn't know it at the time, but this was the first occasion he had allowed a party of any description to take place in his home. Apart from Sheila, he had six sons, aged from nineteen down to twelve, and he must have been concerned that things could get out of hand. They did. At eleven o'clock the call came from Billy Kelly. The place fell silent. We hadn't won the Esso Trophy. Hadn't finished in the first three. In fact, we'd come last. Last of twelve. All our hopes then were on Vinnie for best actor, or Timmy Dunne for best support. There wasn't an acting award in it, we didn't even get a mention. Apart from the donkey, nothing. A passing reference to the donkey and nothing else. Beaten into last place and the top award to a group who'd finished second to us in Killarney. Ignominy.

'You'll win the Esso Trophy.'

John B.'s words echoed in my brain. And as always, Shea put a positive spin on it.

'Isn't it better to finish last than to finish second?'

Sheila put her arm on my shoulder and squeezed it.

'Hard luck. Your time will come, I know it will.'

It was different for Sheila. She operated lights and made the interval coffee and sold programmes. I was in it, emotionally connected to the play, part of its heartbeat. I felt we'd let Marlowe down.

'Would you like to dance?' Sheila said.

I laughed at her.

'Come on, I'd like to dance with you.'

I remembered back to New Year's Eve '68, when I was too small. I was still too small.

'I don't need you to take pity on me, honestly.'

'It's just a dance, come on.'

So we had a dance and I didn't care about the height difference because I was disappointed we'd come last in Athlone. Shea broke into ballitarse and I joined him in it. Then he pulled his trousers down and mooned at the room. Everyone went wild. Sheila's father came in and asked us to stop the music. Someone pulled the plug and the record died a slow death. So did the party. People got their coats and started to leave. I could hear Sheila and her father in the kitchen as I left.

'They're a crowd of homosexuals, that's all they are.'

'They're not homosexuals, they're my friends and they're normal people.'

'Taking your trousers down is not normal.'

'It was just a bit of fun, that's all.'

'I don't think it's one bit funny.'

* * *

Four days after the party, I got a call from Sheila asking me to help her with an essay. She was in her final year at Froebel Teacher Training College and had taken John Millington Synge as the subject of her thesis in English literature. I was flattered to be asked and agreed to meet her, even though I had no in-depth knowledge of Synge. I had a history essay to submit for Trinity but I gladly abandoned it and threw myself into reading *Playboy*. I was blown away by the play. Christy Mahon was a creation of pure genius. I loved the pace at which the story unfolded and how, layer by layer, the true nature of the Irish character was laid bare before us in the play.

Armed with a plethora of ideas and bags of theory, I headed out to Hollybrook Road. I read what she'd written and began to feed some of my own ideas to her. I couldn't believe she was sitting there not taking notes. I asked her did she want me to put something down on paper for her. She thought that was a great idea. I got up to go and she asked me to show her some chords on the guitar. She ran down the kitchen stairs and came back with her brother's guitar.

She sat on a chair with the guitar across her lap. I put her fingers in the shape of the D chord. I took her right hand and led it across the strings. Her hair was only a few inches from my chin. I could see down along her nose to her lips. I started to sing Bob Dylan. Bob Dylan in the key of D. *She's Got Everything She Needs.* I became conscious of my hand on her shoulder. I pulled it away and couldn't get it back.

I went away and wrote reams of material on *The Playboy of the Western World.* I brought it back to her the following week. She didn't want to read it. I asked her if she wanted a guitar lesson. She declined that, too. There was something the matter but I didn't know what it was.

'Do you want me to go?' I asked her.

'No, I want you to stay.'

'Are you upset things didn't work out with Billy Kelly?'

She shook her head and I thought she was going to cry.

'Maybe if you gave him a bit more time he'd get over his shyness,' I said.

'I don't care about Billy. This is not about Billy.'

For a split second I thought she was coming on to me. I looked away. I was still half an inch short of five foot six. That half an inch could make all the difference, I thought. I looked back at her.

'This is about you,' she said.

'What about me?'

'I fancy you.'

'What about Billy Kelly?'

'I don't fancy Billy Kelly.'

I took a step towards her. My heart was racing. I leaned in and kissed her on the lips. It didn't stop. It just went on and on. Sheila unleashed a passion in me I didn't know was there. All of the sexual frustration and confusion of my teens found release and understanding through her. We consummated our relationship that night. From then on, we were never apart. We made love whenever we could. We never talked or thought about protection. I felt that she had saved my life and I wanted to tell her and the only way I found to do that was through poetry:

Shall you and I equally share the poisoned cup?
Shall we commit the sin of Naoise and Deirdre
Or is it a sin to love each other and destroy?
Shall we say goodbye and leave our married minds
To linger here and there.
Return in old age perhaps
Alone maybe, and say we walked
The path of life triumphantly?
Could we force the marriage of our bodies
And call it a common love affair,
A young man's anxiety and a mother's care!
Or would it make new worlds for us to use
And purge our souls of fear;
Turn our mating into months and years
Till we have made grey hairs
And say triumphantly we have walked the path of life.

* * *

Sheila invited me to tea and I formally met her six brothers and her parents. I'd seen them at the party but it was so different to sit down at a table and eat fried eggs, watched by them, trying not to spill the yolk on my shirt. Her family were six boys and a girl, the same as us, only we were now five since Frankie's passing. Frankie was Sheila's dad, too, and it was funny for me to hear her mother Eileen call him by his name at every opportunity.

'Frankie, put on another sausage there for our visitor. Would you like another sausage, Peter?'

'Frankie, cut more bread for the table and would you sit down for your own tea too when you're ready.'

My da never cooked. Never cut bread. Never poured out tea. That was ma's domain. The O'Donoghues were different, more middle class. Frankie was a bookmaker, and I could tell by the furniture and the baby grand piano that they had money. I knew da would love to meet him for inside information on the horses. In between sausages and fried egg, I dropped as many hints as I could.

I must have made an impression, a few weeks later, because Frankie asked me to meet him on my own. We arranged it for Sheries Restaurant, opposite Wynne's hotel in Middle Abbey Street. Frankie was there when I arrived. There were three cigarette butts in the ashtray. He seemed nervous. He offered me a cigarette and I took one, even though it didn't have a filter on it.

'They're an awful bloody price the fags. I should give them up but I can't.'

I agreed with him.

'Sheila is very high maintenance, do you know that?'

It was a question, but it wasn't inviting an answer.

'You're only a student. You have your degree to think about. You need to be a bit selfish, do you understand me?'

'I love your daughter. I love Sheila, just like you do.'

'Love never put a meal on the table.'

She was his only daughter and his eldest child. He wanted the best for her, I understood that.

'There's a lad up the road, he's a teacher. I think they'd make a good match.'

I didn't know him. I'd heard Sheila talk about him, but not as a boyfriend. They'd played together as kids. The O'Donoghues and the Teelings. As well as the Farrells and the Collinses. The up-the-road gang and the down-the-road gang, and Sheila in the middle of it all like the tomboy she was.

'I'm not giving up on Sheila. Not unless she gives up on me first.'

He was making me fight for her. I was from the docks and the other boy was from Clontarf. I wasn't about to let a middle-class teacher get one over on me. I had dreams and Sheila made me feel I could realise them. She made me feel loved.

It turned out that Frankie's biggest problem was not my address but my poetry. He'd found one I'd written for her and was disgusted by it. I wrote it for Sheila's twenty-first birthday, July 19th, July:

I am a man again
You a Queen are
I a King am.
We are complements.
You said so yourself,
When, one night you held me
Deftly in your grasp
And sweet pepette and no pepette
Pettered on your lips
That gave me life.
Your lips have melted

The glassy ice-front
That glazed before me
And you have found me
And I, I.
Your eyes have flushed
Tears from eyes that were cold as poles
And we have sucked water
From eye and eye,
But softer than either eye
Your breasts
Pillowing an arm that had lost all touch
But from your touch
Powdered blood has fused
And an animal lust
Like torrents rushes through my veins.
Animal instincts in me
Surge to a climax.
Your lips
Your lips that gave me life.

* * *

Sheila's parents asked her to end the relationship, but she refused and left home in defiance. I turned up to help her move her things. Her mother came to the door and slapped me across the face, full force. I was shaken but it made me even more determined to protect Sheila and make things work between us. Sheila moved in with married friends of ours in Whitehall and I spent a lot of time there with her. My parents weren't too happy with developments and felt that the relationship was interfering with my studies at Trinity. They were right, but they didn't know that

I had decided to abandon my degree course. I went to see my tutor and told him I was sick of being discriminated against. From now on it was Sheila and me against the world. That night, we went for a drink in O'Neill's pub on Pearse Street at the back of Trinity and something happened that almost ended the relationship.

I had a severe panic attack, only I didn't understand at the time what it was. It started after I switched from Guinness to Jameson whiskey. I began to have weird thoughts. A voice was telling me that I had to destroy the relationship. If I didn't kill it, it would kill me. I loved Sheila, I knew that, I was certain of that, but I had loved Frankie too, and look what had happened to him. When I loved something, it died. It was a punishment from God and the only way to reverse it was to kill first. Destroy love and walk away. I had to get away from her, she was going to smother me, I had to be on my own.

We came out of the pub and walked towards the number three bus stop. I took all the money I had in my pocket and held it out to her.

'Take this, I'm going home to my parents' house,' I said.

'What are you talking about, Peter?'

'I can't be with you any more, I have to be on my own.'

'I thought you loved me, I thought we loved each other.'

'I don't love you any more. It's over.'

I threw the money on the ground and started to run. All the way down Pearse Street and into Tara Street. Past the swimming baths where I'd gone as a kid, onto Butt Bridge and over the river towards Liberty Hall. The sound of the Liffey caught my attention. If only I had the courage to slip into it, all these thoughts in my head would disappear. I could hear it calling me.

'Peter, Peter…'

It was Sheila, standing two feet from me, and she was crying. 'Don't run away, please don't run away.'

I was glad she'd caught up with me and still I tried to push her away. All she wanted to do was put her arms around me. In the end, I gave in and we stood on the bridge until it was too cold to stand there any longer. The last bus was gone and I had thrown all our money away. We ended up walking home, wrapped around each other. I had suffered my first major panic attack, but I made no connection between that and my drinking. The truth is that I didn't want to. It would take many more years and a lot more heartache before I came to any understanding about that.

* * *

I brought Sheila's urine sample to the Rotunda Hospital and I asked her to marry me while we were waiting for the result. The pregnancy test was positive and that decided things. We were delighted. We wanted to live together and this provided the perfect excuse. I needed to get out of Seville Place. It was hard living there with the lodgers. Always people coming and going, making it feel more like a bus depot than a home. I wanted my own place, my own family and Sheila had come into my life to make it possible. We were married on Oscar Wilde's birthday, October 16th – in truth, it was the only Saturday the Grand Hotel in Malahide was available – and we had a great party for our family and friends. I was nineteen, going on twenty, and Sheila had just turned twenty-one.

We set up home in a caravan – or a mobile home, to give it its posh name – situated with twelve others in the back garden of a council house in Crumlin. We were number 12, or site 12 to be official, the second caravan in from the road. Both sets of parents were horrified, of course. Frankie was so tall his head hit off the ceiling, and Da was convinced the caravan was lopsided, but we loved having our own space and making our own rules, free from interference. The only negative was having to acclimatise to living on the south side of the city, hardened northsiders that we were. Sheila had found a job in Basin Lane School, where her grandmother had taught in the turbulent years of 1913-1916. Indeed, her class of 1971, 6th class girls, provided the choir at our wedding in St Anthony's Church, Clontarf.

I left Trinity and enrolled in UCD, Arts, where I lost my scholarship because I was repeating first year. That meant I had to come up with the college fees, in addition to all the other expenses (books, travel, meals) that went with being a full-time student. There is always a price to be paid for taking a stand, and as O'Casey put it in *Juno and the Paycock*, 'You can't eat a principle, now can you?' As well as college, there was the impending birth of our first child. I needed a job, and with da's help I secured one as a bus conductor in CIE. It was full time, of course, and meant that my attendance at lectures was erratic, to say the least. Whenever possible, I worked the first shift on the Blessington route (number 65) because that meant an early finish, 11.15, from a 6.00 a.m. start. I could almost squeeze in a full college day after that. It was some transformation from my Trinity days when ma had to throw cold water at me to get me out of bed!

I loved working on the buses – the camaraderie and the craic were ninety – and I would have sacrificed college for it, only Sheila was adamant that I finish my degree. I knew that we would struggle to make ends meet if I quit my job.

'I didn't marry you for your money, I married you for your mind,' Sheila said.

I liked having money in my pocket. It's always been one of those things that put an extra inch on my height, the feeling that I could pay my way, that I was in hock to no one. Eventually, an incident in work precipitated my decision to quit. There was a practice among bus conductors called 'making the rent.' Like many things to do with the job, it goes back to the days of the trams, when workers had no union. It took Jim Larkin standing up to William Martin Murphy to change that, of course. Conductors at the time were so badly paid that a practice developed whereby passengers, rather than paying their fare and receiving a ticket, would wait until they were getting off and then drop the fare, or a portion of it, into the conductor's bag for him to pocket for himself.

I was working on the Walkinstown bus, the number 55. Like all routes, it was patrolled by inspectors. As a kid, I'd always assumed that inspectors were there to make sure that passengers had paid their fare. However, their real focus was to ensure that the conductors were not defrauding the company, either by not issuing tickets or interfering with the ticket machine. The principal inspector on the Walkinstown route was Tom Smith, better known as Batman, because he wore a cloak. He had a habit of running from one bus to another, causing his cloak to billow up behind him like the character in the comic strip. On the day in question, I was standing at the back of the bus. We were two stops from the terminus. I didn't see Tom Smith approach. The passengers were getting off the bus. A man dropped money in my bag and waved away the ticket. The woman behind him did the same thing. The next thing, I saw Tom Smith staring up at me. He hopped up onto the platform and stood beside me, wearing a big grin.

'Do you know who I am?' he asked.

'Yeah,' I said, 'you're Batman and I'm robbin'.'

Tom Smith was despised among the men. He had been a conductor himself but now used all his inside knowledge on behalf of the management. He was known as a union basher. He asked me for my machine and suspended me on the spot. I was to take three days off work. I went to see Tom Darby of the National Busmen's Union. My only concerns were that, firstly, my father would find out, and secondly that my situation would in any way affect him. Tom Darby reassured me that I had nothing to worry about. He had enough on Batman to hang him three times over. My story was going nowhere. He was confident he could fight my three-day suspension and get it overturned, with pay.

'I can shut down Ringsend garage with a click of my fingers and Batman and the CIE management know that.'

We went for a drink in the union club together. Tom Darby had a bit of Jim Larkin in him, and a bit of James Connolly too. He had a bright red baby face that concealed a burning resentment at officialdom. He was made for confrontation. He loved a good fight. I didn't want the men coming out on my behalf; that was the last thing I wanted. I opened up to Darby and told him what my real situation was – that I was in first year in UCD.

'You get back to university, do you hear me? We need fellows like you with degrees. That's my one big regret in life: that I didn't get an education.'

* * *

I left the job after six months on Friday, January 28ᵗʰ, 1972. The following Sunday, Sheila and I were having a drink with Shea and Fran in Byrne's pub on the North Wall – we were supposed to be at six o'clock mass in Laurence O'Toole's church, but hadn't yet mustered the courage to tell our parents that we didn't go any more – when the television news came on with the unforgettable images of what had happened in Derry a few hours earlier. It was a defining moment; an afternoon when the troubles lost their innocence and the words Bloody Sunday came into our vocabulary and shaped our thinking and our emotions. There was universal outrage in nationalist Ireland. After Bloody Sunday, we were all Catholics.

UCD was rife with talk of revolution. Shea was supposed to be auditioning for the dramsoc show he was directing that spring. I couldn't really get involved, not with all the catching up I had to do for the exams. The baby was due in May. I had to knuckle down and stay focused. I went to my first lecture: Professor Jim O'Malley on John Osborne, Harold Pinter and the angry generation of British dramatists. A student member of the Sinn Féin cumann stood up and led a walkout over Bloody Sunday. I met Shea with Neil Jordan on the concourse in front of the library. He'd abandoned auditions. There was a protest march to the British Embassy in Merrion Square. Sheila joined me straight from school and we went together. The anger in the crowd was palpable. It was the first time I realised that a crowd has a mind, and when that mind fixes on something it is an unstoppable force. We weren't going home until our voice had been heard. We would have taken that Georgian building apart brick by brick, but some petrol bombs did the work and we burned it to the ground. Our collective anger had left it in ashes.

Shea decided to do a modern version of *Oedipus Rex*. It felt like the Greek myth offered possibilities to parallel a corrupt ancient civilisation with a corrupt modern one. Northern Ireland, the six-county state, was the embodiment of failure.

The political and social malaise endemic there was akin to the blighted landscape threatening Greece at the opening of *Oedipus Rex*. The city of Thebes and its inhabitants are facing destruction because the crops won't grow. It is a punishment meted out by the gods because they are unhappy. There is something rotten at the heart of society and only a purge will appease the gods and restore peace.

For Thebes read Belfast and for repression look no further than internment without trial, introduced to quell political opposition but ending in the deaths of innocent civilians, most notably in Derry on that January Sunday. For Oedipus read Brian Faulkner, the diminutive Prime Minister of a society built on a crude sectarian head-count. In order to preserve the status quo, the truth about the past must never be revealed. Such repression, however, is the cornerstone on which empires crumble: Belfast, Thebes, Rome and Alexandria.

I loved the idea for the show and I was flattered that he wanted me to play Oedipus.

'It has to be someone small, someone who can represent Faulkner.'

I had to say no. Fatherhood loomed. Sheila was five months pregnant.

'I don't know that I have anyone else who can play it.'

'What about Neil?'

'I think he's more of a Tiresias than an Oedipus. Look, think about it.'

I tried not to. I tried to suppress it. I was sitting in lecture theatres hearing stories about Beowulf and thinking about Brian Faulkner and how I might crack that waspish accent of his. I was thinking of his blond hair and the way he held his head, with his nose in the air, always looking down. I was thinking about Sheila and how she might react if I took it on. That night, over dinner in the caravan, I slipped it into the conversation.

'Are you looking for my permission?'

'Yeah, sort of, I suppose.'

'I'm not going to stand in your way.'

'What about the baby?'

'What about the baby? You're not the one who's having it.'

'What if I'm on-stage some night and you go into labour and I can't make it to the hospital with you.'

'That won't happen.'

'How can you be so sure?'

'You promised me you were going to be there so you're going to be there. Play or no play, you're going to be at the birth.'

(Fathers were not allowed at the births of their children in 1972. I was going to be there because Sheila had lied to her consultant Mr Jim Feeney, who was a brother of John Feeney, one of the UCD radicals. She told him I was a student, and when he asked if that was a medical student Sheila said yes with a teacher's authority. The consultant seemed happy and opined that I could help with the delivery. That was the deal and there was no turning back.)

Oedipus Rex is a gigantic scream against incest and ends in a bloodbath. There were many versions floating around ancient Greece and the Sophocles text is regarded as the best of them. There are Irish versions of the story too, and *Playboy of the Western World* is one such. In the murder scene – the Sophocles version doesn't show it but reports it only – Oedipus fells his father Laius and his three minders with a wooden pole. In our version we staged the murder. As Laius lay on the ground I went over to inspect the body. I crouched down beside him and reached my hand out. As I did, blood oozed out from Laius's head and made a pool around him on the floor. One of his minders nearby raised a white handkerchief in the air. He tried to get to his feet, and as he did I went over and bludgeoned him to death.

We had a heated discussion in rehearsal about what to do with the bodies. The normal convention is that you wait for a blackout and then the actors get up and leave, as unobtrusively as they can. Shea felt that it was a cop-out. I agreed with him. If we were referencing Bloody Sunday, then we had to remove them in a different way. I felt that as Oedipus/Faulkner, it was up to me to take responsibility for the deaths. So, one by one, I got each of the four bodies into a standing position and hoisted them onto my shoulder. I carried them to a platform and threw them onto it, like meat carcasses. At that point, Neil entered the action as Tiresias, sniffing all about him, smelling death. He was brilliantly eccentric, owing not a little to the character from the T.S. Eliot poem *The Waste Land*:

> *I who sat by Thebes below the wall*
> *And walked among the lowest of the dead*

He was a cross between Eliot's 'an old man with wrinkled breasts' and Beckett's Hamm from *Endgame*. Neil was also a key member of the rock band that played throughout the show, alternating easily between guitar and saxophone. The finale was my favourite sequence when, having torn my eyes out on discovering the truth of what I had done – killed my father and married my mother – I got to sing The Doors song, *The End*. Jim Morrison's apocalyptic anthem is, of course, a version of the Oedipus story, both political and personal. In it, Morrison marries his rage to what his country is doing in Vietnam at the disgust he feels towards his father who, as a military man, supported what America did in south-east Asia.

The killer awoke before dawn, he put his boots on
He took a face from the ancient gallery
And he walked on down the hall
He went into the room where his sister lived, and...then he
Paid a visit to his brother, and then he
He walked on down the hall, and
And he came to a door...and he looked inside
Father, yes son, I want to kill you
Mother...I want to...WAAAAAA

The show went well in Newman House and we entered it in the inter-university drama competition to be held in Galway. However, there was no venue in the city that could house the show. The problem was the set. In Dublin, we erected scaffolding around the sides of Newman House to represent the walls of Thebes. The audience were seated on the scaffolding, and we played the drama courtyard style on the floor beneath them. In order to enhance the atmosphere of danger and repression, the ushers who guided the audience to their places carried rifles. Throughout the performance, they patrolled the walls, like wardens in a high-security gaol.

The organisers in Galway suggested an old hangar in a field in Salthill. A generator was brought in to give us power. That Saturday afternoon, as the audience were being shown to their seats, a row broke out when the adjudicators for the event, John Arden and Margaretta D'Arcy, took exception to having rifles pointed in their faces. They refused to take their seats. Shea and a few of the cast, including Desmond Hogan (the novelist) and Frank Macken (who played Creon), went out to negotiate with them. The rest of us backstage – a posh word to describe where we were – were getting ready to go on. In the end, it was decided that we would perform but not as part of the festival. In solidarity with the nationalist people of Northern Ireland, all prize-giving was abandoned. We had to declare a truce and hand over our arms – the first act of decommissioning in Irish theatre history.

The Saturday of the following week, May 6th, was FA Cup final day. It was a big event in the sporting calendar, a competition full of history, legend and romance. Before I'd fallen in love with the theatre, my dream was to play for Manchester United alongside Charlton, Kidd, Best and Law. The 1972 showpiece was down to Arsenal and Leeds United, with John Giles of Ormond Square in Dublin playing for Leeds. I was in Sheila's parents' house watching the game because we had no television in the mobile home. There was a definite thaw in the hostility towards me, and because Sheila had been open with her mother about her pregnancy, the atmosphere between them had improved greatly too. Into the second half and with no score, a phone call came from Shea. He was in the student bar on the Belfield campus. He'd hitched out to college that lunchtime because there was some problem with the buses. An Irish American in a big Mercedes had picked him up on O'Connell Bridge; his name was George Murphy and he had something to do with the Catholic Church. It appeared that he'd loaned the credit union some money when it was trying to get off the ground here. Shea mentioned Saint Laurence O'Toole's and the Oriel Hall, which we shared with the old folks and the credit union. He told Murphy about his interest in the theatre and the larger than life American seemed interested in taking that discussion further. Shea was meeting him later in his hotel, the Burlington, and he wanted me to come and join them. At that point, Alan Clarke scored a goal for Leeds and the student bar in UCD exploded, as did Hollybrook Road, Clontarf, with Sheila's younger brothers Peter and Paul running up to the hall to fill me in on what had happened at Wembley.

I never made it to the Burlington. Sheila thought she felt a movement. It turned out to be a false alarm, brought on by the excitement of the Cup Final. I had an English exam on Monday, May 8th, my mother's fiftieth birthday. The exam went well; a question on O'Casey came up, which suited me greatly. Sheila was supposed to go in to the Coombe Hospital to be induced on the Wednesday but she declared herself unavailable because it was Shea and Fran's wedding day. We had a wonderful day and a wonderful party. The entire cast of *Oedipus Rex* showed up and we played some songs and enacted scenes from the show.

As Mr Feeney was unavailable on the Thursday, we checked into the Coombe on the Friday morning. They broke Sheila's waters and we waited for labour, which never came. I went out for a walk to clear my head. I walked along the canal to Harold's Cross and on to Ranelagh. When I came back, they had her on a drip. Things started to move and by three o'clock they were talking about sending for Mr Feeney. The drama of it was starting to get to me. I felt like I had no control. This was much more demanding than playing Oedipus. Sheila was whisked away to the labour ward and I was sent to an ante-room to await further instructions. Mr Feeney came in, and I made small talk with him while he washed his hands at the sink. A nurse held out the gown for me to put on and I stupidly turned my back to her as if I was putting on a coat. The nurse coughed and I turned around. Luckily for me, Mr Feeney didn't see it.

'You're some medical student,' the nurse whispered at me as I put my arms through the gown.

I held Sheila's hand. My pride in her was just bursting from me. Our son was born at 9.45p.m. on the evening of Friday, May 12th, 1972. We called him Rossa because we wanted an Irish name. We gave him the second name of Francis, which acknowledged Sheila's dad and my dead brother. We brought our baby back to the mobile home with great intentions to be nothing less than perfect parents.

5

Three weeks into parenthood and the two of us were like zombies. We kept a diary with the same entry repeated page after page:

Put baby down. Cried after ten minutes. Tried soother, wouldn't take it. Seems to be hungry. Took him up and tried him for wind. Could he have colic? Must check Doctor Spock. Must get some sleep first. Checked his nappy and he was dirty. No wonder he didn't sleep.

Sheila persisted with the breast, and I knew things were coming good when we stopped writing in the diary. The truth is that we were getting some sleep. Apart from sleep, our biggest problem was lack of money. Paid maternity leave was still some time into the future, and Sheila, in order to mind Rossa, had to employ a substitute teacher and pay her. I was looking to the building sites for a summer job. I still hadn't paid my first year college fees to UCD. Sheila wanted me to stay at home and help her, but I had no option but to carry on looking for work. One of our fellow residents on the mobile home site,

Harry Armstrong, worked for Semperit Tyres in Ballyfermot and, at his suggestion, I went over to the factory to put my name down. On my return, Shea and Fran were in the mobile home with the startling news that George Murphy was bringing a group of us to America to.

It was fairytale stuff. He was bringing twelve members of the group to Chicago to perform plays. We would be staying on a farm he owned outside the city. We would have cars and drivers and fridges full of food. We would be performing in universities and theatres in Indiana and Illinois. We would be returning to Ireland with pockets full of dollars, and we didn't know in advance how much, but it would be lots. It seemed churlish to ask for specifics when he was laying out so much to bring us there. We weren't hanging around Ireland to stare the gift horse in the mouth, we were on our way. We lost no time in putting Rossa on our passport and organising visas through USIT, the travel arm of the students' union. The flight tickets duly arrived and I brought mine out to the bank in UCD, where I secured a loan (to tide us over) from a suitably impressed bank manager.

The travelling party consisted of five couples – Shea and Fran; Neil Jordan and Vivienne Sheils; Vinnie McCabe and Felicia Foley; Frank Macken and Cass Finn; Sheila and Peter and baby Rossa; and two single men: my younger brother John and Galway native Brendan Conroy. We rehearsed *The Shadow of a Gunman* and *Waiting for Godot* before we left for America in the first week in July. Our plane left Dublin late and we missed our connecting flight to Chicago from New York. Fortunately, Vivienne had an aunt living near JFK so that we had somewhere to stay with the baby. The rest weren't so lucky. We arrived in Chicago the next day where it was one hundred and five degrees. We were picked up in cars that had no air-conditioning. We fanned Rossa all the way to our country residence, fearful that he would die from the heat, and sat him in a bath of cool water when we eventually got there.

We had arrived on what was a working farm with fields of corn everywhere. There were chickens on the driveway and pigs in a pen. A large house dominated with a smaller cottage a hundred yards further up the driveway. It had a big, smiling yellow face painted on a side wall. That was to be for Sheila, myself and the baby. But it had no air-conditioning, so we opted for the big house and Vinnie and Felicia took the smiley house. There was a big, live oak tree between the two houses.

The following day, we went to a reception at George's private country estate. He also had a mansion in the suburb of Wilmette, but it was too warm to stay in the city. The country estate was the equivalent of an Irish castle with its own golf club attached. There were peacocks roaming everywhere. A group of his friends had assembled to meet us. George was on a lilo in the swimming pool. He was reading the IRA newspaper *An Phoblacht*. He got out of the pool and put on a robe, then he made a speech of welcome. As soon as he referred to Rossa, the place went hysterical with people wanting to touch a 'real Irish baby.' There was plenty of Irishness in America, but it was of a different order. Everyone at the party recommended us to O'Leary's restaurant and bar in the city, called after the owner of the cow that started the infamous Chicago fire of 1871. George thought it a wonderful suggestion, but he had to clear it with the 'war department' first.

The war department turned out to be his wife. He called her and they had a discussion about their dogs, and the need to leave all the doors in the house open for them so they were free to roam.

'Yes, I know how they feel if they're hemmed in, honey. I know they get upset. I won't lock the doors on them, promise.'

Then we piled into several cars and headed for O'Leary's. On arrival, he brought out the proprietor, a Japanese man named Tommy O'Leary who spoke fluent Gaelic.

'*Tá céad míle failte romhat isteach.*'

George Murphy broke his heart laughing at Tommy O'Leary's Japanese *blas*. Tommy shook us each individually by the hand.

'*Dia dhuit,*' I said when he got to me.

'*Dia is Muire dhuit,*' he replied, prompting George to break into his Santa Claus laugh once again.

* * *

We rehearsed *Shadow of a Gunman* intensively for four days. The tension in the group was starting to make itself felt. Sheila never considered herself an actress, but we needed her to play one of the parts in the play. I talked her into taking on Mrs Henderson, but she was not happy. The role is not a small one, and rehearsing it while trying to look after and breastfeed a six-week-old baby in temperatures of one hundred degrees was taking its toll.

A shooting incident involving members of the Black Panther Party twenty miles up the road made us nervous. The television reported it as a racist attack on a vulnerable farmer and his wife. The Panthers issued an immediate denial, but that did nothing to allay our fears. We were sitting ducks for any lunatics out there. They might even think we were related to George Murphy, the millionaire lawyer who'd given money to white Irish people. There were photographs of him in his army uniform dotted around the house – an officer, smiling at having helped

America win the Second World War. Someone suggested that, in the event of an unwanted intrusion, it might be prudent to hide the photos under the beds upstairs.

On the next day, Sheila withdrew from the play, and it took me two hours and all of my persuasive powers to make her change her mind. At one point Vinnie, who was directing, thought it was personal, but that wasn't so. It was just nerves, uncertainty and fear. I took Rossa off for a long walk in his pram, hoping that the break might help Sheila relax into things. It seemed to work, and that night, at our communal dinner, things appeared to be back to normal, especially when the television seemed to confirm the lack of Black Panther involvement in the shooting up the road.

We travelled to George Murphy's alma mater, Notre Dame College, home of the Fighting Irish, to première *Shadow of a Gunman*. George had made an endowment to the Theology Department in the college, and all of the department staff and students turned out to see the show. It seemed to be a free gig. That was the way he wanted it, perhaps. He was so wealthy he could afford not to charge. We got a standing ovation at the end, not realising at the time that American audiences nearly always get to their feet, out of respect. At the backstage gathering post-curtain, George was effusive and had only one note for us on the performance:

'Does the girl have to die at the end?'

He was talking about Minnie Powell, the heroine of the play, who dies in an off-stage explosion at the end of the drama.

'Can you work it next time so the girl gets away?'

It was such an outrageous suggestion that we all thought he was joking. But he wasn't. He wanted a happy ending. He wanted to subvert O'Casey with Hollywood. He wanted to change the course of twentieth century drama and he had no shame or guilt suggesting it. It was a Tommy O'Leary moment, terrifying and refreshing at the same time.

George hated our second offering, *Waiting for Godot*, but it had nothing to do with the dialogue or plot.

'Goddamn it, I paid for twelve of you to come and there's only five in the play.'

He did have a point, in fairness. And whatever about introducing extra characters into Beckett, the main thing for all of us was getting paid. Our artistic integrity was not in question. Rossa was sleeping in a drawer lined with towels, Sheila was feeding him in the wings before going on-stage and we wanted a monetary return for our sacrifice. All we had to do was figure out what Mr Murphy wanted. Could we do better than an amended Sean O'Casey for him? And the answer, of course, was yes. It was keening. Neil came up with the idea. He thought that crying over corpses in the old Irish tradition would go down a bomb, for didn't all Americans love an Irish wake?

Ochón, ochón, ochón go deo.

We started to work on a musical called *Dear Dirty Dublin*. The opening number was Finnegan's Wake. Neil on the mandolin and me on the guitar. We were back as strolling players and this time there would be no recasting: we were Valdes and Cornelius, aka Skin the Goat and Zozimus, and we would play them to the death. And beyond. We taught each other the Our Father and the Hail Mary in Irish, the more authentically to pray across a corpse.

'Sé do bheatha, a Mhuire, atá lán de grásta, tá an Tiarna leat....'

And there was crying and weeping and gnashing of teeth, it was an orgy of wailing, a plethora of tears and a barrel of songs,

The Night Before Larry was Stretched, Monto, The Ballad of Humpty Dumpty, *An Puc Ar Buille*, Poor Old Admiral Nelson; we made a harpsicord of the heart strings and a mush of the emotions, it was pure, unadulterated nostalgia.

George loved it. So did Tommy O' Leary. We got a free meal in his restaurant for our troubles. But there was no sign of any dollars, and we were getting to the point where we had to ask. If nobody was paying into our shows, how did George intend to pay us? Would it be cheque or cash? The fridge was running out of supplies and we were eyeing up a few chickens on the farm. We held a group meeting and discussed our situation. A delegation was selected to go and confront George – me, Shea, Neil and Frank – at his house in Wilmette. Our driver, Brooks, dropped us at the front door. We rang the bell. A servant opened it and called him. He came out with a glass of whiskey in his hand. As we stepped across the threshold, a voice boomed out over the intercom.

'Who is it, honey?'

It was the war department. George fixed us with a stare.

'It's the lynch mob,' he said, and turned to walk down the hall.

We followed him into a dining-room. A table and over a dozen chairs. Two large candelabras in the centre. He sat on one side, and we four on the other. He asked us what we wanted to drink, but we politely declined. I got straight to the point and asked about payment. He looked surprised.

'I brought you over here, I paid your fares.'

'We want to get paid,' I said, 'we're students.'

George couldn't see what the problem was. There was lots of work for students in America. What was stopping us? We were free to get work. He'd given us a house, rent free, and a freezer full of food. We had a car and a driver. We had it made.

107

We tried to steer the conversation back towards his responsibilities, and the fact that we'd provided a service for him and needed to be paid. We were trying to save our summer, we needed cash.

'If you're not happy you can always go back to Ireland.'

'Yes, but we don't have return tickets,' I said, 'and we don't have the money to buy them.'

'You want me to fork out for them, is that it? That why you came here tonight? To twist my arm?'

We were going to end up stuck in America. We had come on a one-way ticket and had no way back. There was disbelief in the room mixed with nausea. The intercom crackled into life and Mrs Murphy's voice addressed us.

'The dogs are in the hallway and they're crying, George. They need human contact.'

'That's all right, you go back to sleep, honey.'

'I can't sleep when I know the dogs are upset.'

George got up from his seat on the far side of the table and came around to open the door. As he approached it, the whining of the dogs intensified. I crossed my fingers that there were no German Shepherds in the pack – I had a terrible fear of them since I was bitten as a child on my aunt's farm outside Dundalk. The Irish Wolfhound that bounded into the room almost caused me to pee in my pants. Initially, I thought there were twenty dogs, but in fact it turned out there were seven, ranging from a pair of cavalier King Charles, a poodle, a black labrador, a golden retriever, a boxer and the wolfhound. They leapt all over us vying for attention and their entrance brought our meeting with George to a strange and inconclusive end.

On the way out to the car, Frank suggested that we put pressure on Murphy by contacting the Irish consul in Chicago.

I didn't know such an office existed. Frank understood the diplomatic world. He came from a political family. His father Matthew was Dublin city manager, the top post in local government. Frank knew the right moves to make. Brooks drove us back, and we had to suppress our conversation in his presence. We didn't want Murphy getting any advance notice of our plans.

We got back to the house bursting to let everyone know what had happened. The others were all on a high from a séance they had conducted in our absence. A Blackfoot Indian named Denumbas had spoken to them through a Ouija board. He had delivered a message specifically for Shea.

'Beware the magpie in the room right next to you.'

Everyone was busy trying to decipher the meaning of this cryptic message when Vinnie declared that he had controlled the whole thing.

'I was telling the glass what letters to go to,' he said.

'You were outside the circle,' Sheila said, 'you had nothing to do with it.'

'I did it with my mind. Mental telepathy.'

A fierce row broke out that ended up with people shouting and screaming at one another. Our American odyssey was over. And maybe it was all over, full stop. We took a vote. Of the twelve members of the group, only four wanted to stay on in America and look for work – Vinnie, Felicia, Frank and Cass. The rest of us wanted to cut our losses and run.

The following day, Vivienne drove Frank and Shea into Chicago in Brooks's car – she was the only one with a driver's licence. They got to see an official in the Irish Consulate who agreed to ring Murphy on our behalf. While they were in the city, Neil, Brendan, Johnny and I took a taxi into Antioch. It was a middle-sized town about four miles from the farm. They had a theatre called the Pallet, Masque and Lyre, PM&L. They didn't perform shows in the summer because of the heat. They were amused and surprised that an Irish 'dramatic troupe' was in the vicinity looking for a venue.

We booked it on the spot, even though we didn't have the deposit. Opposite the theatre were the offices of the *Antioch News*. We went there looking for publicity. They needed production shots but we didn't have any. Back at the farm, we rounded up the troops. We threw what spare cash we had on the table. It came to seventy-eight dollars. We needed sixty. That left eighteen dollars for everything else. Shea and Fran had photos of their honeymoon on the Aran Islands. There was one of them standing on the deck of a boat with the island in the near distance. The Antioch News thought it was wonderful and published it as part of a piece on Slot Players' recent tour of the Aran Islands!

Dear Dirty Dublin played for a week at the PM&L. We got a rave review in the *Antioch News*, which made special mention of the keening and the prayers in Irish, but more importantly we sold out the last three nights and ended up with a small pot of gold to split between the ten of us. By that stage, Vinnie and Felicia had opted out of the collective. They went their own way, and rumour had it that Murphy had offered them a job elsewhere. After the American experience, it took several years for our relationship to get back to anything like an even keel; and it was 1976 before I worked with Vinnie again.

We left America older and wiser. It took all of our powers of persuasion and the intervention of the Irish Consulate to convince Murphy to buy our return tickets. As a parting gift, we treated ourselves to a movie, one that was to have a profound effect on all of us, in different ways. The movie was *The Godfather*, and to experience that in the context of all that had happened to us was eerie. Marlon Brando as Don Corleone rules with an iron fist in order to help the business prosper. For him, it is all about family and keeping it together, safeguarding it against all outside interference. We weren't a family but we had just fallen apart; Slot Players had come to a natural end and there was nothing to keep us together anymore, either as friends or as artists. *Dear Dirty Dublin* was us prostituting ourselves, it didn't represent any kind of artistic vision. *The Godfather*, on the other hand, was the real thing. It was contemporary, it was visceral, it was upsetting, it was moving. And it wasn't on the stage, it was on celluloid.

'Fuck the theatre,' was Shea's immediate response, 'why would you want to do plays when you can do that?'

Neil was in total agreement. 'I love the fact that it's so accessible. No one dresses up. Everyone eats popcorn. I love that. I love the popcorn, yeah?'

I loved the way he asked a question that wasn't a question. It was the quality that made him such a compelling Tiresias. He wasn't a great actor, but he was compelling. He also laughed like it was a question. He was unique. From that day on, Shea and he talked about film a lot. It became their cultural reference point. But it would take another ten years or more for them to make their breakthrough into that medium. In the meantime, we had university fees to think about and we came home from America with very few dollars – some presents for family was all we could afford. Our dream was in ruins.

Back in Dublin, I got a job in Coca Cola on the night shift – Semperit Tyres were not taking anyone on – I loaded bottles, two by two, into wooden boxes, and my fingers bled from the metal caps and I wondered what it might be like to have a nice, cushy job, like that of a bus conductor, or an actor. I was three weeks at Coca Cola and just settling in when the company dropped a bombshell and announced that they'd come up with a machine for loading bottles into boxes. They didn't need humans any more and we were free to go. Voila!

6

Neil and I tried our hand on the cabaret circuit. We put a set together that included Buddy Holly's Rave On and That'll Be The Day, George Formby's When I'm Cleaning Windows and Fanlight Fanny as well as some traditional Irish ballads from *Dear Dirty Dublin*. For the cognoscenti we threw in Oscar Brown Junior's I Was Cool and Neil played a solo Spanish piece by Segovia. Our first public performance was in the New Inn on Clanbrassil Street, just down from St Patrick's Cathedral. It was a disaster. The entertainment manager of the venue, Des Smyth, thought our biggest problem was our appearance.

'You need to have matching outfits. Red shirts and black waistcoats. The clothes you've on look like what you'd wear around the house.'

We'd never thought about outfits. The idea of the two of us looking the same seemed preposterous. We were individuals, the last thing we wanted was to merge our identities. The punters in the New Inn didn't care what we looked like, they just wanted to sing along. We hadn't given them the songs to do that. Well, we'd given them snatches, a chorus here and there, but no anthems.

We'd frustrated them, in truth. Des Smyth gave us a fiver and told us to go out and buy some shirts.

We never overcame that first reverse, even though we strutted our stuff a couple of times more. We played at student gigs and parties but we were never going to threaten Simon and Garfunkel or the Everly Brothers. We weren't even competition for Foster and Allen. Neil was a serious musician, however, and Niall Stokes, a fellow student at UCD (and later the founder of Hot Press magazine) put out feelers to see if he would play saxophone in a rock band he was putting together.

I couldn't afford to go back to college and Sheila wanted to stay at home and mind Rossa rather than continue teaching. So we sat down and made the definitive plan of the rest of our lives. What's more, we put it into action. Sheila took over a pre-school playgroup at the back of Saint Gabriel's church, Clontarf, which gave her the opportunity to keep Rossa with her all day. It was a long way from our mobile home site in Crumlin to Clontarf, so we put a deposit down on our first car, a grey Mini, MZO 663. Her dad, Frankie O'Donoghue, who was too tall to sit into the car, offered to go guarantor for us but the hire purchase company turned him down on the basis of his profession – he was a bookmaker. In the end, Da stepped into the breach and signed the forms.

I wrote to Dublin Corporation and argued that, as a married student not living at home, I was entitled to a maintenance grant on a par with students coming to college from the country. In order to bolster my case, I went to see the Professor of Metaphysics, Father Des Connell, who would later become Archbishop of Dublin and a cardinal. I asked him for a letter of support. He took out his pipe, lit it and stared into midspace. He ruminated for a long time. The silence was awful. My request, unintentionally, had given him metaphysical anxiety. He pondered the question, like Socrates of old.

'You should have thought of this before you got married,' he said finally, through a pall of smoke.

'We have a baby, father….'

The words were travelling towards his ears and I wanted to reach out and pull them back. I didn't want him to hear them. 'We have a baby,' like it was some sort of excuse, that I was looking for his pity, poor me saddled with a son. Rossa was the best thing that had ever happened to me. I never wanted to give the impression that he was a burden, but the words just slipped out….

'I don't live at home, father, I live with my wife.'

'Your personal situation is your own, of your own making. You can't ask the grant-giver to pick up the slack for that. Nobody forced your hand. (Pause) I hope.'

It was almost a perfect syllogism. Three statements, A, B and C. If A equals B and B equals C, then, of course, A also equals C. Logical thinking at its best, with a little Christian 'I hope' to finish it off, a final flourish to get the good philosopher off the hook.

Father Connell understood the letter of the law, but nothing of its spirit. I wasn't trying to defraud Dublin Corporation. It was just a unique situation. I didn't know of one other married student on campus. I was just trying to make college possible; I wasn't setting out to commit a crime.

He didn't have any empathy with me. I thought he looked lonely, behind the celibate smoke. A man with no one to relate to. No intimacy. It turned me against metaphysics forever. Well, it turned me against Aquinas, who was Father Connell's hero. I felt myself move towards the existentialists. They might be atheists, I thought, but they had compassion. Jean Paul Sartre had it for Simone de Beauvoir, but who had Father Connell got? An abstract, loveless God?

'My baby is a boy,' I said as I left his rooms, but it was for me I said it, not for him.

'That's nice, a boy.'

'Yeah, his name is Rossa. Rossa Francis Sheridan. Maybe you'll have him as a student some day.'

Michael Paul Gallagher, who was almost a Jesuit priest (he would be ordained later that year) and a teacher in the English department, came to my rescue. He framed a letter with me for Dublin Corporation that sparkled with common sense – at least that's how it seemed to me – it was written on headed notepaper from the Jesuit Centre, Milltown Park and I sent it to the Corporation grants' department along with a letter from me. While I waited for a response, I went looking for work. As per the plan of the rest of our lives I'd drawn up with Sheila, I started my search in Crumlin on the assumption that a job in the local area would save on bus fares. I headed out from the mobile home looking for building sites. There were men repairing a wall at the local swimming pool on Windmill Road. It was less than four hundred yards from our home. I made enquiries. They were employees of Dublin Corporation. I figured it might complicate things with the grants section if I was found to be in the employ of the swimming pools section.

I headed around the corner, past the boys' school on Armagh Road. From the outside it looked like a replica of the school I'd attended on Seville Place. The same grey, two-storey rectangle of drabness. They were both run by the Irish Christian Brothers, of course. I went in and asked for the Principal, hoping that they might need a handyman or a janitor. As it happened, they needed a substitute teacher for fifth class. Someone had let them down and they were stuck.

'Could you come in here tomorrow? I might need you for a week,' Brother Owens said.

'I don't have a degree, I only have a Leaving Cert.'

'That's fine. You don't need a degree for primary school, not as a sub. Your Leaving Cert will do you fine.'

I couldn't believe I was starting work as a teacher. In a Christian Brothers school, to boot. The more I thought about it, the more I wanted to back out. I wasn't cut out to be a teacher. I didn't have the experience. Sheila wouldn't hear of me backing away. She thought I was more than up to the challenge. The following morning at nine o'clock, I found myself standing in front of forty-nine eleven and twelve year olds, wondering what in the name of God I was going to do with them. It was only eight years since I had been sitting in their place. Brother Owens showed me where all of the teaching aids were kept – chalk, dusters, copy books, roll books etc. Then he pointed to the leather strap, the same that I had encountered in my schooling in St Laurence O'Toole's.

'There's the strap, don't be afraid to use it,' he said, loud enough for the boys to hear him.

It was strange to be in charge of the leather. I knew what it was to feel it across the palm, the hot sting that brought tears to your eyes, tears you wanted to hide but couldn't, tears that made you foolish in front of your friends, tears that rendered you a snivelling coward. I knew the hatred you felt towards the punisher, how in that moment of pain you wished that he could feel as you felt, vulnerable, exposed and abused. Now I had the instrument at my disposal. How could I use it and look myself in the mirror again?

I survived without the strap until the tea break. I was welcomed in the staff room, and former teachers of the children in fifth class marked my card.

'Watch out for Murphy, he's from a long line of bastards that fella.'

'Put plenty of marks on Murphy's hand and the rest will toe the line.'

'Show them who's boss at the start and you won't have any trouble.'

I found it almost impossible to control the class. It felt like they wanted and expected me to use the strap. Paul Murphy, in particular, seemed to challenge my authority at every turn. I tried to engage with him and he looked out the window. In the end, I threatened him with the strap. But I had no intention of following through on it. It was a fatal mistake. You cannot control with threats you are not prepared to carry out. Kids pick up on it immediately and make you pay. The unrest spread throughout the class. I had anarchy on my hands. There was a glass panel in the door to the corridor and Brother Owens, significantly, appeared at it. I had to regain control or I was out of a job. I called Murphy to the top of the class. I gave him one on each hand and told him to sit down. The mini revolution abated. I had quiet – a quietness of fear. Paul Murphy looked up at me and I could feel the hatred. I saw tears in the corner of his eyes. He thought I'd won, but I'd lost.

I went home feeling sick. I had to get the strap out of the class, whatever else. I couldn't continue to teach in an atmosphere of fear. Sheila put her arms around me and I cried for what I'd done to the boy.

'You can't turn a whole school around in one day. Give yourself a break, for Christ's sake.'

In our plan for the rest of our lives, we devised a system for the rest of the school term. Sheila brought me through a Froebel approach to organising a classroom. It was challenging stuff for me. The first thing we did was to set out a rewards system. It was a simple way to encourage good behaviour by rewarding it. The second important decision was to organise the class into groups, to break up the system of rows and put the boys facing each other to encourage teamwork. The third innovation was to devote all of Friday afternoon to art and craft. To encourage expression that had nothing to do with rote learning and exams but everything to do with creativity and spontaneity. The fourth decision was to draw on my own natural strengths and to teach as much as I could through drama.

The boys took to the new class arrangement with gusto. I had nine groups of five and one of four. Each group had a captain who recorded their star ratings. I gave stars for punctuality, neatness, good behaviour, honesty and so on. If the combined class total at the end of the day was ten, or one star per group, then I cut formal lessons short by fifteen minutes and read to them. Each star over ten secured them an extra two minutes. The first book I chose was the classic *I Am David* by Anne Holm, and it proved a huge success.

The big reward on offer that first term, and they needed one hundred stars to secure it, was a trip into the Peacock Theatre to see a play. *The Blue Demon* by Lin Ford was playing there. I'd been doing drama with them, we even staged scenes from *I Am David*, and they loved the idea of a 'proper play' in a 'proper theatre with lights.' Through my contacts in the Abbey Theatre I secured seats at a knockdown price I knew the boys could afford. The number eighty-one bus stopped on Armagh Road outside the school, so the transport was no problem. I only had to get them from College Green to Lower Abbey Street. I was going over the plan of the day with them when I discovered, to my horror and my amazement, that of the forty-nine in the class, fourteen boys had never been in the city centre. Ever. In their lives, they had never taken a bus into town. They had never walked across O'Connell Bridge, or stood outside the GPO, or looked over the wall into the river Liffey, or counted the storeys on Liberty Hall. They had never experienced the capital city of their Republic.

Corporal punishment was never an option after the class reorganisation. Rewards and the leather strap just didn't go together. I don't know how long it was – it may have been four or five weeks after I started – when a boy called Peter Barry put his hand up to ask a question.

'When are you going to slap us again, sir?' he said.

There were a few titters and I could feel all eyes on me. It was a good question, deserving of an answer.

'Would you like me to use the strap?'

'No, sir,' they answered back in unison.

'Well, if you don't want me to use it, then I won't.'

I looked down at Paul Murphy. He smiled back at me. An idea flashed into my mind. I went to the *cófra* and took out the leather strap. I held it up before the class.

'I think we should get rid of this. What do you think, boys?'

'Yes, sir.'

'I think we could bury it.'

'Yes, sir.'

'Who'd like to bury it?'

No one put their hand up. It felt like something they didn't want to touch, or be associated with in any way.

'Who was the last person to be slapped by it?' I asked.

'Paul Murphy, sir,' Peter Barry said.

Everyone wheeled around to look at him.

'Would you like to take it?' I said.

'I don't mind, sir.'

'It's yours if you want it.'

He got out of his seat and approached me.

'Do you have an open fire at home? One that burns turf or coal?'

'Yes, sir.'

'You can throw that on it. It'll burn.'

'Ok, sir.'

So he sat back down and put the leather strap in his school bag. He had no sooner done it when I thought it was a bad idea. If he produced that at home his parents would think he'd stolen it. He might even get a hiding for his trouble, thanks to me. I was thinking about taking it back when Brother Owens appeared at my door. He caught my eye and then he entered. He swished soutanely up to the top of my class to make an announcement. I've no idea what he was talking about because my attention was inside Murphy's bag with the leather strap. When he finished his address, the boys all got up and left. Brother Owens had let them go early and I'd no idea why. Paul Murphy was gone and I hoped that was the last I'd hear or see of the instrument of torture.

It was. Paul Murphy came to school the next day in good form. He was clean and smiling. He had missed the play in the Peacock, the only one in the class whose parents 'didn't have the money.' He was a troubled and troublesome pupil, the type who brought his domestic dysfunction everywhere with him. He had the worst attendance record in the class but he never missed Friday afternoons, art and craft, which he loved. He would always show even if he hadn't been in that morning.

* * *

It broke my heart to leave the school. I loved the boys and I loved teaching. I was supposed to stay a week and that turned into months. I was to be there until Christmas, but the position stayed vacant after the holidays. So I stayed on until the end of January, and that turned into the end of February, and by mid-March I knew I had to get out or I would fail my second-year university exams. I'd done very little study, knackered as I was each day after work. So, on the first Friday after Saint Patrick's Day, I made my exit. Brother Smith, who had the sixth class, organised a musical farewell in my honour. We crammed the two classes together, his and mine, for the recital.

'You're a great man for the newfangled ideas, you have them at the tips of your fingers,' Brother Smith said.

It sounded like a compliment but, of course, it was anything but. He got his class to play. It was the beautiful El Condor Pasa, made famous by Simon and Garfunkel. On the final note, he conducted them to a stop and we broke into a round of applause.

'I wrote that myself, I call it Bluebird,' he said.

I couldn't hide my surprise.

'I know, it sounds very like a popular tune but that's an original, I wrote that for the boys.'

I smiled at him and let him get away with the lie.

* * *

The grants people of Dublin Corporation, despite Michael Paul Gallagher's intervention, took the Father Connell view and refused to increase my maintenance. I crammed night and day for my second-year exams and did my best to stay away from drama, my primary addiction. I did relapse, however. Word on the grapevine had it that Alan Simpson was directing the Irish premiere of *Jesus Christ Superstar* and would love anyone from Slot Players to audition. He wasn't to know about our American implosion. I turned up at auditions in the Gaiety and sang a few scales for the musical director. Then I did some moves for the choreographer, who turned out to be Alan and Carolyn's daughter, Jessica Swift. By this time in his life, Alan was married to the actress Eileen Colgan, and they had four young children – Cathal, Katy, Clara and Ben.

I went home and told Sheila they'd offered me the chorus in *Jesus Christ Superstar*. She wanted to know what the money was, naturally enough. I'd forgotten to ask. I went back for the first day of rehearsals, but the producer, Noel Pearson, was gone before I had time to corner him. We worked on through the day and I realised that the chorus would be on-stage throughout the show. That meant full-time rehearsals. I'd figured on having lots of time off to study and to help out with Rossa, who was now walking and a handful.

I went in for the second day, but at lunchtime, I quit. It was just too intensive. I wasn't used to that much dance. My legs were hanging off me. And my back hurt, in the place where I'd damaged it some years earlier doing street theatre. Alan was disappointed when I told him, and I was disappointed too. I'd just said goodbye to working with Colm Wilkinson, Tony Kenny, Honor Heffernan and Luke Kelly, all Dubs and people I greatly admired. Nothing in the intervening years has dimmed that admiration.

I sat my second-year exams that summer, and Da got me a part-time job at the dog track. I worked alongside another lad, Tony Ward – he would become a well-known and much-loved soccer and rugby star, playing for Shamrock Rovers, Shelbourne, Munster and Ireland – and our job was to collect the tickets from the totalisator booths and bring them back to the central hub for verification and authorisation. Da had been working at

Shelbourne Park and Harold's Cross for many years and was now in charge of calculating the dividends on each race. It was grist to his mill, gambling addict that he was. He worked out the win, place, forecast and tricast on each race, and also the jackpot on the third, fourth, fifth and sixth races. I never met anyone in my life with a better understanding of permutations and combinations than Da. He invented bets that not even bookmakers understood.

For me it was boring and repetitive work, but the money came in handy at the end of the month. The best part of working at the dogs was the time it gave me with Da. We had a little routine going. I drove the Mini from Crumlin and picked him up in Seville Place. That meant he didn't have to take his own car out of the garage. We chatted on our journey to and from the track. He was always interested in what I was reading for college, especially the plays. I knew he missed Slot Players, even though he was proud that Shea and I were carrying the torch. He loved getting the inside story on our escapades and I gave him a blow by blow on our American odyssey.

'You know the mistake you made there, Pete?' he said on more than one occasion.

'What was that, Da?'

'You should have given him the O'Casey ending he wanted. He might have paid you had you done it.'

I don't think he was right about that. George Murphy never had it on his agenda to pay us. We were naïve, and Murphy didn't understand that we were poor. He assumed that we were middle-class students happy to get a free flight to America. I think he was completely taken aback when we arrived in Chicago with a baby in tow. 'A real Irish baby,' as the Americans called Rossa.

On his first birthday, May 12th, 1973, Sheila and I decided we would try for a second baby. We finished off the birthday cake, put the candle in the kitchen drawer and went to bed. Sheila conceived that night. That date was the anniversary of our first kiss in Hollybrook Road and Rossa's birthday. Our special date, as we came to know it.

I was travelling to Shelbourne Park with Da, hours after we got the confirmation of the pregnancy test.

'You're going to be a grandfather again,' I said to him.

He looked across at me but I knew he didn't cop it.

'Who's expecting?'

'Sheila. We got confirmation today. Baby is due in February.'

He couldn't believe that we'd planned it. Despite the fact that he himself loved children, he couldn't see why we were adding to our family right now. He thought we should at least have waited until I finished college and had a proper job. I explained that we didn't want Rossa growing up as an only child; we wanted a brother or a sister for him, companionship. Sheila was one of seven and I was one of seven and we wanted a house full of children, just like the homes we'd grown up in. It was a compliment to him, but he didn't see it that way, or chose not to.

I wanted to ask him about Frankie but I couldn't find the courage. I could only imagine the pain he must have felt on Frankie's death. I tried to imagine losing Rossa but it was too difficult a feeling to entertain for more than a second. I would love to have been able to talk to him about Frankie but I could never find the right moment. I didn't ever want to re-open that wound. So I prayed that he would bring it up. I tried to put the thought in his head, around Frankie's anniversary in April and his birthday in July, and sometimes out of the blue I would just repeat 'Frankie' like a mantra, hoping that he'd pick it up by osmosis, but he never did. Or if he did, he kept his mouth shut.

By 1974, Ireland was still in the Stone Age and I was barred from the labour ward. Doctor Drumm, Sheila's consultant, wouldn't hear of a father being present at a birth, and the fact that I had previously broken the rule didn't wash with him. He was implacable. Sheila still believed that when the time came I could sneak in. I came from a family of 'sneakers in' – we did it at football matches, racing fixtures, cinemas – but none of us had ever sneaked in to a delivery.

Fiachra was born in the Coombe Hospital on Valentine's Eve, February 13th, 1974, and to my shame, I wasn't there. I had a legitimate excuse, however. I'd taken over the running of Sheila's preschool playgroup in Clontarf. By the time I'd tidied up and dropped Rossa off with my mother, it was mid-afternoon. I dashed to the hospital and Sheila was in the last stages of her labour. Unfortunately, Mr Drumm was in attendance, and even had I succeeded in evading security, I would have been summarily ejected.

Fiachra had the Sheridan look, just as Rossa had been born with the O'Donoghue look. It made him an immediate hit with my mother, who couldn't understand why we were giving him a strange name that sounded like the Irish word for teeth.

'Could you not give him a proper name, son? Why do you have to call him Fiacla?'

'No, Ma, it's Fiachra, not Fiacla.'

'It sounds the same. I can't tell the difference.'

I did my best with Ma. I tried to explain the difference between the 'r' sound in his name and the 'l' sound in fiacla. But she called him fiacla every time, and after a while I was sure she was doing it on purpose. A major gripe for Ma was that she didn't know another living soul called Fiacla – not a jockey, a footballer or a singer, not even a patriot of the past – no one she could look up to and make her proud of her grandson.

'He's called after a saint, Ma.'

'I never heard of him.'

'That's because he went to France and set up a monastery. Near Paris. He's very well known in France.'

'It doesn't sound French.'

'In fact, if you went to Paris….'

'Didn't I go there on my honeymoon, but I didn't meet any Fiaclas.'

'Fiachra is the patron saint of Parisian taximen. A fiacre is a sort of a taxi. That's how they got their name, from the Irish saint Fiachra.'

'Are you telling me he's called after a taxi?'

There was no winning with her when she had her mind made up. Ma had only one brother, Felix, and she was hoping that we might name the baby for him.

'Felix is nice, even for a second name. What do you think, Pete?'

I knew it would mean a great deal to Ma, and I also knew that Sheila wouldn't countenance it. Not that I was in love with the name Felix myself. But events outside our control conspired to consign the discussion to the dustbin. Six weeks after Fiachra's birth, on Saturday, March 23rd, 1974, Sheila's dad Frankie collapsed and died while working at Naas races. He was fifty-eight years old. A man younger than the one who is writing this book. It was totally out of the blue, and shook Sheila and the family to the core of their beings. We left the mobile home and moved in to Hollybrook Road to be close to everyone. It was incredibly stressful. The boys ranged in age from 22 down to 14, and only the eldest, Michael, was working. Sheila's brother

Brian took over the running of the bookmaking business. A business partner of Frankie came to the house and removed the family car, claiming it was his. I drove Brian around in the Mini and we did our best to recover gambling debts owed to his father. In the main, people refused to settle. They argued that as gambling was a gentleman's agreement, not a contract, the liability died with the person. Legally, there was nothing Brian could do to make them pay. My faith in humanity took a severe battering acting as Brian's chauffeur.

The O'Donoghues were steeped in racing. Frankie, and before him his father, Killarney, (so called because Killarney was his birthplace – his actual name was Michael) were among the best known faces at Irish meetings. Their cousin, the legendary Paddy O'Donoghue, one time chief of staff of the Manchester IRA (1916 –1920), had founded Shelbourne Park greyhound stadium and became the leading public figure of that industry. Michael Collins had been his best man when Paddy married Violet Gore in 1919 and a photo of the wedding party, taken in Saint Stephen's Green, adorned the dining room of Hollybrook Road. Frankie O'Donoghue had owned several top dogs, best known among them Splonk, who won several prestigious races at Shelbourne Park. Frankie was an owner of repute and a shareholder in the dog track. Our two families were linked through Shelbourne Park and greyhounds. In death, that linkage mattered and gave extra meaning to our grief. Our son was meant to be named for his grandfather and so we added Michael Francis to Fiachra and left it at that.

Her father's death brought Sheila closer to her mother. In all of the turmoil and the anguish, Sheila was the only daughter and the empathy between the two women was self-evident. She'd been close to her dad and felt his loss in a way that only daughters do. Sheila also had children, sons, and though nothing can ever replace a lost father, Rossa and Fiachra offered continuity.

We eventually returned to the mobile home and I reconnected to my studies, determined not to be distracted any more by the theatre. I was as good as my promise. I sat my third-year exams, my finals, and I felt that I did well enough to be optimistic about graduating in the autumn. The only problem was that my first-year tuition fees were still owing. I crossed my fingers and hoped that they wouldn't use that as an excuse not to confer me. Sheila's playgroup was our only source of income. I scoured Dublin for a job, and while I waited for something to materialise, I looked after Fiachra at home. He was an easy baby, and when I got him to take his nap, I sat down and started to write a play.

I wanted to write about the housing crisis in Dublin. I was a part of that situation but I never felt like a victim. Maybe that had to do with my education. 'Educate that you may be free,' Padraig Pearse had written. I never felt trapped in poverty even though we had no money. I never felt bad about our housing situation even though we lived in a mobile home. I knew that many people were trapped and saw no way out. Housing allocations were based on a points system, awarded across a number of categories. To qualify for the most basic flat – and that usually meant Ballymun – the applicant would need 1) to be living in overcrowded or insanitary accommodation, that is, residing with your parents or with rats, and 2) have a brood of small children, preferably with a mix of boys and girls. The influence of the Catholic Church was never far from social policy in our country; in the area of housing, its footprint was stamped all over it. Its opposition to contraception encouraged large families which, by definition, added to the crisis. The state colluded by doffing its cap to the bishops and banning the sale of condoms.

The living conditions of families in Dublin had been a scandal since the foundation of the state and it took the collapse of houses in Fenian Street in 1963, with the deaths of three occupants, to propel the Government into action. Their answer was to build a modern high-rise town on the outskirts of the city and house people there. The new facilities, while initially welcomed, were never properly maintained – broken lifts were not repaired, there were no greenfield sites or playgrounds for the children and, for the men, there was no work, only welfare. Ballymun, in no time, became a modern slum and a byword for failure.

Many young couples, in the circumstances, preferred to take their chances in the inner city. On the northside, that usually meant Sean McDermott Street or Gardiner Street. These three- and four-storey houses had once been the envy of Georgian Dublin. They were now slums, the majority of the inhabitants living in one room, usually sub-divided by curtains and with limited toilet and washing facilities, often an outdoor WC shared by ten or twelve families. Despite this, many saw it as preferable to Ballymun. One such was my friend Robert Sheeran and his wife Teresa, better known as Tess. Robert had grown up in Sheriff Street but he was sent away to Artane Industrial School for mitching from school when he was ten. He had a tough time there, but he discovered music and threw himself into it to escape the horror of his incarceration. He played rhythm guitar in a garage band called Michael Malteze, which Shea and I had put together in the late sixties. It was very much a forerunner of Slot Players, but as the drama took centre stage, the band faded into the background.

I tracked Robert down to a flat in Sean McDermott Street. He now had three children and an unhappy, pregnant wife. Tess was fed up with the inner city. She was after a house. One with bedrooms and a bathroom. A fourth child gave her an excellent chance of an offer. Or, as she put it to me:

'I won't have four after this one is born, Peter. I'll have five.'

Robert, the fifth baby she was referring to, laughed at her innuendo. He had a great laugh, it was how he survived, big child that he was. He also had copybooks full of songs. After the demise of Michael Malteze he'd kept on writing original material, marked out in block capital letters with the chords above the words. He took out his guitar and played them for me, one after the other, upbeat songs in the vein of 'Hand Jive,' a rockabilly tune that was Robert's all-time favourite.

I know a guy named Way Out Willie
He got a cute little cat name of Rockin Billy...
Hand jive, hand jive, doing that crazy hand jive.

I sat down at the kitchen table of the mobile home with a copybook and a pen and started to write the story of Robert and Tess. The first thing I put down was a task for myself. Find out about the Forcible Entries Act, check the legislation, make sure you have it correct, understand every facet of it before you start. My first scene, I decided, was to have them break into a flat – indeed, that is precisely what Robert and Tess had done – and I was going to have them arrested and charged under the Act. I felt paralysed by my lack of knowledge. I got the bus into town, dropped Fiachra off at my mother's – she had finally managed to get her tongue around his name – and went to the National Library. I trawled through *The Irish Times* for coverage of the Bill on its way through the Dáil. I took copious notes. I spent three days there. I had terrific stuff, great quotes from Noel Browne and Conor Cruise O'Brien. I didn't know how I was going to use it in the play, but I was sure that would come to me in time. I was walking down Kildare Street with my head buzzing when I met one of my college lecturers, the writer Tom Kilroy. He asked me how I was and I told him I was writing a play.

'I'm in the library researching the Forcible Entries Act,' I told him.

'You need that for the play?'

'Yeah. I have to know the legislation. I can't start without it.'

We went for a coffee, at his suggestion, and he offered me some advice.

'I write first and research later,' he said.

'What if you don't know something?'

'Make a stab at it. Take a guess. If I waited to know everything, I'd never start.'

'That makes total sense,' I said.

I was researching out of insecurity, not out of need. I was afraid of the play, and in my fear I was running to the library for solace.

'Do you know the best advice I ever got about the process?' Tom said. 'Put your bum on the seat every day and don't let it move.'

Had I not made the mistake of going to the National Library, I never would have received that gem of wisdom, unparalleled for its simplicity and depth.

I sat on my arse for the following six weeks and wrote a first draft. I only got out of my chair to tend Fiachra when he required feeding and nappy changing. At the end of the process, I had a play called *It's a Fair Squat but Don't Get Caught*. I was delighted but broke. Shea came to the rescue on the work front. Or rather his house did. Like myself and Sheila, he and Fran had bought a mobile home. Unlike us, they hated living in it and couldn't wait to get out. They sold their mobile home and came up with the deposit on a house on Ballybough Road in the north inner city. They also applied and were successful in securing a home improvements grant – they were all the rage at this time, and political parties competed with one another in making them available – giving Shea and Fran enough cash to put a new roof on their second-hand house. Da, being an expert when it came to DIY, was eager to take on the contract. However, the grants scheme debarred family members from carrying out works. They didn't reckon on Da, however, who knew a man who knew a man who did a line in headed notepaper. So he made up a company name, situated it at the rear of 133 Cardiffsbridge Road (his brother Paddy's house in Finglas) and successfully tendered for the work. So with Da acting as foreman – he took three weeks off his job in CIE – Shea and myself laboured for him and learned how to strip, felt, flash and tile a roof.

It was almost an unqualified success. On the last day of work, unfortunately, Da's ladders were stolen from the front of the house. He had brought them into the marriage with him, like a dowry. They'd been tied against the scaffolding when a person or persons unknown had cut their cord and removed them. Da was incredulous. The ladders defined him; they were a part of who he was, an extension as precious as a limb. Every Saturday they facilitated his adventure on the valley roof of Seville Place – 'Get the ladders out!' was his cry in the morning, and 'Take the ladders down!' his cry in the evening – and he went at his roof adventures with the poise and the drive of a Shackleton or a Scott.

They were easily identifiable, being wooden. We drove up and down every estate in Dublin in search of them. He had friends everywhere on the lookout and he missed nights at the dogs when sightings of them were reported, all of which proved false. He kept it up for months before he officially called it off and wound down the search. He couldn't go to the police, having falsified the headed paper. That proved a major drawback in the investigation, the 'pig's mickey of a flaw,' as Da called it. Shea had a new roof and we were proud of it, but it had come at a price to Da's body and his mind.

* * *

I submitted *It's a Fair Squat but Don't Get Caught* to the Abbey Theatre and waited for the rejection, which duly came. I sent it to RTÉ and some independent production companies, but I didn't hold out much hope. Shea thought it had potential, but didn't like the title, thinking that it was a bit fey. He suggested some rewrites and I went at them whenever I could. One good thing was that, in writing the play, I had taught myself to type. I did it using a manual Olivetti. I covered the letters of the keyboard with bits of paper and undertook the following typing exercise:

The quick brown fox jumps over the lazy dog.

That one sentence, containing all 26 letters of the alphabet, was the breakthrough. I typed it out over and over again, hundreds of times, like a man possessed. I practised until my fingers went to the correct keys of their own volition. I figured it was a great skill to have, and so as not to put it to waste, I decided to become a journalist. It felt like a logical follow-on. John Feeney, whose brother Jim had delivered Rossa, had taken over the editorship of the *Catholic Standard* – a strange appointment for a radical who had led the occupation of Hume Street. I wasn't bothered by that. I had delivered the *Catholic Standard* for the Legion of Mary in my younger days, so I figured they owed me something.

I presented myself at the offices of the newspaper in Talbot Street. John Feeney took me to the pub for a drink and a chat. Four hours later we were still there. We never discussed religion, in the private sense, although I quickly ascertained that he had a healthy disrespect for the Catholic hierarchy. He thought they were gangsters with low morals. He also thought they were crazy to appoint him as editor. I liked his anarchic spirit. He liked my working-class credentials. We quickly became drinking pals, me with my pints of Guinness and small Jameson whiskies, he with his penchant for French red wine and lager. He was generous to a fault, and always paid for the drink. He got me to write theatre reviews for the paper – Patrick Kavanagh had once been the drama critic, as had Heno Magee of *Hatchet* fame – and he also introduced me to John Mulcahy, editor of *Hibernia*, the fortnightly review.

It wasn't long before my name was appearing regularly across a range of publications, from *Woman's Way* to *Hibernia*, the *Irish Independent* to *The Irish Times*. I applied and was accepted for membership of the freelance branch of the National Union of Journalists, NUJ. I graduated with a second-class honours from UCD, but I was too principled (stingy, in other words) to pay for a photograph. I have no record of the event, apart from the piece of paper with the Latin writing. Ma was disgusted by my behaviour that day – she had wanted to pay one of the professional photographers there – and she didn't talk to me for weeks afterwards.

Sheila and I started talking seriously about buying a house. One advantage of being on the housing list was that we could apply for a Dublin Corporation mortgage. The terms they offered were far superior to the banks and the building societies. We went looking and fell in love with a two-storey house in Ardilaun Road, Ballybough, not far from Shea and Fran. In 1975, we put the mobile home up for sale and got an immediate offer from, a young married couple. Shea and Fran offered us the front room in Ballybough Road while we waited for the legal process on the house in Ardilaun Road to come to completion.

It was quite a change, living with all of our worldly possessions and two children in one room. We tried to protect Shea and Fran's privacy, so we ate as much as we could in our own room, and watched television there, too. The pressure took its toll on Sheila and she came down with colitis. I tried to be as supportive as I could, but I have never been good around sickness. We had some terrible rows. The fact that I was spending so much time in the pub didn't help matters. I might have been too broke to pay for a graduation photograph, but I always had enough money for alcohol.

Shea asked me to get involved in *The Non-Stop Connolly Show*. It was a cycle of six plays written by John Arden and Margaretta D'Arcy, whom we'd first met at the time of *Oedipus* in Galway. It was hugely ambitious: they were bringing an actor over from Scotland, Terence McGinty, to play Connolly; a mask and prop maker from England, Maggie Howarth; a director from London, Rob Walker. They had pulled in the support of the Irish trade union movement (Mickey Mullen was a great help), the Irish Workers Cultural Centre, the Communist Party of Ireland and the Official Republican Movement. Shea was going to play a part in it, and help out with the direction where he could.

It sounded exciting and ground breaking, but I knew that if I said yes it might spell the end of my journalistic career. I couldn't get involved, but I'd help out where I could. In that respect, I found a house for John and Margaretta to rent in Artane. On the day they moved in, I noticed a house four doors down having its roof repaired. Leaning against the front of the house were a set of ladders. Da's ladders. Wooden with a red paint mark on the fifth rung. I went to check them at closer quarters. Someone shouted down from the roof.

'What do you want?'

'I'm helping some friends move in. I need to get some keys cut. Is there anywhere around here I can get it done?'

'Haven't a clue.'

I walked back towards John and Margaretta's house, thinking about what I should do. One of the men shouted after me.

'Are you one of the Sheridans from Seville Place?'

'Yeah,' I said. 'I'm Peter.'

'I went to school with Sheamie.'

I was going to ask them about the ladders, where they got them, or borrowed them, or came by them. But I held my counsel. I drove down to Da's and gave him the news. He got his car out of the garage. He checked the petrol tank with his home-made dipstick: there was about two pints in it. We stopped at Stafford's in Amiens Street and he put a gallon in, double his normal purchase. We drove out to Artane and the ladders were gone. So were the roofers. They must have known we were on the trail. We'd missed our opportunity, and Da felt that we would not get another one. The ladders would be kept hidden away, repainted perhaps, or transported over to the southside and sold.

Living with Shea meant that I was at close quarters with the trials and tribulations of the *Non-Stop Connolly Show*. It was a military operation of a production, not unlike the events it depicted. There were times when I was sure it would not see an opening night, particularly after Rob Walker, the director, left his briefcase, containing uncopied pages of dialogue involving Vladimir Lenin and Rosa Luxembourg, in a pub. Margaretta, who was playing Rosa, lay down on Ballybough Road in front of Rob Walker's Landrover and said that she would not get up until the pages were retrieved. But the pages were lost. John tried to calm the situation down, peacemaker that he was.

'Look, Margaretta, it doesn't matter because it is not historically accurate anyway,' he said.

'I'm not moving until he finds those rewrites.'

'Lenin was in Moscow in March, 1914 and Rosa Luxembourg was in Germany, so they couldn't have met. They couldn't have spoken.'

'I don't care where they were, they are meeting in our play.'

'Very well, Margaretta, as long as you understand it's a fiction. Now get up off the ground before you catch a cold.'

The Non-Stop Connolly Show was the theatrical event of 1975. The curtain rose at noon on the morning of Easter Saturday, April 5th and it came down at 2.30 in the afternoon of Easter Sunday, April 6th. A running time of twenty-six and a half hours, the longest play ever staged in Ireland and possibly the world. At the finale, the audience rose with the actors and they cheered, clapped, banged the backs of their seats and stomped their feet. I had been there for most of it. My review appeared the following week in the *Catholic Standard*. I have to confess I nodded off once or twice. In the middle of the night, I remembered Shea running onto the stage and shouting that the police had drawn their batons.

'Take cover, the police are on the rampage,' he shouted.

He stood centre stage, waiting for a baton to strike him across the head. But it never came. The policeman missed his entrance. Undaunted, Shea ran off and came back on wielding a baton. He removed his cap and whacked himself over the head and fell to the ground. It got one of the biggest cheers of the night.

In scale and ambition, the show was a landmark. In the middle of the worst communal and sectarian violence in the history of our country, it celebrated a republican who sought to unite the Catholic and Protestant working class in a common cause. The show travelled to Belfast, where performances were organised by Billy McMillen and his colleagues in Official Sinn Fein. A week later, in an appalling and cruel irony, Billy McMillen was murdered. No one was ever charged in connection with his death. It is widely believed that he was shot by Gregory Steenson, a member of the breakaway IRSP who were feuding with the Official IRA at the time. Billy McMillen, like James Connolly, was a great socialist. He paid for it with his life.

7

We moved into our new, old house at number 2 Ardilaun Road in the Spring of 1975. The road was named for Lord Ardilaun, one of the Guinness family, who had once owned large tracts in the area including St Anne's Park in Raheny. There were four houses in our row, and they nestled in the shadow of Croke Park's Cusack Stand. All that stood between us and the stadium was a field used by the boys of Belvedere College for rugby and athletics.

The residents of the road were elderly. The occupant of number 1 was a retired watchmaker, Michael Dunne, who had lived there since the house was built in 1907. He was born in 1898, but still had a keen intellect. By way of demonstrating this, he recalled for me the names of all the people to whom his father administered first aid on Bloody Sunday, November 21st, 1920. That was the day the British Army rolled into Croke Park and opened fire on spectators and players – the attack was in reprisal for a series of assassinations carried out that morning on the British Secret Service by a crack squad of Michael Collins' known as the Twelve Apostles. Fourteen agents were murdered and fourteen civilians died in Croke Park, among them Michael Hogan, the Tipperary footballer after whom the stand on the northside of the ground was named. Michael Dunne recited the litany of the injured who were tended to in the house, adding that only one, a Padraig Timmons of Rialto, returned later to say 'thank you.'

I was intrigued by Michael. He had lived his whole life in that house, which was now in a state of some disrepair. As a boy he'd gone to school out of there. He'd trained as a watchmaker, cycling across the city to O'Connor's Jewellers in Harold's Cross every day. He'd buried both his parents and seen his younger brother, now deceased, emigrate from it. He'd never married and was now living out his final years alone, no one for company apart from some old photographs and a radio. He loved the 'wireless' as he called it. He didn't have a television and had no interest in owning one.

'I'm too old for television,' he said to me, 'it's too bright for my eyes.'

As the evening shadows drew in, he listened to radio and he read. Dickens, Thackeray, Tennyson and particularly Shakespeare. He had copies of the plays and a *Collected Works*, too. He read them propped up in bed with a fire raging in the grate. He lived and slept in the one room now, because it meant he didn't have to heat the whole house. Among his favourite plays were *Hamlet* and *Macbeth*. He could recite whole sections of them by heart:

Out, out brief candle, life's but a walking shadow. A poor player that frets and struts his hour upon the stage and then is heard no more.

He could go straight from the Scottish tyrant to the Danish Prince:

To be, or not to be, that is the question. Whether 'tis nobler in the mind to suffer the slings and arrows of outrageous fortune, or to take up arms against a sea of troubles and by opposing, end them.

His diction was perfect, his emotion true. The lines felt like they encapsulated his life; that Shakespeare had written them for him. I sat by his bed in the shadow of the room and watched the glow of the fire on his face, now strong, now weak.

'Where did you learn to speak like that?' I asked him.

'My father was a great man for the drama. He had an academy, pupils galore.'

'Where did he teach them?'

'Here, in this house. In the back room. He had a little area, curtained off.'

Michael pulled back the blankets, got out of the bed and struggled into the back room. I followed him, and he showed me the arch from which the curtain hung before the actors stepped out to enunciate their lines.

'Do you know Willie Shields?' he said.

'Willie Shields?'

'Yes. Do you know who I'm talking about?'

'I think I do. Is it Barry Fitzgerald?'

'The very one. He was only five feet four, did you know that?'

'He was a scene stealer, isn't that what they say about him?'

'He had a brother, Arthur. He was one of James Connolly's stretcher-bearers when he was taken from the GPO to Moore Street, number 16. He was an actor too. But Willie was the star pupil. My father trained him right here.'

Michael's father, James H. Dunne, was a real force in Dublin theatre at the end of the nineteenth and the beginning of the twentieth century. He was so well known and respected that Yeats invited him to join the Abbey Company for the presentation of *On Baile's Strand,* the first production at the new theatre in December, 1904. Six-year-old Michael and his mother sat beside Yeats on the opening night. I was completely taken aback that this now seventy-seven-year-old man, my next door neighbour, was living out his life in poverty and obscurity. He provided a link between Ardilaun Road and the foundation of our most important theatre and arguably one of the world's most famous cultural establishments.

It was forty years or more since he'd last set foot inside the Abbey. It was before the fire that had occurred in 1951. I told Michael about my love/hate relationship with the place. I let him know that they had rejected my first play.

'What's the name of your play?'

'It's called *It's a Fair Squat but Don't Get Caught.*'

'That's a terrible name, they were right to reject it.'

I determined to write something on Michael Dunne. Like most things with me, it became an obsession. I decided on a television format. I couldn't think of any way to encapsulate his life working within the restrictions of the stage. I wanted him to be able to walk down O'Connell Street and see himself as a young boy. I wanted him to stand outside the new Abbey Theatre and for the picture to dissolve into the old Abbey. I wanted Yeats to take him by the hand and show him to his seat. I wanted Michael to see his father live on the stage. I wanted him, as an old man, to go in search of the man who came back to say thank you after Bloody Sunday. I wanted him to stop outside a television shop and see the image of Father

Edward Daly with the white handkerchief on Derry's Bloody Sunday.

It was the mix of past and present that fascinated me. In my mind, Michael was in love with the Countess Markiewicz. He turns up in St Stephen's Green on Easter Monday to lend what support he can. He sees her in the park, commanding her men. He follows her in and has his encounter with her. He declares himself for the Republic. She asks him to round up all the kids in the York Street area and bring them to a soccer match in Dalymount Park. He does what he's asked. He gets the kids out of harm's way by taking them to Phibsboro to see Bohemians play. He returns to the scene of the action. The Countess and her colleagues have now taken over the College of Surgeons. Michael can't get near the garrison. The British Army have taken up positions in the Shelbourne Hotel and are shelling the college.

Michael walks through St Stephen's Green as an old man. He sees a woman sitting on a bench. She reminds him of the Countess. He stops and stares at her. The woman gets frightened. She starts to leave and Michael appeals to her but in vain. He walks home to Ballybough. He lights the fire and gets into bed with his book. He hears voices from the back room. He gets out of bed and goes to check. He sees his father and the Countess act out a section from Yeats's *The Countess Cathleen*. He watches, and as he does, he starts to cry.

I decided there was only one actor in Ireland who could play Michael and that was Cyril Cusack. As luck would have it, he was appearing in the Abbey. Armed with my rough draft of *A Kind Of Patriot* as I'd called it, I headed into town to meet him. I had no appointment. I figured he would be in the bar of the Abbey after the show, and if not there, he was sure to be in the Plough or The Flowing Tide. My plan was to walk up to him, introduce myself and hand him the script. Once he read it, I figured, it was only a question of shooting it around his busy schedule. It never crossed my mind that he might reject it. Or ask for rewrites. Or not be interested in the role.

He was standing in a circle of people when I got there. He was wearing a rather flamboyant yellow jacket with leather elbow patches. I sat down and observed him for a few minutes. He was smaller than I imagined. It made me think of Barry FitzGerald. Or Willie Shields, as Michael called him. I wondered about Cyril. Was that his real name? Maybe it was a stage name. It would be so good to call him by his proper name. That would certainly get under his defences. I lit a cigarette and drew heavily on it. I'd have to call him Mr Cusack. I didn't have an option. I started to resent the people in his company. Why didn't they bugger off home and leave the man alone. I had the manuscript under my right arm, cigarette in my left hand. I made my way to the edge of the circle. One of the women in his company noticed me. She smiled and nodded at me. He turned and his lips made a sound.

'Hmm….'

'Mr Cusack…?'

'Yes…?'

'My name is Peter Sheridan.'

'Hmm….'

'I'm a writer and a journalist.'

'Is that so?'

'I've written this piece about a man who gets involved in the Easter Rebellion….'

'You're burning my jacket.'

I looked down. My cigarette had burned a hole in his jacket. He didn't do anything, he just made the observation. A simple statement of fact. Under-acted, a simple reality, verified. No histrionics. That was him. As for me, I panicked. I told him I would get him something. I didn't know what it was. A fire extinguisher? A glass of water? A damp cloth? The only thing he needed was for me to disappear. To be gone from his life and never to appear in it again. He needed a new jacket. I'd destroyed the one he had. I ran away to get him a new jacket. That was my only thought. I'd find out where he bought his clothes and I'd get him a replacement.

I never got the jacket and he never got the script. I put *A Kind of Patriot* in a drawer, knowing that it wasn't ready, that it's time had not come. Scripts are strange things. Some don't want to be born, or need to be born. My relationship with Michael was more important than any script. He was a true patriot and my duty was to honour him by being a good friend and neighbour. I didn't need to put him on the stage, or the screen, at least not yet.

* * *

In 1975, money was the burning issue. Or rather, the lack of it. Our hire-purchase payments on the mobile home had been nine pounds a month. Our mortgage on Ardilaun Road was forty-five. That represented a five-fold increase. When we got together, Shea, Fran, Sheila and me, the great topic of conversation was how we might rob a bank. We planned several robberies, always with Sheila as the getaway driver. Jer O'Leary, who'd played Jim Larkin in the *Non-Stop Connolly Show*, had raided several banks on behalf of the IRA. He was caught and sentenced after a botched attempt on Wynn's Hotel in Middle Abbey Street. In the course of the robbery, he was confronted by an American tourist staying in the hotel. The gun he was carrying discharged and sprayed the ceiling. The tourist bashed him over the head with a chair and Jer stumbled onto the street, concussed. He was spotted by a uniformed Garda on point duty in nearby O'Connell Street and arrested. Jer served four years for his commitment to the cause.

Sheila was our definitive choice for behind the wheel of the car. She had developed into a brilliant city driver. She knew every back lane and short cut on the northside. The Mini wasn't a fast car, however. In a chase against the Gardai, it stood no chance. Four years in Mountjoy was a long time for me to be minding the kids on my own. I'd have no time for writing or directing plays if that were to happen. We looked at several other options, including a scam on the foreign exchange end of things. Shea had worked for Bank of Ireland before going to college and had good inside information. His scheme sounded attractive, but it always went over my head, in truth. I wondered if it was possible to get the banks to sponsor us, to gamble on our success. We had the ideas, they had the money.

I went to see my bank manager in Talbot Street. He sponsored us for fifty pounds. It was a start. We were planning to form a theatre group to go around schools. They were a ready-made audience, and if we could manage to extract ten pence for every pupil in every primary school we could make a killing. It was such thinking that led to the creation of the Children's Theatre Company, that soon became simply the T Company. We were socialists, and operated on the principle of a box office divided equally among us. We were nomadic, too. We travelled on buses, carrying our costumes and props in suitcases. The minimum fare was our guiding principle. We paid it for all journeys, in all circumstances.

Susie Kennedy was the exception. She was from Chicago and didn't understand the drill. She had arrived in Ireland with a sleeping bag and an electric typewriter. When asked for her fare, she told the bus conductor where she was going. That was information that no Irish person would ever divulge.

'Ballyfermot, please,' Susie said.

We all moved away from her. She wasn't with us.

We arrived at St Louise's Primary School in Ballyfermot for the world premiere of *The Unhappy Birthday*, a play in which I played the young hero, Tatty Matty, and Susie played the feisty Fiona. Two sold-out performances in front of a captive audience. Four hundred children at ten pence a head. That was a total box-office take of forty pounds. Not bad for our first day.

By the end of the tour, Susie was more Irish than the Irish themselves. She was the heart and soul of the T Company. She cared deeply about the work and hated shoddiness of any kind. On the Monday of the second week, she called a company meeting. The issue was the birthday cake had. The cake appeared on-stage with a slice gone. Susie was furious. Des Hogan, who played the evil genius, Leabharlann, owned up that it was him.

'I was hungry. I had a coffee but nothing to go with it. I took a slice, it's no big deal.'

'It is a big deal,' Susie said. 'It's a big deal for the kids.'

'Look, you can't see there's a slice missing,' Des said. 'If you keep the gap to the back you don't even notice.'

Shea suggested that you could eat half the cake and get away with it. Susie was against trying it out. We did. We ate half the cake. The children didn't notice. One day, there was less than half a cake. Someone had crossed the line. The children could see that it wasn't a proper birthday cake.

'We're cheating the kids,' Susie said. 'I can't be involved in fraud, simple as that.'

'Everything in this country is a fraud,' Des said.

'I love you, Des. I love everyone in the T Company, but it's over for me. After this, I'm done,' Susie said.

* * *

Ironically, Susie stayed with the group and I moved on. I helped with the touring, but I hung up my acting boots and took on an administrative role instead. I had an idea to invite the President of Ireland, Cearbhaill Ó Dàlaigh, to our new show, *Launcelot Versus the Dragon,* he was going to grace us on our opening night. I knew he had been to the Abbey a few times. Indeed, I'd once attended a seminar in the Peacock Theatre at which he spoke. He had made a comment in relation to *Waiting for Godot*, suggesting that as Beckett was a master of language, with fluency in several European tongues, he may have been making a pun on the Gaelic word, *go deo*, which translated as waiting for 'forever.' I thought it a brilliant observation, even if it wasn't true. I wrote him a flattering letter and invited him to the opening performance at the Town Hall, Dun Laoghaire. The following day, a letter bearing the seal of the President of Ireland arrived in my letter-box in Ardilaun Road. He was coming to *Launcelot Versus the Dragon.*

Buoyed by my success in snaring the President, I rang Gay Byrne in RTÉ. Well, I rang the offices of *the Late Late Show* looking for him. I didn't know that he had researchers who booked his acts. I left a number and was rung later by a man called Tony Boland. I organised for him to come to rehearsals. I rushed in to tell the company of our good luck. Some people felt we should pass on *the Late Late Show*, that we weren't ready. I hit the roof. A television appearance would set up the tour, we couldn't turn it down. Tony Boland was outside the door, listening. In the end, I was sent out to bring him in.

'I suppose you heard some of that,' I said to him.

'Look, Peter, I understand. They're artists.'

'I think they're mad, this is the best publicity we can get.'

'But you want it to be right. That's really important.'

We took up our slot on *The Late Late* and Susie performed the cat song from *Launcelot Versus the Dragon*.

Miaow, I'm a pussy
Miaow, I'm a cat....

The impact on the box office was immediate and sustained, and the tour sold itself. In a sense, the T Company had arrived.

We got an invitation to perform at the new Project Arts Centre in East Essex Street, part of the area that is now called Temple Bar. After its tenure in the basement opposite the Peacock Theatre in Abbey Street, Project had moved to premises in South King Street near the Dandelion Market. The building that housed it was sold for redevelopment and the Centre had then moved to a vacant factory – the old Dollard Print Works – in East Essex Street. We got an afternoon slot in the fledgling theatre. A group of activists including Alan Stanford, Agnes Bernelle, Ann O'Driscoll (she had found the building), Tom Hickey, Chris O'Neill, Lee Gallagher, James McKenna, Mike Bulfin and many more were trying to make the building usable at the same time that we were engaged in a tech rehearsal for our show. They had built frames for two wooden banks of seats, and were covering them with foam and leather while another work party were hanging doors in the ladies' and gents' toilets.

A group of visual artists were turning a space adjacent to the theatre into a gallery. On the roof, a firm of contractors were burning tar and spreading it in an attempt to seal the building – a problem that would bedevil the Project for years to come. Patsy O'Shannon, the Centre's administrator, was trying to organise an upstairs office, while underneath her the constant thrum of a kango hammer signalled the advent of an art house cinema.

As always, it came together. The T Company opened on time, even though not every member of the audience had foam under their backsides. The Fire Officer came to visit and luckily the rain held off, although he did insist on us widening the gap between the banks of seats that led to the exit. The collective that was the Project Arts Centre was reconstituted into its new Essex Street home. The various disciplines fought with one another from day one. But they were good fights, creative ones. We had a very modest grant from the Arts Council, two and a half thousand pounds. There was a board of directors, but no one wanted to be on it. You couldn't be on the board and earn money from the Centre. No one wanted power if it meant you had to starve. Shea suggested to me that we get ourselves onto the board.

'Why would we do that, it's only a talking shop?'

'You have to go to where the power is.'

'I just want to put on plays.'

'Let's get onto the board and change the rules.'

At the AGM, Shea let his name go forward and he was duly elected by the membership. The plan was that I would be co-opted later. At his first board meeting, Shea put forward an artistic programme that included *It's a Fair Squat But Don't Get Caught*, a play he'd been working on himself called *Mobile Homes* and *The Risen People*, James Plunkett's highly regarded play on the

1913 Lockout. It was a season of socially and politically engaged work that nailed the Project's colours firmly to the mast. Shea put my name forward to direct *Mobile Homes*, with him taking charge of the other two shows. The board properly said that under their articles and letters of association, he could not be paid. Shea agreed and told the board that I could be paid instead. It was a solution, unique and slightly bizarre, but not one with which the board was comfortable. The only other way forward, of course, was to change the articles and letters of association. A solicitor, James Hickey, was brought in to advise and Shea immediately proposed his co-option onto the board.

While we waited for a legal solution to the payment conundrum, we got on with trying to realise the programme. In reality, the money issue was largely academic because Project had none. They put a small fund at our disposal for the set and the advertising. Apart from that, we all worked for shares. It is one of those great illusions of the theatre, the idea that you will make a week's wages from the door take. It's a principle that never works out in practice and leads to massive rows and people not talking to one another for the rest of their lives, or longer. Before the box office can be split, there is the rent to the theatre (enough to cover lights, heat and newspaper ads); actors never believe these costs are true. It is part of a universal belief that venues are corrupt and that actors never get their just reward. If the show does badly, the theatre is at fault for not publicising it properly. If the show does well, the actors are appalled at the amount spent on advertising – the audience would have come regardless, they say. The box-office split is socialism, and it can't work because we live in a capitalist world.

I was coming home from Project one day with Shea in the Mini. I took a short cut down Eustace Street to get onto Dame

Street. A Garda stood out on the cobblestones and stopped me. I rolled down the window.

'You know this is a one-way street?' he said.

I feigned ignorance.

'Did you not see the "No Entry" sign at the bottom there?'

I shrugged my shoulders and tried to look penitential. He wasn't in a forgiving mood. He told me to produce my tax, driving licence and insurance at the first available opportunity, and that failure to do so would result in a gaol sentence as well as a fine. He instructed me to reverse down the street, which I did.

'You better get Project to pay that fine,' I said to Shea.

'No chance. Not a snowball's in hell. But I have an idea.'

'Yeah, don't pay the fine and go to gaol, is that it?'

'No, what about "No Entry" as a title for your play?'

No Entry it became. Shea brought a great cast together, and one of the actors, John Olohan, also designed the set. He put barrels everywhere and one of them contained a pole with a 'No Entry' street sign in it. For the tenement house, he hung the frame of a Georgian window from the lighting rig. He'd found it in a skip on Henrietta Street. Don Foley, who played the Dublin Corporation official, designed the lights. He always claimed that his interest in lighting came from the fact that he was blind in one eye. Don's mantra was 'too hot, too hot.' He would stare up into a light with the good eye, looking like a demented genius who had just discovered the origin of the universe.

'Are you at six on the board there? Too hot, too hot. Give me four, or three, give me three, the good eye says it's a three.'

It cracked Shea up every time.

No Entry opened in March, 1976 to mixed reviews. David Nowlan in *The Irish Times*, while welcoming the 'savage attack on our housing situation,' did not like the use of the children's street songs that bridged the scenes. Shea had introduced them into rehearsals – we were indebted to Eilis Brady's wonderful book on the subject, *All In, All In!* I thought they brilliantly juxtaposed the innocence of the child's world with the awfulness of the adults' predicament. In the scenes that take place in Artane Industrial School (comprising much of the play's first act), we see the boys stripped of their identity by the Christian Brothers. Thus Robert, the central character, is known as Sheriff Street and the other boys follow a similar designation – Raheny, Foley Street, and so on. They are stripped of their Christian names by those charged with their Christian education. On the day he is due to leave Artane, Robert is blocked by the other boys who link arms and won't let him through. He knows the game. He knows the rhyme. He sings it out.

> ROBERT: *Open the gates and let me through.*
> BOYS: *Not 'til you show your black and blue.*

Robert pulls up his shirt and shows the boys where he was beaten earlier in the drama.

> ROBERT: *Here's me black and here's me blue.*
> BOYS: *Open the gates and let him through.*

This presentation of the children's rhyme is a subversion. The world of the play is an upside-down one. Children are sent to a State institution for protection, but are abused. Everything is the opposite of what it should be. Innocence is corrupted. The promise of the Proclamation to protect all of the children equally is a sham. The Republic is a failure. The only triumph is that of Robert and Tess, with their humour and their determination to survive, to offer something better and nobler to their own off-spring.

That first season in Project was exhilarating. We followed *No Entry* with a new play by Mary Manning entitled *Outlook Unsettled*. There was also a series of lunchtime plays that started with Pascal Finnan's *The Swine and the Potwalloper*, followed by Mary Maher's *Women at Work*, then Des Hogan's *Squat* and Christy Hudson's *Guilty 'Cause We're Filthy*, which caused an uproar. The piece was directed by Dave McKenna of the T Company, and he used an ensemble of four actors. The show was a series of sketches, political and saucy. One of them was a spoof on *Last Tango in Paris* called *Last Célà in Mullingar*. It featured the great Irish dancer, Michael O'Twinkletoes, who was no Michael Flatley, let it be said. Father Fabian Smooth, on the other hand, was a definite progenitor of Father Ted. The sketch in which he appeared was a spoof on *The Late Late Show* and featured the song, 'I Wanna Hear Your Confession, Baby!' However, the one that caused all the trouble was about masturbation. It had Vinnie McCabe as a balaclava- wearing leader of the Wire Pullers Liberation Front. There was a theory, expounded by Hudson in the writing, that masturbation didn't exist in Ireland until it was brought in by the British. The piece ended with Vinnie McCabe declaring that he was going to scale one of the Ballymun Towers and 'toss himself off for Ireland.'

The League of Decency picketed Project and called for the show to be closed. Some of them gained entry to the theatre and heckled the performers. After their removal, the show continued on. The publicity in the press was extensive, and *Guilty 'Cause We're Filty* sold out. We had to put it on late night as well as lunchtime to accommodate audiences. It became the big hit of that first season. The League of Decency didn't go away,

155

however, and they picketed City Hall because we were in receipt of a grant from Dublin Corporation. They hassled councillors and started a letter-writing campaign to the papers. They were dotty, certainly, but they were dangerous. Several politicians jumped on the bandwagon and came out against us. They were interviewed by the press but none of them had seen the show. We had our defenders too, of course, and Pat Carroll of the Labour Party was brilliant in upholding the right to 'creative and artistic freedom.' We survived the vote, but the lines were drawn and we knew that trouble and interference were never going to be far away.

8

The late summer of 1976, I was walking down Dame Street with the actor Paul Bennett, when a young man blocked my path. He stood in front of me, having come from the direction of Dame Lane, to my left. There was something about him, a street energy, something that said 'don't mess with me'. I saw a tough, working-class kid and I saw vulnerability too. He was nervous; he had his hands in his pockets.

'My name is Gerard Mannix Flynn,' he said. 'I'm just out of prison and I want to be an actor.'

Paul Bennett and I looked at one another, amazed at the balls of this young man.

'How do you think I can help you?' I asked.

'You're Peter Sheridan. I saw your photograph in the newspaper. Peter Caffrey told me to speak to you.'

Peter Caffrey was an actor friend, known to Paul Bennett and myself.

'How do you know Peter Caffrey?' Paul said.

'I met him in prison. He came in and done a play for us. I spoke to him after it. Told me there was a place behind the Olympia that put on plays.'

'It's called the Project Arts Centre,' I said. 'It's on East Essex Street.'

'I know it. Used to be a printing place.'

'It's a theatre now. And an art gallery. I'm holding auditions for a play called *Mobile Homes*. Come down tomorrow at two o'clock and I'll have a look at you.'

'Do I need to bring anything?'

'No, just bring yourself.'

He took his hands from his pockets and proffered one for me to shake. It was such a confident gesture, I was unnerved by it. He shook my hand and then he shook Paul's. He turned to go back down Dame Lane.

'What were you in prison for?' I asked.

'A policeman wouldn't ask me that,' he said.

He paused and smiled. There was real mischief in him.

'I got four years for burning down Dockrell's,' he said, nodding his head in the direction of South Great George's Street where the department store once stood. 'I didn't do it though. I'm innocent.'

He disappeared down Dame Lane.

Dockrell's had been one of the biggest fires ever seen in the city. The newspapers said it was arson and the young man we had just met had been convicted for it. Paul Bennett turned to me and shrugged his shoulders.

'Only in Dublin, only in fucking Dublin,' he said. 'Where else in the world could you meet someone like that? Only in fucking Dublin.'

I had cast Paul Bennett to play the lead in *Mobile Homes*. We were seeing people for the minor roles now, including that of a pervert who stole women's underwear from a clothesline on the site and a wife beater who was squaring up for a fight with the landlord. I'd cast Tom Irwin in the landlord role. He was an actor of the old school who referred to every show as a concert.

'It's a lovely concert, son,' he'd say, 'gritty but good, a good concert.'

Tom was the only actor I ever worked with who wore a dicky bow to rehearsals.

Gerard Mannix Flynn arrived on time for his two o'clock audition. They were taking place in the theatre, and the atmosphere was pretty informal. Tom Irwin was on the floor, reading against the aspiring young actors. I was sitting in the front row. Mannix asked me what I wanted him to do.

'Just go over there to the man wearing the dickie bow and let him know that he can't push you around.'

'Do you want me to say anything?'

'Only if you want to. Just throw a few shapes. Act tough.'

Mannix didn't walk over to Tom Irwin, he circled him, like an animal surveying its prey, never taking his eyes off him, not for a second or any part of a second. I could see that Tom was unsettled. Mannix, very slowly, approached him. He made a sudden movement with his head and shoulders. From where I was sitting it looked like he'd head-butted him. Tom Irwin slumped to the floor, like a balloon that had lost its air. I ran across to him, suspecting there'd been a clash of heads. He was clutching his chest with his hand.

'Jesus, Mary and Joseph...' he was saying, gasping for breath.

I thought he was having a heart attack. I pulled at his dickie bow and loosened the top button of his shirt. I ran out to the box office and told Patsy O'Shannon, our administrator, to ring for an ambulance. I grabbed a glass and filled it with water in the bathroom. I ran back into the theatre, and Mannix had made a pillow from his jacket and had it under Tom's head.

'He got a fright, that's all,' Mannix said, 'he's going to be all right.'

Tom sat up momentarily and took a sip of water. I could see his face, there was no bruising on it. Thank God, he seemed to be recovering. I walked Tom out to the foyer and cancelled the ambulance. Tom turned to me:

'That boy is terrifying, but he's perfect for the concert, perfect.'

Mannix Flynn had found his calling. He had arrived onto the stage and into my life.

* * *

Shea and I were putting an enormous amount of time into Project for very little return. Our ambition was to put together a company of actors and to hold on to them from show to show. We had huge artistic plans, but to realise our ambition we needed to pay everyone the Equity minimum wage. Otherwise the actors had to go off and work for the subsidised companies like the Abbey, the Gate and the RTÉ Rep – or worse still they had to take non-acting jobs. A year into our tenure at Project and we were still working off box-office shares.

I supplemented the theatre work with freelance journalism, and Shea taught part-time in Sutton Park School where Ruairc Gahan, the great libertarian and opponent of corporal punishment, was the headmaster. (We were still working out a plan to rob a bank, but the IRA were killing that option by taking out the easy ones and making the rest uber security conscious.) I got a regular column writing on DIY for *The Irish Times*. Mary Maher, who'd written *Women At Work*, which we produced in our first lunchtime season at Project, secured the commission for me and it was a godsend. I also continued to write regularly for *Hibernia*, the *Irish Press* and the *Catholic Standard*, in addition to which I edited a number of small magazines including the *Progressive Farmer* for Tara Publications, a company run by the Farrell family, old neighbours of Sheila's from Hollybrook Road, Clontarf. I was, without doubt, the most unlikely agricultural correspondent in Ireland, hailing as I did from the north inner city. Despite my journalism work, I considered the theatre my vocation and I pined for it to be my full-time occupation.

No Entry was invited to do a two-week season at the Institute of Contemporary Arts (ICA) in London. We had the ambition, but not the money to go. Ambition won out and we travelled by boat, third class, and the actors slept on mattresses, on couches or with family or friends, and one even managed to lodge on the stage of the ICA itself. We wanted to say we had 'played London,' and we endured the hardship for that sobriquet. We thought it would do our profile good with the decision-makers back home, and we were correct in that assumption. The maxim was true that to be successful in Ireland, you must first be successful abroad.

The big news at the ICA in 1976 was the emergence of Gay Sweatshop. They were the first exclusively 'gay' theatre company to be established in Britain and their lunchtime season was breaking all box-office records at the venue. I saw their show, *Mister X*, a piece they had put together collaboratively, inspired by the book *With Downcast Gays: Aspects of Homosexual Self-Oppression* by Andrew Hodges and David Hutter. It blew me off my seat, particularly the performance of Drew Griffiths, who did a turn as a drag queen replete with feather boa, encouraging audience participation on a level I had never seen before. The companion

piece to *Mister X*, Jill Posener's *Any Woman Can,* was equally brilliant and equally ground breaking.

On my return to Dublin, I put a plan together to bring
Gay Sweatshop to Project. I contacted the Hirschfield Centre,
the hub of the gay movement in Ireland, who resided around
the corner from us in Fownes Street. I met David Norris, as
unlikely a gay activist as you were ever likely to meet – he was a
Protestant, an academic, had a long beard, lived in North Great
George's Street, spoke posh and taught at Trinity College – and
he committed himself immediately to organising a fund-raiser
at the Hirschfield Centre. He also threw in a bed in his house
for one of the cast. Not to be outdone, I went down to Ma's
and persuaded her to take two of the Sweatshop girls and their
young baby, never once letting the words lesbian or gay pass
from my lips.

In November – usually a dull and lethargic month in the
theatre – we presented *Mister X* and *Any Woman Can* as a
double bill. We were sitting on a homophobic time bomb in
Ireland. Gay Sweatshop lit the fuse. We handed the League of
Decency the event they'd been waiting and praying for. Gay
men on an Irish stage, declaring their sexuality; and not just gay
men, but lesbians too. In the furore and debate that followed,
it turned out that lesbianism was not a crime under Irish law. It
was not an offence because it didn't exist on the statute books.
It was never imagined by those who framed the laws in the
late nineteenth century that women could engage in same-sex
depravity. So the League of Decency had to leave the women
alone and go after the men. They wanted them brought before
the courts and charged. They wanted the den of iniquity that
was the Project Arts Centre closed, and any monies given or
due to us taken away.

Ned Brennan of Fianna Fáil led the attack in City Hall. In the Chamber, he referred to the members of the Gay Sweatshop company as 'funny bunnies from across the water.' Homosexuality, and the gross acts in which homosexuals engaged, wasn't an Irish thing; we were better than that, holier. Ned Brennan's words were a crude appeal to nationalist sentiment. Ma was having none of it. She'd taken a shine to her new lodgers and thought they were terrific mothers. She was a card-carrying member of Fianna Fáil and one of their best canvassers in the North Central constituency. She presented herself at George Colley's office on Amiens Street and asked him who the hell this councillor was who was attacking her two sons.

Meanwhile, the chairman of the Arts Council, James White, asked to see Shea. They met privately in the Council's offices on Merrion Square. Straight off the bat, James White told Shea that he was not a fan of the Project Arts Centre.

'I don't like what you do down there. I'm not a fan. But I do value it.'

He went on to offer the Voltaire defence: 'I may not like what you say but I will defend your right to say it.'

As the meeting went on, Shea realised that James White was angry, but that his anger was not reserved for Project or Gay Sweatshop.

'I had a call from Mr Haughey. He suggested I take your grant and give it to the Dublin Theatre Festival.'

In that moment, Shea knew we were safe. If the Project grant was under threat, we would have received a letter. That was how things worked when you were being dropped in the shit. You didn't get a meeting to tell you the bad news.

James White was a civil servant of great integrity. He took his independence and the independence of his office very seriously. Mr Haughey had impeccable credentials in the Arts. It was he who had introduced the tax exemption for writers and artists in 1969, a ground-breaking piece of legislation that put Ireland on the world map in how we treated our creative community. At the time of the Gay Sweatshop controversy, Mr Haughey was engaged in a backroom campaign to take over the leadership of Fianna Fáil and become Taoiseach. He made no moves that didn't enhance his prospects of achieving that ambition. To be seen as a friend of the Dublin Theatre Festival was far more beneficial and astute than championing Project or Gay Sweatshop. Haughey was a bully, but in James White he'd met his match.

In addition to our grant from the Arts Council, Project also received an annual subvention from Dublin Corporation via its Cultural Committee. In the wake of developments, the Committee froze our grant pending an investigation. On the day our case was to be debated, John Stephenson, secretary to the Project board, wrote a letter to the councillors. Its content felt like a commitment to sin no more. One paragraph of it read:

I realise that there has been an unfortunate history in this regard in the last year but, as you can see from the list of events held this year, we in Project learned from that to be more responsible in our choice of work. We have worked hard to organise and present the maximum number of events to the public which were of a high standard and which cause no gratuitous offence.

John had written the letter off his own bat, and had shown it to no one before sending it. It reflected the desperation of a man who knew how perilous our finances were. We could not, however, sacrifice our principles on the altar of financial expediency. The issue was just too important for us to don sackcloth and ashes. An emergency meeting of the Project board was held. It asked for John's resignation and he tendered it. An immediate press release was issued restating Project's right to determine its artistic programme free from outside interference. We were apologising to no one.

The League of Decency picketed Project for the run of the show. Dublin's gay community came out in their hundreds and tried to hug and kiss the protesters on their way into the venue. The legendary Tom McGinty and his friend Hugo McManus told everyone that they were 'funny bunnies,' but they were Irish, not from across the water, and they were available for parties, whatever their orientation (Tom, of course, was Scottish, which made his declaration all the funnier). Inside the venue, there wasn't a seat to be had. Gay Sweatshop received a standing ovation, and that was before the show started. They had never experienced an atmosphere like it. By the end of the performance, it was bedlam. The audience refused to go home. Project became the erstwhile centre of the gay universe. A drunken Drew Griffiths threw his arms around me and pulled me outside onto East Essex Street.

'I want to come and work here, Peter,' he said. 'I've had it with England.'

I was a huge admirer of Drew's, and I was flattered by the compliment, but I knew he didn't understand our situation, either financial or artistic.

'I don't have a play I could put you in right now....'

'No, no, you don't understand me. I'm not talking about plays. I'll clean the toilets. Paint the walls. Fix the roof. I'm not bad with my hands, you know.'

'You're a writer, Drew, and an actor.'

'No, I'm a tramp first and foremost. I'm a down-and-out, a vagrant. I'm like Wilde at the end of his life, a person of no fixed abode.'

'You're drunk is what you are.'

'That, too. Here, have a slug.'

He produced a half bottle of whiskey from his inside pocket. We drank it and Drew went on about how frustrated he was in his life. The success of *Mister X* meant nothing to him. He wanted desperately to be anonymous, and failing that, a toilet cleaner at the Project Arts Centre. I laughed it off and told him we'd talk about it some other time. He asked me for an 'official appointment' and I suggested eleven o'clock the following day, knowing that he would still be in his bed. To my surprise, he turned up at eleven o'clock on the dot.

'I thought you'd still be in bed,' I said.

'I haven't been to bed. I'm here to see you.'

He was determined to get out of England. It was Dublin, or failing that, Paris. We had a lady who cleaned the toilets at Project and I couldn't replace her with Drew Griffiths. It was just too insane.

'Why don't you write a play for me?' I said. 'Something on Oscar Wilde.'

'You write it, Peter. You're an Irishman.'

'Yeah, but I'm not gay.'

'You're married. Oscar Wilde was married. He had children. I'm never going to have children. I'm a queer, a sad queer, that's all.'

As it turned out, Drew and his writing partner, Noel Greig, were already writing a play on the history of the gay movement, beginning with Oscar Wilde in the post-trial period, 1896, and going from there through Weimar Germany of the 1930s and concluding with the birth of the Gay Rights movement in 1969. *As Time Goes By*, as it became known, opened in London and went on tour throughout the UK, coming to Dublin under the auspices of the Project, playing Trinity College Dublin, Oscar's old alma mater, to great critical response and sell-out audiences. Gay Sweatshop went from Dublin to Amsterdam, and while they were there, the Company split in two and imploded. After many rows and much soul searching, Drew Griffiths was expelled from Gay Sweatshop and went to live in Paris as a tramp. After some time there living rough, he got himself together and returned to London. He started to rebuild his life in the theatre and took on some writing commissions. Unfortunately, it didn't last. He was found murdered after he picked up a man in the Elephant and Castle district of south London in June, 1984. He was thirty-seven years old.

* * *

Mobile Homes proved a popular success, and after its premiere in the Dublin Theatre Festival we transferred the show to the Eblana Theatre, situated in the basement of Busáras, the bus depot in Amiens Street. It was a claustrophobic space, and smelly to boot. The passenger toilets were housed no more than a stone's throw from the auditorium, along the same corridor. This unfortunate juxtaposition led to a thousand bad jokes about the quality of the entertainment on show; but it didn't deter the public, who came in good numbers to support the Eblana and its productions.

Mannix Flynn quickly became an important member of the emerging Project theatre company. His real name was Gerard, and that was what I called him in those days. He had a younger brother, Mannix, which made things confusing, but deliberately so. As a young boy, Gerard was constantly in trouble, and when the Garda, or any authority figures, came knocking on his door, he assumed his brother's identity.

'I'm Mannix. Gerard's not here,' he'd tell all callers to his door.

So he was Gerard to some, Mannix to others, and Gerard Mannix if you wanted to be posh. I called him Gerard most of the time because I felt slightly odd using a name that wasn't his. He didn't seem to mind, however, he was comfortable in the confusion it engendered. He enjoyed having masks to hide behind. Above all else, he loved being bold, and the question of his name fed into that boldness and added to the sense of mystery. Ironically, his brother Mannix died in an accident on Valentine's night, 1981, a date that is etched in the memory of all Irish people because it was the night of the Stardust tragedy in which forty-eight young people lost their lives in Dublin's worst ever nightclub fire.

Throughout the run of *Mobile Homes*, Gerard and I talked about a play based on his experiences of St Patrick's Institution, the juvenile prison where he'd spent the guts of three years for arson. Prior to his incarceration there, he'd spent time in Marlborough House, a lock-up for young offenders; and before that he'd been sent away to St Joseph's Industrial School in Letterfrack, Connemara, for non-attendance at school. He was a bright, intelligent person, but the system had utterly failed him. Not only that, it had brutalised him, stripping him of his identity and subjecting him to physical and sexual abuse. Yet he had survived all that, and was carving a career for himself as an actor, standing shoulder to shoulder with the finest emerging talent in

Ireland. He had overcome colossal disadvantage to get where he was. He was living proof, if it were needed, of the indomitability of the human spirit.

I felt it incumbent on me to reflect his spirit in the writing. Gerard had learned how to play the guitar inside and was now writing original songs. Indeed, he had won prison entertainer of the year and had the trophy to prove it. Ironically, the prisoner he had beaten into second place came from the Sheriff Street flats and had attended Saint Laurence O'Toole's CBS school, as I had done myself. I knew him and his family. I thought it might be wise, and safer, to change all the names in the play. So I started with Gerard, and called the character based on him Jonnie Curley. I never imagined that Gerard would end up playing him. That wasn't in my consciousness at the start. The ambition was to get a play written, get it staged and to use the publicity surrounding it to have the case re-opened so that Gerard could prove his innocence and clear his name.

It was exhilarating working on the play with Gerard. He had the toughest, most amazing growing-up story I had ever come across. It seemed that from the moment he came out of his mother's womb, the first thing he'd heard was a police siren. He took an immediate and profound dislike to that sound. By the age of six, he knew every Garda and detective on the south side of the city. Whatever problems the family had in coping with life, he took them on and internalised them. He wanted to protect his family so he put himself out there and fought their fight. It made him fiercely protective and fiercely passionate. It also made him fearsome and attractive. His contempt for society and its ills was never far from the surface. He was a ball of energy, an unstoppable life force and I did my best to capture that in the writing.

The similarities and parallels to Robert Nolan's journey in *No Entry* were obvious. I was loath to write the same play twice, and did everything to avoid it. An early decision was to avoid the industrial school, to stay away from Justice Eileen Kennedy, the children's court and Marlborough House. It felt like the drama began with the burning of Dockrell's – or rather Sockett's, as it became, in this new world of *The Liberty Suit* – and the incarceration of Jonnie Curley, on the most circumstantial of evidence, for this crime. I saw it as a classic prison drama where the protagonist goes in as one person and comes out as another. He undergoes a transformation, not because of the system, but despite it. His real education is that he becomes politicised. He realises that his anger, if it is not properly channelled, will condemn him to life as a recidivist prisoner. He must reinvent himself if he is to triumph and beat the system.

The development of Jonnie Curley in the drama was greatly helped by the introduction of Vinnie Lane, a Provisional IRA prisoner with lots of attitude and opinions. I was taking a licence here because IRA prisoners were housed together in Mountjoy, down the road from St Patrick's. IRA remand prisoners, how-ever, sometimes found themselves in the juvenile wing because no accommodation was available in the main prison. I wasn't overly concerned that I was taking liberties. I just kept seeing a prisoner wearing his own clothes – the IRA inmates had that privilege – and that this fact would provide an essential trig-ger for Jonnie Curley on his journey of self-discovery. Having introduced the character of Lane, I found it impossible to let him go. He was such a great foil to have there. The truth is, he could not have spent two years in the juvenile prison. There was an old adage about not letting the truth get in the way of a good story, and that was always in the back of my mind. But more than that, it was a drama I was writing, not a documentary, and I wanted to be bound by the rules of dramatic, rather than literal, truth.

Alan Simpson had once said to me that a writer had to punish his heroes. It was a comment he made after he came to see *No Entry* at the Project. (After I moved into Ballybough I found myself living only a few hundred yards from his home on Clonliffe Road). There was an implied criticism in his comment that maybe I hadn't pushed Robert Nolan far enough, that he hadn't struggled enough, to be a great protagonist. The question surrounding Jonnie Curley was to find a way for him to reveal his true, vulnerable self to us. To do that, it had to be a place where he was in some distress but safe to communicate. The only credible location for that was the punishment cell. The basement. Chokey.

The Liberty Suit first draft consisted of four acts and twenty characters. That quickly became two acts and sixteen characters. The chokey scene opens the second act, representing the mid-way point of the drama. Jonnie Curley finds himself there because of a riot started by him and his nemesis, Kava – the result of a row at a Legion of Mary meeting in the recreation hall. After the energy and camaraderie of act one, the chokey cell is the first time we see Jonnie, isolated and alone. I wanted to show his abandonment and how it felt having no one to comfort and console him. I'd spent a week in hospital having my tonsils taken out when I was nine. I was inconsolable. Gerard Flynn had been taken from his family and transported to the other side of the country at the same age. I wanted him to remember that now in the chokey cell. I wanted him to cry out. I wanted his pain to be felt by us, the audience.

JONNIE. *Why did you send me away, Ma? Why did you let them take me? I was only eight years old. I wasn't a criminal. It was no crime not to go to school. You don't have to go. You don't have to go in here but I do. They don't give you any medals. It was the same before. You didn't have to let them. They fooled you 'cos you didn't want me. Nobody wants me now.*

The Liberty Suit, both in scale and ambition, was too big for the small space of the Project. It needed a stage with wings and flies. It needed a company with resources and a track record of staging large productions. It needed a producer who could take the financial risk. For those reasons, I felt I had to take it elsewhere. The Abbey was the obvious first port of call. They'd taken an interest in *No Entry* and were aware of me. I typed a letter to their Artistic Director, Tomás MacAnna, asking him to consider it for production. I put the letter inside the script. I looked at the title page. It read: The Liberty Suit by Peter Sheridan with the co-operation of Gerard Flynn. I thought it was confusing to have two names on the title page. I changed it so that my name alone appeared under the title.

* * *

The plays that opened our Spring season, 1977, were dominated by two giant figures of the twentieth century – Jim Larkin and Eamon De Valera. Shea had always wanted to do a production of Jim Plunkett's *The Risen People*, the story of the 1913 Lockout. It had begun life as a radio play, produced by RTÉ radio in 1957 – indeed, Jim Plunkett was a senior producer at the station, having moved there from the Irish Transport and General Worker's Union, ITGWU, where he'd worked as a union official.

In that capacity he had met with Larkin and become fascinated by him. The radio play was produced on the tenth anniversary of Larkin's death (he died in 1947 and his funeral was one of the largest ever seen in the city). It proved so popular on radio that the Abbey Theatre staged it the following year, 1958, in a production directed by Jim Fitzgerald, who later became one of the founders of the Project Arts Centre. Buoyed by this success, Jim Plunkett spent the next twelve years writing a novel, *Strumpet City*, inspired by the same events. It was Plunkett's masterpiece. It quickly became a classic and almost every house in Ireland owned a copy of the book.

In coming to the play twenty years after its premiere, Shea wanted to do something radical with it. I'd read it and found it brilliant in places, but it was wordy and static, betraying its radio origins.

'It needs a kick in the arse as a play,' I said to Shea.

'I think it needs to come out of that tenement room. It's a street play, for fuck's sake. What's the action doing stuck in a room? I want to *see* the baton charge in Sackville Street, not hear about it second hand.'

Shea (or Jim as he had become known by then) relocated the play and discovered a hidden energy to it. He introduced a street singer to give it atmosphere. He cast Mil Fleming in the role, and with the possible exception of Luke Kelly she was the finest singer of protest songs ever to come out of Dublin. She was also a member of the Bread and Butter Theatre Company, which made a vital contribution to the production. Jer O'Leary, of their number, who'd played Larkin in the *Non-Stop Connolly Show*, reprised the role in *The Risen People*.

There was a tremendous energy about Project at the start of 1977. Actors were coming in to the Centre, telling us they wanted to work with us. Peter Caffrey and Olwen Fouéré (her father was the Breton separatist leader Yann Fouéré), who'd started to make reputations elsewhere, auditioned for the new season. Johnny Murphy, who'd acted with the Focus, and Maureen Toal, highly regarded in the business, agreed to play Mr and Mrs Hennessy. John Molloy, who'd acted with everyone and been in several films – indeed, he had his own one-man show, *From the Vikings to Bang Bang* – came in to be seen for Rashers Tierney, and told us that if he didn't get the part he'd shoot us. He wasn't joking. Ena May came in to be seen for Mrs Mulhall. I read against her.

'You should change your name,' she said to me, after we'd finished.

'Why is that?' I asked.

'There's a fella with the same name as you writes a column for *The Irish Times*. It's a DIY thing, but he hasn't a clue. Do you know him? I'd change it if I were you,' she said.

Shea looked at me and laughed.

A week after the encounter with Ena May, I got a call from Mary Maher to tell me that *The Irish Times* didn't require the column any more. They were reorganising the 'homepage' and DIY didn't fit into the new plan. Mary was being kind to me. My work was perfunctory and not up to scratch. I continued with other freelance commitments, including my editorship of the *Progressive Farmer*, but my heart was becoming more and more calibrated to that of the Project.

The Risen People became a hit. It was the only show we did that never played to an empty seat. We revived it five times over the years, and each time it worked its magic with audiences. It had a very special, secret ingredient, but what it had more than anything else was soul. It was about something that mattered – the right to belong to a trade union – and while the Lockout was a failure on paper, the spirit of Larkin's 'rabble of carters and dockers' reflected an image of ourselves that people wanted to see. Indeed, it was something they couldn't get enough of. On the back of the success of the play, we introduced a policy of paying equity minimum to all actors who worked in Project. It was a big step forward, and it felt we were paying real and practical homage to Larkin and his crusade for workers' rights.

I directed Gerry Gallivan's *Dev,* which rehearsed by day while *The Risen People* played by night. In the process, we broke every rule in the trade union handbook. Seven of the actors – Olwen Fouéré, Ena May, Gerard Flynn, Garret Keogh, Johnny Murphy, Peter Caffrey and Alan Stanford – worked a full day in rehearsal before heading off to perform in *The Risen People* at night. I tried to facilitate them with long breaks, but it was a logistical nightmare because our Arthur Griffith, played by Gabriel Byrne, was teaching at a school in Crumlin, and I had to work around his availability too. The play was very technical – it used captions, slides and 35mm film, long before the term multi-media had entered the lexicon – and the day we began the tech rehearsal, Gabriel Byrne, who turned out to be the company joker, opened a sweep on how long it would take to complete. The actors put fifty pence each in a hat – they made their guesses and the last time posted was eleven p.m. At midnight, we abandoned the tech due to the failure of the projector. At that stage, we were still in act one. We reconvened the following morning and went at it again. At ten o'clock that night, we had just started act two. The show was opening in less than twenty-four hours. I called the actors together and everyone agreed we had to keep going. Six hours later, at four in the morning, I called a halt to proceedings. Gerry Gallivan, who had sat in the theatre throughout, looked across at me with the saddest face I had ever seen on a human being. I knew what he was thinking. I'd made an orang-utan's arse of his play. I should have staged it as he'd written it – no slides, no captions, no moving images, just characters telling their story in words.

'I don't suppose there's anywhere we'd get a pint at this hour,' Peter Caffrey said, and the room broke into hysterical laughter.

'There might still be somebody in the Arts Club in Fitzwilliam Street,' Johnny Murphy said. 'Follow me.'

'I have the money from the sweep,' Gabriel Byrne piped up.

'I won that,' Garret Keogh said.

'Yeah, but you were out by two days,' Gabriel answered.

* * *

Dev got an invitation to the Listowel Writers' Festival, to be held in June 1977, and I got a reply from the Abbey Theatre concerning *The Liberty Suit*. Tomás Mac Anna, the then Artistic Director, who'd been very encouraging when I had submitted *No Entry*, sent me the readers' opinions on the play. On the top of each page were the words 'PRIVATE AND CONFIDENTIAL' in block capital letters. I had no idea when I received the readers' reports that they were not actually for my eyes. They were for in-house consumption only. Hugh Leonard, the then Literary Manager of the theatre, expressed himself thus:

> *I do think the play could be worth doing in the Abbey, but it shouldn't be rushed at. I have a hunch that the writer is not the kind who can reshape and rework his material: any amendments will have to be a collaboration between him, the play editor and the artistic director. First, a fair copy would have to be knocked out*

by someone intelligent enough to make clarifications and corrections along the way. Then the play would need to be sorted out into scenes and the dialogue well-trimmed….

I think the playwright is a 'oncer', but it could be a splendid 'once', if the play he had in mind to write is dug out of what is here. But basically, the first question to be answered is: is its similarity to the Behan play a practical deterrent? This could kill the play if the comparisons were unfavourable, and it is a question worth asking and arguing… it would be a shame to produce the play in its present sprawling and half-baked state, and I visualise that Tomás, the author – if he is amenable – and myself could come up with a text by, say, late Summer.

I rang the theatre to see what they wanted to do and was put straight through to Tomás Mac Anna.

'Jack is very embarrassed. Very embarrassed. You weren't supposed to see those opinions.'

I had no idea who Jack was.

'Who's Jack?' I asked.

'Jack is Hugh Leonard. Hugh Leonard is what he writes under. His real name is Jack Keyes Byrne.'

It was the first time I became aware that Hugh Leonard was a pseudonym. It made me think about him in a different way. I knew from his newspaper columns that he was irascible, combative and highly opinionated. I also knew from his newspaper column that he could write.

Tomás Mac Anna asked for permission to pass my details on to Jack. At Jack's suggestion, we met in the Plough Bar, across the road from the Abbey Theatre. He seemed nervous, dropped his money at the bar when ordering the drink and ended up on his knees retrieving coins from under the seats. He made some reference to the readers' opinions and I brushed it off saying that I wasn't concerned about any of that.

'I know about the Project Arts Centre, I know who you are, you and your brother,' he said.

'I never saw your play *Da* but I read it. Just the other day. I thought it was brilliant, really brilliant,' I replied.

It was nice to pay him a compliment and mean it. He lit up. We talked about *The Liberty Suit* and I told Jack the story of meeting Mannix and how the play came into being. We drank, pints of Harp and pints of Guinness, and he wouldn't let me put my hand in my pocket. As the evening wore on, he became more and more relaxed. I couldn't help feeling that I wasn't what he expected – maybe he thought I'd be angry and difficult. The truth is, I'd never written anything as good as *Da* and I wanted to learn from the master. I made a reference to one of Madge's lines in *Da*, the scene where she reveals to us that Charlie is not hers, that he is adopted:

MADGE: *I took him out of Holles Street Hospital when he was ten days old… my mother said to me… you don't know where he was got, or how he was got, and you'll rue the day. He'll turn on you.*

I asked him had he heard that growing up, and was it painful writing it down? Jack got very animated. He turned to me, and I realised something. It was the first time that he had looked into my eyes. For the first time in our encounter, he was himself, letting down his guard. It had nothing to do with being smart or clever; it had to do with the light of his eyes, with letting them seek me out, like a lighthouse.

'I spent a quarter of my life looking for my mother, a quarter of my life not looking for her, a quarter loving her, and a quarter hating her, and that's what has driven me, the need to search for her and the need to block her out.'

The mother is the absent figure that hovers over *Da*, and creates the psychological crux, the turmoil that Young Charlie needs to overcome. It wasn't a million miles from Johnny Curley's predicament in the chokey cell. Two characters abandoned by their mothers, trying to make sense of their worlds. Outside the Plough Bar, I hugged Jack and saw him safely into the back of his Rolls Royce. He wanted to take me home but I needed to walk. I was drunk and beat to the world. Sheila would be at home looking forward to a blow-by-blow account of my meeting. All I could think of was the lighthouse, flashing its beam, looking for Jack and looking for Hugh.

Tomás Mac Anna wrote and offered me £100 as an option on the play. He told me that the director of the Peacock, Joe Dowling, was very interested in staging it there. I wrote back immediately and told him that had I wanted a 'small theatre' production, the facilities of the Project were always available to me. Tomás wrote back by return post.

… I was not aware that you are submitting your play for the Abbey Stage only… if you fail to get what you desire for the play elsewhere then perhaps you might wish to take the matter up with us again….

Two days later, I was standing at the bus stop on the North Strand trying to make it to Project for ten o'clock. The coach taking the cast and crew of *Dev* to Listowel was leaving East Essex Street on the hour. Apart from my directing responsibilities, I'd taken over the part of John Devoy from Johnny Murphy, who'd gotten a lucrative gig with RTÉ television. I was keeping my fingers crossed for a 54 bus when a car pulled in to the stop. It was Tomás Mac Anna. He shouted at me to get in. I sat in the front seat, not knowing what to say.

'I think your play could be a big hit. Have you got a producer yet?'

I told him that Noel Pearson and Phyllis Ryan were looking at it. I'd sent them copies but they'd both baulked at the idea of a play with sixteen characters. Tomás asked me where I was headed, and I told him about Listowel and taking over the part.

'Don't worry, there won't be a problem, we'll get you there on time.'

He drove across the city and dropped me outside Project. I was touched by his generosity. Maybe I should have given him the play, I thought. The truth was that we were in negotiations with the Dublin Theatre Festival. We'd had a meeting between Brendan Smith, Director of the Festival, Shea, myself and John Stephenson, Project's administrator. John had resigned, of course, after the ill-judged letter to the city fathers, but we had found a way to bring him back and resume his administrative duties.

Brendan Smith liked the play, apart from the opening scene where the prisoners are processed.

'We can't have them taking off their clothes. They'll have to have a towel or underpants, we can't have them showing their bits to the audience.'

'It's a shower scene,' I said, 'we can't have them wearing underpants in the shower.'

'Nudity is out. I have enough problems as it is,' Brendan Smith said. 'I don't want the League of Decency outside the theatre. Or the Catholic Church.'

'We can have them facing upstage,' John Stephenson said, 'that won't offend anyone.'

'The rules of the Olympia Theatre don't allow for nudity.'

'I thought there was no censorship in the theatre,' I said.

'No, but there are traditions. And good manners,' Brendan Smith said.

'We can rehearse it two ways,' Shea said. 'We can rehearse it using towels, and we can rehearse it not using towels, and we can see what looks the best.'

'As long as we don't see their bits and pieces, that's all, I'm happy, we're all happy.'

After the meeting with Brendan Smith, Shea, John Stephenson and I went back to Project.

'I'm not happy,' I said. 'This nudity thing is going to backfire.'

'He's putting your play into the Olympia Theatre,' John said. 'The fucking Olympia Theatre.'

'It's the best venue in the city,' Shea said. 'Especially during the Festival.'

'What are we going to do about them taking their clothes off?' I said.

'Let's get our foot in the door first,' John said.

* * *

Listowel proved an interesting experience. In my first appearance as John Devoy, there is a party scene welcoming Eamon de Valera to America. I stepped forward to propose a toast. I was wearing pince-nez. As I spoke the words of salutation, the glasses fell from my nose. I thought they had fallen to the floor and I proceeded to look for them. They had, in fact, fallen into the glass of champagne I was holding in my hand. I had no idea why the audience were in convulsions. Alan Stanford, who was playing Judge Cohalan, retrieved the glasses and handed them back to me. It brought the house down.

The second act focused largely on the negotiations leading up to the signing of the Treaty and the positions adopted by Michael Collins and Dev. As soon as we got into the heart of this, the tension in the hall was palpable. There were one or two shouts of 'traitor, traitor,' when Collins questioned being part of the delegation to London. This was countered from the other side with shouts of 'Dev's the traitor.'

You know as well as I that you're the man for London, Dev. I'm no bloody politician.

The house erupted. The Fine Gael crowd were on one side of the hall and the Fianna Fáil shower on the other. They traded insults, while the Parish Priest did his best to restore order. The passion on both sides was frightening. In addition to John Devoy, I was also playing Lloyd George, and when I made my first entrance there was a chorus of 'ya Welsh bastard', which sort of united the opposing sides, momentarily. After the show, we retired for a drink to John B. Keane's bar. I saw Paul Bennett (who played Dev) surrounded in a corner with a man pointing a finger into his face.

'Now listen to me, Dev, you didn't have the courage of your convictions. You didn't go to London because you knew what was on offer.'

Art and reality. In Listowel, the distinction meant nothing. There was no doubt that the play was real for this audience. *Dev* was not an escape; it was part of who they were. It resurrected the old debate about who was responsible for the partition of

Ireland. In that sense, it was inflammatory and invigorating in equal measure.

* * *

The big decision in the summer of 1977 was casting Gerard Mannix Flynn to play the lead in *The Liberty Suit*. The show was utterly dependent on Jonnie Curley and the ability of the actor to take the audience into his world and make them care about him. The fact that the play was based on Gerard would count for nothing if he didn't command the stage and deliver a knock-out performance. Throughout August, we auditioned dozens of potential leads. None of them had Gerard's visceral, working-class quality. The only question in our minds was his technical ability to project himself in a theatre the size of the Olympia. So we booked it for an afternoon to test him out. I sat in the back row of the Dress Circle and Shea sat in the Gods. We put Gerard in the centre of the stage and asked him to read from the monologue at the opening of act two. His voice was crystal clear. When he sang the lines from Bohemian Rhapsody, it was chilling – a lone voice in a vast wilderness looking for his Ma.

'Can you hear me all right?' Gerard shouted from the stage.

There was a silence.

'Are youse out there?' he shouted.

'We're here.'

'I thought I was back in gaol there for a minute,' he said.

We went back to Project and Shea told him he was cast.

In the world of the theatre, casting decisions are always a mix of euphoria and sadness. There are disappointed actors and happy actors, that's the nature of it. In the case of *The Liberty Suit*, everyone, to a man, was delighted that Gerard was cast.

There was no doubt that he was ready to take this on. He had made enormous strides as an actor in the nine months he'd been with us. He'd played Pat Bannister in *The Risen People* and Cathal Brugha in *Dev*, acquitting himself with distinction in those supporting but substantial roles.

Taking the show into the Olympia (a theatre with over 1,000 seats) was a huge financial risk for Project. We essentially gambled our Arts Council grant on the venture. If it failed, then Project would have to close, at least temporarily. That meant that the gallery, cinema and music side of things were implicated in the decision. After all, we were an arts centre, and the various disciplines fed off and sustained one another. In 1976 the Arts Council grant was £16,000. By 1977, our subvention from the Council had risen to £34,000, but our expenditure, in tandem, had gone through the roof. We were not in a position to publicly declare the nature of the gamble, but many people privately thought we were certifiably insane.

The media couldn't get enough of the arsonist-turned-actor story. The tabloids went to town – there were fewer of them then, making them all the more powerful – and 90 per cent of the coverage focused on Gerard, his past misdemeanours and his chance at stardom. The other 10 per cent went on Noel V. Ginnity, the diminutive and well-known comic who was guesting (as Benny Morelli) at the Christmas concert in the second act of the play. Noel's assistant was the brave Claire Mullan, who'd taken the role knowing she had to bare her breasts – or at least attempt to – at the very same moment that, elsewhere in the prison, the young traveller Furey was tying a sheet around his neck, preparing to hang himself.

The play opened on Monday, October 3rd, in what was really a dress rehearsal. Shea and I stood nervously at the back of the stalls. On one side of us was John Stephenson, and on the other Brendan Smith. We wished each other broken legs as the lights went down. Curley (Gerard Flynn) and Grennell (Gabriel Byrne) were discovered in a light centre stage. Curley puffing on a cigarette and Grennell squinting at him. Beside them the screw, Carson, played by Kevin Flood. Carson tells Curley to finish the cigarette and exits. Curley drops it on the floor and Grennell gets down on his knees, retrieves it and sticks it in his mouth. There are ripples of laughter. Shea digs me in the side, I dig him back. The train has left the station and we're on our way. Grennell sucks on the cigarette butt and turns to Curley.

> GRENNELL: *I'm a common thief. You're a fire-bomber or whatever you call it.*
> CURLEY: *Look it, I'm in here for nothing, remember that, nothing. I'm an innocent victim of Irish law. And for your knowledge it's called arson, not fire-bombing.*

The audience laugh at the dialogue.

They start to strip. They get down to their underpants. In tandem, they pull them off and stay as they are, staring front. Brendan Smith comes over to Shea and myself and berates us for breaking our agreement with him. Patrons in the back row turn around and tell him to 'shut up.' On-stage, the screw Martin tells Curley and Grennell to get into the showers and 'wash some of the Dublin scum off yourselves'. It's all over in a matter of seconds. No member of the audience has walked out in disgust or shouted abuse at the stage.

At the interval, I leave the theatre to avoid people. It's a bit like half time in a football match. I don't want to accept the

congratulations of victory and neither do I want the commisera-
tions of defeat. I don't want to deal with 'small talk.' I walk up
Dame Street in the direction of South Great George's Street. Just
around the corner is where Dockrell's stood, on the corner of
Fade Street. Four and a half years earlier the building was ablaze.
Tonight, something else is burning. Gerard Flynn's star is lighting up the Olympia. Across the city in St Patrick's Institution, the
prisoners are looking out their cell windows. Eighteen months
earlier, Gerard Flynn had been among them.

Noel V. Ginnity looks tiny on the Olympia stage, but he
loves the interaction with the audience. It is his life blood. He'd
told us in rehearsal that people love to abuse small people; they
feel they have that right, part of the belief that small people are
the progeny of the devil.

'You're only a fucking leprechaun,' a man shouts up from the
second row of the stalls.

Noel V. fixes him with a stare. Then he points at him.

'Do you see you,' Noel V. says. 'The last time I saw a mouth
like yours, Lester Piggott was beating the arse off it.'

The audience applaud the put down.

'Get off the stage, there's a smell of manure off you,' Kava
(Peter Caffrey) shouts, entering into the spirit of the occasion.
With that, the audience realise that the prisoners have come
down and are in the auditorium.

'The fellow who just said that, me and him were a double
act one time,' Noel V. retorts. 'We were called the Symbolics. My
name was Sym.'

The prisoners jeer Kava, who is not best pleased. But it helps
to settle the audience. The concert is great craic and Johnny Curley
wins the trophy for entertainer of the year. Ironically, Gerard

Flynn had brought the real trophy into rehearsals but everyone thought it was too small for the play, that it would look silly. So, in the interests of 'truth,' we went for a bigger cup! Curley, with his own song, beats Kava's Elvis Presley impersonation and wins the trophy. On the way back to the cells, the curtain rises and the figure of Furey is revealed, hanging from a sheet in his cell. The reality of suicide intrudes and destroys the atmosphere.

Emotions are running high. The final scene is Curley's departure, having completed his sentence. He's saying his goodbyes when he stops. It looks like he's forgotten his lines. I can tell the occasion has got to him. He tries to speak but he can't get the words out. I can sense the other actors wondering what they should do. A member of the audience shouts out:

'Go on, Mannix.'

There is a whistle and then some applause. It gives Gerard the opportunity to compose himself. Billybow (Paul Bennett), manages to quieten the house.

BILLYBOW: *Go on, Johnny Curley, give us a song.*
CURLEY: *All right, I'll sing a song for you, Billybow.*
                 On the day of my departure
                 They gave me the snot green suit
                 Two piece imitation tweed
                 With flecks of yellow and blue
                 Two strings vests big fish in the sea
                 White underpants for virginity
                 Two green stockings to cheer me up
                 Two handkerchiefs come blow me nose
                 The release form said it was a fact
                 I was a liberty boy

CHORUS

So all young offenders please take note
There's a typewritten card on your prison door
And when that day it comes at last
You'll be a liberty boy

On the day of my departure
They gave me the liberty suit
But I didn't like the look of it
So I gave it to the Vincent de Paul
Then I got me own clothes back
Brown double-breasted pin-striped suit
The buttons wouldn't button
And the stripes wouldn't match
I didn't know that me gear was small
Or maybe I was growing tall
I was a liberty boy

The play was supposed to end there. But Ger Hogan (Garret Keogh) had organised a surprise. He got a bucket of water. On the final beat of the song, he and Billybow dump the water over Curley's head. Then Ger Hogan pushes the parcel containing the liberty suit into Curley's hand.

GER HOGAN: *Jonnie Curley… you're going to need that now.*

Blackout.

9

I was awarded the Rooney Prize for Literature at the end of 1977. I had no idea it was coming, which made it all the sweeter. It felt like a vindication of all the work I'd put in at the Project and the T Company. It was also nice because my good friend Neil Jordan had won it the previous year for his collection of short stories, *Night in Tunisia*. The book had been published by the Irish Writers Co-Operative, of which I had been a founding member. It felt like our generation were finally coming to the fore and being recognised. Shea had been awarded the Macauley Fellowship in 1976, which made it a literary hat trick, so to speak.

Sheila and I went into town and bought our first suite of furniture. There was a sale in Arnotts, and we forked out a large portion of the £2,500 prize money on the best sofas and armchairs they had to offer. We paid cash and Arnotts presented us with a special store card that gave us access to all that they had to offer. It was a credit card before credit cards had been invented, and we used it often because it was a powerful feeling, knowing that anything we saw could be ours.

It should have made us happy but it didn't. Newfangled gadgets fell into our laps and made our lives easier only for our lives to get much more difficult. I was spending more and more time on my career and less and less time at home. I rarely made it back to read my sons a bedtime story. I didn't know that their childhoods would be over in a heartbeat. I thought that there would always be time to retrieve something, that I would have the opportunity to make it up to them. I thought they would understand that my career was important.

Sheila and I were seeing less and less of one another. We were sharing a bed but little else. Her concerns centred on the family, mine on the theatre. I couldn't work up any enthusiasm for the latest Mothercare catalogue and Sheila wasn't bothered whether we could afford to pay Equity rates to the actors or not. We were living in separate universes, in different emotional spheres, but the big row, when it came, was about my drinking.

'Do you have to come home smelling of drink?' Sheila said.

'I'm entitled to a pint after a hard day's work.'

'When was the last time you went into a pub and had a pint? One pint?' Sheila said. 'You're sitting in the pub when you should be at home telling the boys a story.'

'I meet people in pubs. That's where business is conducted. Everyone does it.'

'I don't.'

'You're looking after the boys.'

'Exactly.'

'You've no business being in a pub,' I said.

As the words left my mouth I realised how ridiculous they sounded.

'Neither do you. You're a writer. You should be at your desk, not talking shite in a pub.'

'Who's talking shite?'

'You know what I mean.'

'I don't know what you mean.'

'You'll never write anything decent sitting in a pub. Anyhow, you should be at home telling the boys a story. They notice everything.'

It descended into an argument, and we said awful things to one another. I told her I'd only married her because she was pregnant and she said that I was too small for her and that she should have gone with her gut instinct and refused my entreaties at the start. We decided to separate and spent the whole night trying to work out the practicalities. We hadn't resolved things by morning and I went with her to the playgroup. I was so incensed that I cancelled two meetings at Project so that I could continue the row with her. We tried to finalise our separation in between picking building blocks up off the floor and organising sand play. We collected Rossa – Fiachra attended the playgroup – and went into town and had lunch in the Bad Ass Café. We bought a loaf of bread and headed to Stephen's Green to feed the ducks. The boys amused themselves while we tried to finalise splitting up.

'I don't want to lose you,' I said. 'I don't want to lose the boys. I love you. I love our family.'

'You're killing the family, killing it stone dead.'

I tried to imagine what it would be like not seeing them again and it brought up stuff I hadn't felt since Frankie's death. I didn't want my heart broken again, once in a lifetime was enough for that.

'Please don't leave me,' I said.

'You're the one doing the leaving. You're never at home, Peter.'

We went home, bathed the kids and I told them a story. Sheila and I went to bed but we were beyond arguing by that stage. Everything that needed to be said had been said. She lay with her head on my chest and I held her close. I thought about running away. To London or New York. But I knew that wasn't a solution. That was a cop out. My boys needed me and I needed them. I needed Sheila, too.

I decided to cut back on my drinking. The following morning, I told Sheila that I would not be coming home any more smelling of drink. The boys would get their bedtime story, and if drink was to be consumed, we could have one together in the house or in the pub, depending on the availability of babysitters. I wanted us to be a proper family, and if that required change, then I was ready to embrace it. I was determined that alcohol was not going to take my family away from me. I loved them too much to let that happen. I put a plan in place to control my intake, because I knew that without a plan I might have to abandon alcohol altogether, and that was a price I was not prepared to pay.

* * *

The tensions at home were mirrored at work. A row between two of our actors, Jer O'Leary and Alan Stanford, almost brought the production of *Marat/Sade* to a premature close. The play's full title – *The Persecution and Assassination of Marat as Performed by the Inmates of the Asylum of Charenton Under the Direction of the Marquis de Sade* – embodied what happened. Towards the end of the play, M Coulmier, the director of the asylum, addresses the audience on the corruption at the heart of contemporary French society. Jer O'Leary, who played M Coulmier, took the liberty of addressing the Project audience on the corruption at the heart of the Irish judicial system, specifically, the arrests of

Osgur Breathnach, Nicky Kelly, Mick Plunkett, John Fitzpatrick and Brian McNally for the Sallins mail train robbery. 'The Sallins Four', as they were known, (the charges against Plunkett were dropped because he held out against signing a confession), members of the Irish Republican Socialist Party, had formerly been a part of the Official Republican movement. The two groups had been shooting at one another as part of their deadly feud. On the day of their convictions, however, Jer felt it incumbent to make a speech in defence of his political enemies.

Alan Stanford, who played de Sade, was outraged. He felt that the context made it appear that Jer was speaking on behalf of the cast of *Marat/Sade*. In the dressing-room he confronted Jer, and before they knew it both of them were rolling on the floor, headlocked together. The rest of the cast were on-stage, singing the final number. At the curtain, they ran to the dressing-room and separated the two men.

Stanford assumed that Jer was part of the IRSP, and was amazed to find that such was not the case. Jer, for his part, assumed that what he had done was within the tradition of the theatre, taking a liberty in the context of it being the last night of the show.

'I was just being a bit loose with things,' Jer said. 'You once said to me that was in the tradition of the theatre, Alan.'

'A bit loose, maybe,' Alan said, 'but not that bloody loose.'

It didn't take long for the row to become the stuff of legend. I've met thousands of people who were there on the night, even though Project only held one hundred and fifty. It took the Sallins 4 many years to clear their names. They did, and in the end Nicky Kelly was offered a Presidential pardon. Christy Moore wrote a song about him, and I taught it to my children:

Give the Wicklow boy his freedom
We must give him back his liberty
Or are we going to keep him in chains
While those who framed him up hold the key.

* * *

There's an old gag about a Paddy going into a barber's shop in England with a pig under his arm. The barber asks where he got him and the pig says, 'I won him in a raffle.' It's a crude put-down, eighteenth century in origin and tells us a lot about the plight of the Irish at that time. Many of those who survived the Famine and the coffin ships did so precisely because they had pigs – the warmth of the animal kept their owners alive – so the newly arrived Irish who survived the journey were the ones seen carrying pigs under their arms.

The pig joke provided the starting point for a play. I'd wanted to write something about the relationship between Ireland and England, or rather, the lack of a relationship, how our perceptions of one another were based on misunderstanding, fear and ignorance. Things were at an all-time low in the mid-seventies, the IRA had taken their bombing campaign to England, making any kind of *rapprochement* impossible. This was nothing new, of course; anti-Irish sentiment was fuelled in the nineteenth century by the migrations of starving, uneducated peasants from famine-racked Ireland. So on the one hand England proved to be our saviour, and on the other our tormentor. We blamed the British Parliament for the conditions that led to the catastrophe of the Famine in the first place. Due to the prevailing economic wisdom of the time, enshrined in the Corn Laws, food was exported from Ireland while people died of starvation. It was argued, with a great deal of validity, that the Act of Union of 1801, which abolished the Irish Parliament and brought us under the direct control of London, was a political decision that made us incapable of action when catastrophe struck.

I set out to write a play that would parallel then and now. The volunteer with the pig becomes the peasant with the gelignite. They are part of a continuum. The violence of the contemporary period is not an isolated thing. It has its roots in history and until the causes of the conflict are faced up to and confronted, nothing will be resolved. However, once I started to write about the Famine, I couldn't stop. I knew that it was too big a subject to deal with in one half of a play. I couldn't get from the nineteenth to the twentieth century in the course of two hours. John McGrath (of the 7:84 Theatre Company – 7 per cent of the people own 84 per cent of the wealth) had commissioned me to write the play, and he felt it was imperative to bring the action up to date. He thought that without that juxtaposition the piece was a history lesson. I disagreed with him, and John was difficult to have a row with. Apart from being a thoroughly decent person, he was one of the brightest and best-read individuals I have ever come across.

We agreed to disagree on my Famine play, now called *Emigrants*, and John let it go, without rancour. I brought it to a London-based company, Pirate Jenny. Their artistic director, Jenny Rees – I thought initially that the company was called after her, but the name owed itself to the character in Brecht's *Threepenny Opera* – was intrigued by the subject matter and particularly the character of the Scarecrow, who was the play's narrator. I created him because I couldn't think of anything more redundant than someone charged with protecting the crops in a landscape where the crops have failed.

I had great fun with the Scarecrow, and loved writing him. He was opinionated, funny, annoying, perverse, abrasive and gross, a great foil for the apocalyptic awfulness of Ireland's great catastrophe. He owed a great deal to the Greek chorus with a nod to *The Wizard of Oz* along the way. I knew that the casting of the Scarecrow was crucial to the success of the play. Pam Brighton, the director, had previously worked with Irish actor, Alan Devlin (only ever known as Devlin) at the Half Moon Theatre in London's East End. He'd played the lead in *George Davis Is Innocent OK*, a play by Shane Connaughton (from Finglas in Dublin by way of Redhills in Cavan) that had helped secure the release of Davis, who'd been stitched up by the Metropolitan Police. As it happened, Shane Connaughton also joined the cast of *Emigrants*.

Devlin was just like the Scarecrow, funny and annoying, brilliant and dangerous. He was a Jekyll and Hyde; he could charm you in the morning and torment you in the afternoon. You never knew, on any given day, which Devlin would show up for rehearsals; and there were the days when he didn't show up at all.

'I was in the pub, I'm not going to lie,' he said arriving at rehearsals one afternoon smelling of drink. 'The second act is a pile of shite. I mean, I'm a fucking Scarecrow, what am I doing in England? I belong in Ireland, I'm an Irish Scarecrow.'

Devlin was extremely agitated, and yet you couldn't help feeling that he was talking from the heart. He cared about the play and the role. He wanted it to be right and he'd fight anyone and anything to get it there. He'd even fight himself.

'Tell me to shut up if I'm not making sense. Please tell me to shut fucking up.'

It was impossible to rehearse with him in the room. So we abandoned rehearsals and Pam Brighton and I went to Sheehan's pub in Chatham Street to talk things through. We were considering our options – to sack Devlin or not to sack Devlin – when the aforementioned burst into the bar.

'I know you're going to sack me. Buy me a drink if you're going to sack me, that's the least you can do.'

Dermot Sheehan was behind the counter, and I could see that he was nervous. The sight of Devlin in full flow often had that effect on him, as it did on many of the city's bar owners.

'If you've any backbone you'll buy me a drink. One for the road, isn't that what they say? One drink for the Scarecrow and I won't bother you again.'

Dermot Sheehan was out from behind the counter and over to us, all hands and whispers.

'I can't serve you any more drink, Devlin, so please don't ask.'

'I wouldn't ask you for the steam off your piss,' Devlin said.

'Now language, please, I have customers in the bar.'

'Order a drink for me Mr Playwright,' Devlin said. 'He won't take an order off me but he might take an order off you.'

'No more drink, I'm giving you no more drink.'

Devlin turned on Dermot Sheehan and started to assault him with quotes from the 1916 Proclamation, Emmet's speech from the dock, Brendan Behan's *Borstal Boy*, all the while gaining in intensity as he went along. By the end of it, he was frothing at the mouth. All conversation in the bar had ceased. Everyone's eyes were fixed on the crazed Devlin. He had lost control. Pam Brighton shouted at him, at the top of her Yorkshire voice:

'Devlin... Devlin... you'll bloody give yourself a heart attack.'

He stopped dead in his tracks.

'My heart would never attack me,' he said.

Everyone laughed. Dermot Sheehan cracked, despite himself. Devlin surveyed the bar, like a great performer who'd won over his audience, who'd turned disaster to victory.

'I'll give you one drink and that's it, one drink and you must leave the bar,' Dermot Sheehan said.

'I'll have a pint of Guinness and a small whiskey, Irish, with a drop of water on the side.'

Devlin sat down beside us and grinned.

'I know you're going to sack me,' he said. 'If I was in your place I'd sack me, too.'

He never made it to rehearsals the following day, even though we'd offered him one last chance. As it turned out, Devlin's non-appearance was the least of our problems. There always comes a point with a new play where the actors lose faith. They start to doubt themselves and then they start to doubt the play. When this happens, it is imperative that the creative team – director, writer, designer – hold steadfast to the belief that the play is the most important new drama since *Look Back In Anger* or *Hamlet* or *Waiting for Godot* or *Death of a Salesman* or whatever. Once that wobbly period of uncertainty is navigated, the play returns to calmer waters and becomes, once again, the masterpiece it was always destined to be.

Pam Brighton, for reasons I could not understand, either then or now, allowed all of her doubts regarding the play to surface in the rehearsal room. At the point when we needed her strength and conviction, she fed only our uncertainties. She picked up and repeated Devlin's mantra that the second act was 'a pile of shite.' I don't know why she did this because it served no useful purpose. The only thought that made sense was that she wanted to follow Devlin out the door. But she could have come to me or Jenny Rees and asked to be relieved of her duties. She didn't have to bring the entire edifice down around her. She was an experienced director and it didn't make sense.

Her behaviour made me very angry. She had done irreparable damage to the show, and if it was to survive, then she had to go. Jenny Rees and I met with Shea and asked him to take over as director. He agreed, with the caveat that I would have to play the Scarecrow. I had no choice. We held a late night meeting with Pam and told her she was fired. Her surprise surprised me. I had to inform her that company morale was on the floor because of her. Her position was untenable.

The following morning, Jenny, Shea and I came to the Bricklayers Hall in Cuffe Street, where we were rehearsing. We presented the actors with the news. Veronica Quilligan, who was playing Maurya, immediately said that she could not continue without Pam. The Canadian actor, Peter McNeill, whom Pam had brought over to play Michael Pat (I had no idea why the part was not cast from the hundreds of available actors in Ireland, none of whom would have struggled with the accent) said that he would have to consider his position. Nora Connolly, a London-based Irish actress and former girlfriend of Devlin's, came in to replace Veronica Quilligan. We were back in business.

Sheila was upset that the tour was going to take me away unexpectedly. I was sad that I was going to miss out on Fiachra's first day in big school. Mannix Flynn, who was playing Ronan Furey, was set to miss out on the birth of his first child. Indeed, the new arrival came in the middle of our run at the Royal Court in London. He and Christine, his girlfriend, called the baby Sheridan. He was not, as some people assumed, named after me. It was called after Christine, who was also a Sheridan.

Her brother Michael had directed *Marat/Sade* in Project earlier that year.

Emigrants opened at the Clifden Labour Club in Blackpool. Having spent many summers there as a child with my mother and father, it was weird to go back in the guise of a Scarecrow, spouting aphorisms about the ills meted out to Ireland by absentee English landlords. The play toured around the north of England before heading to London. I stayed with the show until after it opened at the Royal Court, when Vinnie McCabe, my old friend, took over the role from me. I watched his opening performance and then got so drunk that I have no idea how I got back to my digs in Earls Court. The night is completely erased from my memory.

Two weeks later the cast arrived in Dublin. The play was slotted into Project for the Dublin Theatre Festival. Peter McNeill came to see me.

'I have no way of getting back to Canada,' he said. 'I'm feeling very vulnerable right now.'

I understood that his deal involved return air travel to Canada.

'Yes, but I don't have a return ticket right now,' he said.

'You'll get your return ticket when the show finishes in Project,' I said.

'Do you know what a panic attack is?' he said.

I was aware of panic attacks because I suffered with them when I drank. It was not something I talked about because I didn't want to acknowledge, not even to myself, that alcohol had this effect on me.

'No, I don't know about panic attacks,' I said.

Peter McNeill described them. He couldn't sleep at night, worrying that he'd never get back home. All he wanted was something that would alleviate his stress. He felt that a plane ticket might just make his life bearable for the remainder of the run of the play.

Jenny Rees could be tough, but Peter McNeill won her over with his arguments. She bought him a ticket to Toronto. At the tech rehearsal the following morning, there was no sign of Peter McNeill. At twelve o'clock we got a call. He was in London, about to board a plane for Toronto. He was sorry but he'd had enough of Ireland; enough of Devlin and Pam; enough of famine and death; he needed to get home to his girlfriend; he was sorry to dump us in it. He wished us well and hung up.

That night I appeared as Michael Pat in *Emigrants*. I got blind drunk after the show and suffered a panic attack. I had to get out of the pub. I stood outside the Granary in Essex Street in the rain. Shea followed me out and asked me what was wrong.

'It's stress. Taking over this part. I'll be all right in a minute.'

I never made it back inside and Shea never understood the reason why.

* * *

Things improved at home after the near collapse of our relationship earlier in the year. I'd had to admit I was a workaholic and make changes accordingly. I got home more regularly and cut back on the drinking. The result was that Sheila and I spent more time together and we decided to have another baby. We were both delighted when she became pregnant again. It was a welcome distraction from the travails of *Emigrants* and the Project Arts Centre.

Sheila hated hospitals and I wanted to see the baby being born. It was a perfect recipe for a home birth. We got all the latest books and studied them. It was so exciting, the idea of a birth taking place in our own bed, in our own house, at our own pace, with the boys around, and no one shouting that visiting time was up. On Friday, December 29th 1978, Hannah Barlow, the midwife, arrived to induce the baby as it was two weeks overdue. I had a huge fire blazing in the front room. The Christmas smell had given way to the smell of talcum powder. There was a new baby bath, and lots of little vests and babygros. The television, with the sound down, flickered in the corner. RTÉ were showing a new version of Bram Stoker's *Dracula*, starring Irish actor Bosco Hogan.

Hannah Barlow, as well as being a midwife, was a member of Dublin Corporation. She was a non-party, Independent Councillor. In the battle over Gay Sweatshop, she had voted with Ned Brennan to withdraw the grant to Project. I was under strict instructions from Sheila not to mention the war; I had no intention of bringing it up. I went upstairs to tell the boys a bedtime story and Hannah broke Sheila's waters. I came down and we sat around waiting for nature to take its course. Nothing much happened. After a couple of hours, she administered a series of pitocin injections to speed things up. Again, the result was disappointing. There was no movement. She placed her hands on Sheila's tummy and examined her bump.

'Oh!'

For the first time, I felt a concern.

'I think this baby may be breach,' she said. 'I can't be certain but I think the head is above and the feet are below.'

She took Sheila upstairs to the bedroom for an internal examination. I tried to distract myself with the goings-on of *Dracula* but it wasn't distraction enough. Hannah Barlow came down and told me that she was going to look for a second opinion. She called our family doctor, Ita Killeen. By this stage it was snowing outside. Hannah was very assertive on the phone. It added to my unease. Less than twenty minutes later, a knock came to the hall door. It was Ita Killeen and her husband Colm, himself a doctor too. She was wearing an evening gown and he was in a tuxedo and bow-tie. They were on their way to a gala dinner. They stepped out of their car and came in. They went straight upstairs to Sheila. I followed them up. They both examined her. There was a disagreement. Colm thought the baby was breach but Ita was fairly certain it was in the correct position. There was much discussion as to whether the baby's head was the head or the bum.

'I think that's the bum,' Colm said.

'Well, if that's the head, there's no nose,' Ita said.

Hannah seemed to agree with Colm. It was two against one. They were agreed on one thing, however. I had to get Sheila to the hospital ASAP. The Rotunda. This was no longer a home birth. The situation required everything a hospital had to offer. Colm took me outside into the hall.

'Do you know what anancephalus is?' he said.

I shook my head. I'd never heard the term before.

It's an abnormality where the brain doesn't form as it should.

'Are you telling me that the baby is not going to survive?'

'Not if it's anancephalic, no. It won't make it, I'm afraid.'

'And Sheila?'

'She'll be fine. But you need to get her to the hospital.'

The Killeens left and Hannah started to pack up her stuff. All I could think about was the large head and Sheila's reaction when it came out dead. Hannah was saying something about delivering breach babies in the old days but I wasn't really listening. My only thought was how was I going to keep this awful news from Sheila. She was such a motherly mother. I couldn't let her know what I knew. It was my secret and I had to keep it that way. I had to keep normal, had to stay casual, put up a front and not give anything away. I had to let nature takes its course, its bloody awful course.

Hannah was stepping out the hall door saying goodbye and I didn't even notice. I heard her car engine turn over and ran out after her. I waved at her and wasn't sure if she saw me through the falling snow. Sheila came down the stairs with her small bag packed. I picked up the phone.

'I'll call the ambulance,' I said.

'No,' Sheila said. 'I don't want to go by ambulance. I want you to drive me in. I want you to stay with me. Is that ok?'

'Yes, of course,' I said trying to be normal.

'You'll have to get a babysitter for the boys.'

'Of course I will.'

'What would I do without you?' Sheila said. 'I don't know what I'd do without you. You're a life saver.'

If only that were true. I ran down to Shea's house on the Ballybough Road, less than two minutes away. I explained the situation, but said nothing about the baby's head. We ran back up the road. Shea settled himself in downstairs and Sheila and I headed out in the car. The roads were treacherous. Despite the gravity of the situation, I took my time. The Rotunda was quiet and we were seen immediately. A very personable junior doctor from Sri Lanka attended to us. He filled out a form with our address, occupation, medical card details, Sheila's history and so on.

'What religion are you, Mrs Sheridan?' he asked.

'None,' Sheila answered.

The junior doctor laughed. He looked at me and I smiled but inside I was shaking. We went over the events of the day and he listened and took notes. He admitted Sheila to the ante-natal ward and he put her on a drip. I stayed with her for a few hours and then I went home to relieve Shea. I didn't meet one other car on the road.

It was near four o'clock when I got to bed. I didn't sleep a wink. I prayed a lot. I even said the rosary, something I hadn't done since I was a child. I prayed that the baby would be ok, and Sheila too. The last time I'd prayed with such desperation was in the weeks leading up to Frankie's death. I blamed God at the time for letting him die. I was sure He'd save him but it hadn't worked out. I turned to Him again now, in my hour of need. I was hopeful He wouldn't do it to me twice. He couldn't do it to me twice, I figured.

The following morning, I organised the boys, dropped them off at Shea and Fran's and went to the hospital. The weather had improved somewhat. Sheila was sitting up in bed, no visible sign of labour. She introduced me to Veronica, a hospital administrator, who was standing beside the bed to the right.

'I'm having trouble with this woman of yours, Mr Sheridan,' Veronica said.

Sheila threw her eyes to heaven and shook her head.

'Do you know what she put down on the form for her religion?' Veronica said.

'None,' I said.

Veronica was surprised that I had the answer at the ready.

'She was raised a Catholic. At worst, she's a lapsed Catholic, am I right?'

'I'm not putting down lapsed Catholic,' Sheila said.

'But what if something were to happen to you?'

'What do you mean?' Sheila said. 'Do you mean while I'm giving birth?'

'I mean if you were in a traffic accident. Wouldn't you like to have a priest with you? Wouldn't you like to receive the sacraments?'

'I'd hate to have a priest with me. I'd want Peter with me if I was in an accident.'

'You really have turned your back on your religion, haven't you?'

'To be perfectly honest, Veronika, I think it's the other way around. I think religion turned its back on me. It turned its back on women. When the Church treats us as equals, I might think about joining again.'

Veronica tried to suppress a smile. There was a great deal of admiration in the way she looked at Sheila. She turned her attention to me.

'You're married to a real women's libber, aren't you?' she said.

'Yes, I am, thank God,' I said.

'Thank God, indeed,' Veronica said and walked off holding the form in her hand.

The Master of the hospital had been down to see Sheila. He was not a happy man. He wanted to prepare a full report on everything that had happened in the house. Now was not the time for finger pointing. He wanted a safe delivery, that was the important thing. The questions could come later. Sheila had signed a form authorising a Caesarean section if it was required. I was relieved but I couldn't tell Sheila. I couldn't tell her about the baby's head. Thank God for a C section, I thought. Thank God for the Rotunda hospital, the same hospital where I'd been born twenty-six years earlier. I felt nothing bad would happen in the hospital where I'd drawn my first breath. I clung on to that hope. I was not going to let any negative thoughts take hold. It was New Year's Eve, December 31st. The end of the old and the start of the new.

The boys were excited about staying up for the New Year and hearing the fireworks and the ships' horns and the people coming out onto the road to sing. By nine o'clock, however, they were unable to keep their eyes open. All they wanted was a story and bed. By nine-thirty, they were soundly asleep. I called the Rotunda. There was no change, Sheila was still on the drip and there was no labour. As the clock ticked towards twelve, I started to feel very sorry for myself. I was alone, stuck in front of the television. At a quarter to twelve I decided to pop over to Shea and Fran's. I checked on the boys, they were unconscious. I would only be a half an hour. They'd be safe for a half an hour, I told myself. I put the spark guard in front of the fire and left.

There was a party in full swing in Shea and Fran's and the atmosphere was intoxicating. I knocked back two large whiskies, one after the other. It made me dizzy. Once the wave passed through me, I was at ease. All the worry and concern that had been occupying my brain vanished. I was myself again, my true self. I wanted more of this feeling so I knocked back another whiskey. In no time at all, I was drunk. I started to get morbid, thinking of Sheila. That gave way to paranoia about the boys. I couldn't remember if I'd put the spark guard in front of the fire or not. I went home to check. Coming around the corner of Ardilaun Road where I lived, I saw Ned and Eileen Kennedy, my next door neighbours, on the footpath.

'Congratulations, we heard your good news on the radio,' Ned said.

I didn't know what he was talking about.

'The first baby of the new year, I wouldn't doubt you,' Eileen said.

'They announced it on the radio, gave your address and all, two Ardilaun Road. You're after putting us on the map,' Ned said.

Sheila had given birth to a baby girl, at one minute past midnight, by Caesarean section, the first baby girl of the new year, 1979. The news sobered me up, in a fashion, but not enough to drive the car into town. I rang the hospital and spoke to a nurse who'd assisted in the delivery. The baby was normal. There was no enlarged head. Six pounds even and perfectly formed. Mother doing well but exhausted.

He hadn't let me down. I said a prayer, kneeling by the bed, and thought about my daughter, not yet a day old. In twenty-three hours she would reach that milestone. We had decided on Doireann if it was a girl. It was Sheila's choice. I liked the name, too. I thanked God for bringing Doireann safely to us. I'd missed her birth but she was all right, that was the main thing. I wanted her to be normal, that was all. To grow up and prosper. In the year 2000, she would be twenty-one, the first Irish girl to reach that age in the new millennium. It made me smile to think about it. I was so happy, I fell asleep laughing.

10

My sister, Ita, gave me a present of *Down All the Days* by Christy Brown for Christmas of 1978. It didn't take me long to fall in love with this magnificent book and the struggle of its paraplegic author to communicate with the world. It is such an emotional book, and after the trauma of Doireann's birth, it felt like it had been written for me. It is quintessential Dublin working class, one of the great books in that tradition, on a par with James Plunkett's *Strumpet City*, Paul Smith's *The Countrywoman* and Brendan Behan's *Borstal Boy*.

I read it quickly and then I started it again. I read it more slowly the second time. I drank it in and savoured it. I was plotting an outline in my head. It was an unselfconscious thing because I had never adapted a book before. I was consumed by the material. I took notes in a jotter and christened it my Christy Brown notebook. I went out to the house where he had lived on Captains Road in Crumlin. It wasn't far from the mobile home site where I'd lived for three and a half years. I walked along the paths where he had been pushed in his 'chariot,' the ramshackle trolley knocked together by his father when he was a boy. I studied the window of the upstairs bedroom from where he had seen his sister Mona kiss her boyfriend under the street lamp below; and the excitement and guilt he felt at the stirring it engendered in his groin.

Christy was living in Ballyheigue, County Kerry, with his wife Mary, who was formerly his nurse. I found this out from the producer, Noel Pearson, a font of knowledge when it came to these things. He told me that Mary was very protective when it came to Christy's work. He urged caution in how I approached them. Undeterred, I wrote to Christy at Mab Cottage, Ballyheigue and had an immediate response. He wanted to meet me. I showed Sheila the typewritten letter with the signature at the bottom that looked like a child's.

'This is one of my all-time heroes and he wants to meet me,' I said.

I didn't waste any time. I travelled by train to Tralee, and Mary collected me and drove me to Mab Cottage. The location, high up on the mountain overlooking the sea, was spectacular in the extreme. I was too nervous to take it in or appreciate it. Mary brought me into the living-room and she called Christy. Seconds later he came bounding into the room in his wheelchair. He said something to me but I didn't catch a single syllable of it. He threw his head back and repeated it. I looked at Mary.

'He's saying "up the Dubs,"' she said.

I broke into a nervous laugh.

'Up the Dubs,' I said.

A sporting reference was the last thing I expected from him. I never imagined that he would be interested in Gaelic football. I told him that Paddy Cullen, the Dublin goalkeeper, was a neighbour of mine from Seville Place. He seemed delighted and became very animated. I gathered that he had lost a fortune backing Dublin to beat Kerry with the locals. He was a Dub living in the Kingdom and he had to stand up for his native city against the culchies.

'I'm still a Jackeen,' he said.

He had the saddest eyes I have ever seen. They were a piercing blue covered in a film of sadness. He gave the impression of someone with a brilliant mind trapped in a body that had failed him, a failure he could not conceal. There were moments when he seemed far away, as though the effort to engage in conversation was just too painful. It was easier for him to retreat to his own world where the rules of social intercourse didn't apply.

The first item on the agenda was getting out to the pub. He had been savouring it for days in advance of my coming. He'd been on the dry, working on a new book (*A Promising Career*, as it turned out, his final novel) and he'd been looking forward to his reward all week. I needed no persuading to become his accomplice. We hit the local pub and two pints of Guinness and two small whiskies appeared before us. Mary pushed a straw into his pint and he manoeuvred his lips onto it and began to suck. He didn't stop sucking until there was nothing left in the glass. He attacked the whiskey and demolished that too. Then he threw his head back and laughed up at the ceiling like he had outfoxed God Almighty Himself.

The more he drank, the easier it was to understand him. I don't know if that was the effect of the alcohol on his muscles or on my brain. I suspect it was the latter. We were becoming familiar with one another, a familiarity that was about to deepen when he indicated that he needed to use the bathroom. I pushed his wheelchair to the men's toilet only to discover that it didn't fit through the door. I lifted him out of his chariot and carried him in. The cubicle toilet was out of order. The only alternative was a stainless steel urinal that stretched along one wall. I held

him up and I realised what I had to do. I undid his fly and fished
for his willie. I pointed it towards the stainless steel wall before
us. He urinated with gusto. I knew in that moment he would give
me permission to adapt his book.

We headed back to Mab Cottage. Mary went to bed and
Christy and I played LPs on his record player. He was a Chuck
Berry fanatic. I jived with him, spinning his wheelchair around
the living room. *Riding Along in my Automobile* was his favourite. He made me play it four times in a row. We drank some
more whiskey and talked. I was getting more accustomed to
the strange sounds he made. He stopped talking and started to
groan. I realised he was snoring. I'd been asleep, too, I figured. I
called Mary, and she came and collected him and I went to bed
in the spare room.

I had the mother and father of a hangover the next day.
Christy didn't seem too bright either. We talked about *Down All
the Days* and he seemed happy with my thoughts on it. He loved
the idea of the narrator who would communicate the boy's inner
thoughts for the audience. That was how I imagined it might
work when I read the book. Having met Christy, I wasn't so
sure. He was such a powerful presence, the way he tried to talk,
the struggle of it, the movement of his head, and I wondered
was there any way to realise that on-stage. Or to look at it from
another angle, would the narrator pull the attention away from
the boy, would he steal the protagonist's thunder? Christy was so
enthusiastic about the narrator, I felt the time was not right to
raise the deeper question.

Armed with his outline permission, I left Mab Cottage on
the Saturday afternoon to catch the five-thirty train to Dublin.
Mary dropped me at the station. She drove off and I went in
to the barrier to present my ticket. There was no checker and

no passengers waiting. The last train to Dublin had departed at five o'clock. I thought about calling Mary Brown but I was too embarrassed to explain my predicament. I didn't have the price of a bed and breakfast. There was only one thing for it.

I started to hitch. Six lifts later, I arrived in Portlaoise. It was after midnight. I found a hotel and called home. Sheila got her brother, Francis, to babysit the boys and drove to Portlaoise in our Fiat Bambino to collect me with baby Doireann in her Moses Basket on the back seat. On the way home, we stopped for petrol and oil. I poured in the oil but forgot to replace the cap. By the time we arrived back in Dublin at three in the morning, the car smelt like a funeral pyre. I checked the engine. It was covered in a blanket of black gunge. I had managed to write off the car. Somehow I knew that *Down All the Days* was going to be a difficult ride.

* * *

Life at Project seemed like a series of unending conflicts. The ongoing battle with our funders was matched by the war within, the internal struggle to make the building respond to our growing ambition for it. It was difficult trying to sustain a theatre, visual arts and cinema programme while buckets hung from the girders trying to catch the rain that poured through the roof. We were putting serious pressure on the Arts Council to provide funds for the refurbishment of the space. In an effort to ratchet up that pressure, John Stephenson had the toilets in the foyer knocked down – they'd been giving trouble for years – in the belief that it would force the Arts Council's hand.

Shea was on holidays when the demolition took place. He came home and lost it with John.

'You knocked down the fucking toilets. We had toilets and now we have none. How is that progress? Tell me, how does not having a place to piss make us more radical? It's bourgeois, bourgeois crap, that's what it is. I can't believe the toilets are fucking gone. I feel like walking away, that's the truth.'

The conflict over the toilets and their destruction was about class. Shea and I came from a background where it was important to hold on to what you had. In 1956 we had moved from a three-roomed cottage in East Wall to a large house in Seville Place. It was to accommodate our expanding family, two adults, four children and one on the way. The new house had no bathroom or toilet. There was a creepy W.C. at the end of a garage at the back of the house. It had no roof, which made it both indoor and outdoor at the same time. What it did have were cobwebs and spiders. All of us children avoided it except for emergencies and Ma threatened to move back to East Wall if the situation was not resolved. In order to save the marriage and our collective sanity, Da got Uncle Paddy and Uncle Jim (his two brothers) to help him plumb in an inside toilet and bath. They started on Friday night and kept at it until they finished late on Sunday evening, when Ma went into labour and was taken by taxi to the Rotunda. Frankie was born the following day. His coming home and christening coincided with a party to welcome the arrival of our new 'modern conveniences.' So the issue of a toilet was important to our family and the destruction at Project cut to the core of who and what we were.

Shea never bought the argument that the toilets could be used politically and he found it impossible, in his role as chairman of Project, to justify their destruction to the Arts Council.

One good thing did come out of it, however. It was a celebration of punk culture called *Dark Space: 24 Hours* and it was the brainchild of Nigel Rolfe, the centre's visual arts officer. He was essentially a performance artist, determined to put Project at the heart of cutting-edge work. His own practice was ground breaking and innovative. He crossed over and made links between the disciplines (the first one to do so, in my opinion), working with Mannix Flynn on an installation where he built a cell (with breeze blocks and cement) that entombed Mannix, who had to be freed using a sledgehammer. He also used soundscapes in his work, and was a great enthusiast for the modern in all things.

Nigel believed that we could get Johnny Rotten to headline *Dark Space*. After the demise of The Sex Pistols, Rotten was now fronting a band called Public Image Limited (PIL). He'd been born in Dublin (real name John Lydon) and never tired of proclaiming his Irish roots. We were delighted when PIL committed to headline the event. The result was that every band in Ireland wanted to play. In no time, we had signed up The Undertones, The Virgin Prunes, The Atrix, U2, The Radiators and scores more. We had cabaret performers, jugglers, circus acts, performance artists, street acts, poets, a human jukebox, strippers, fire eaters and caterers. We were having food and we were having toilets too. We rented portaloos and put them in the small gallery and on the roof. Every contingency was planned for and taken care of. Then, at the eleventh hour, PIL pulled out.

Shea went to London to find out why we'd been dumped. It was just too easy and too cosy for the band to cancel over the phone. Shea wanted to be told to his face, man to man, and he wanted to be given a reason. Shea was furious with Johnny Rotten because he was furious with John Stephenson. It was all about the toilets being knocked down. Somehow Johnny Rotten became part of that story, even though Johnny Rotten knew nothing about the toilets. We were putting on *Dark Space* because we had a building that didn't work any more and we were celebrating punk culture because the punks were outsiders like us. The last thing we needed was for Johnny Rotten to go back on his word and kick us in the teeth when we were down.

It was a Friday evening when Shea arrived at the house in Gunther Grove where Rotten lived. It was set out in apartments and Shea pressed the bell that said 'Lydon.' A man, not Lydon, answered and refused Shea entry. Shea brushed past him and headed up the stairs, but the man laughed at him and headed for the basement. Shea realised his mistake and went after him. The man blocked his way and shouted down the stairs. Johnny Rotten appeared and said something but he was hard to understand.

'Why are you not coming to Ireland?' Shea shouted down to him.

'What the fuck's going on, mate?' Johnny Rotten shouted back.

'I'm talking about your appearance at the Project, why did you cancel your appearance at the Project?'

'I know nothing about your project, son, nothing.'

'Do you want me to get rid of this geezer, John?' the man blocking him said. He grabbed Shea by the lapels.

'Take your fucking hands off me,' Shea said.

With that, the man pushed Shea and he fell down the stairs and knocked Johnny Rotten to the floor. They wrestled for a minute or two where they'd fallen. Shea felt ridiculous.

'Do you want to go to the pub and talk about this?' Shea said.

It was all he could think of to say. There were four or five of them and one of him. He didn't want to get his head kicked in. Johnny Rotten thought the pub a good idea and they went there and got drunk. Somehow the story of the row filtered back to

Dublin and the *Evening Press* newspaper carried it on their front page. Two hours after it did, the tickets for *Dark Space* sold out.

* * *

The fact that U2 played at *Dark Space* seems seminal. It wasn't, in fact. In the pecking order of the day, they were down the bill to The Undertones, The Atrix, The Virgin Prunes and The Radiators. The thing that struck me about them in those days was how unlike a rock band they were – they were clean and they were Christian. Bono was involved with a sect called the Children of God and they had a place in the dunes in Portrane, not far from where my parents had a summer cottage. I had helped my parents buy it with money I'd received from the Abbey Theatre. They had Bible readings and sang hymns to give thanks for the setting sun and the splendour of the universe. It was respectful. It was sincere. But it wasn't rock 'n roll.

After their appearance at *Dark Space*, Paul McGuinness came to me and organised for the band to do a residency. We had a regular late night slot on Fridays and Saturdays, and the main performers were Scullion, Andy Irvine, Supply Demand and Curve, Freddie White, Christy Moore, Barry Moore – artists that, broadly speaking, came from the folk tradition. U2 brought a whole new audience and a whole new dynamic to the Project. As well as their loyal and growing fans, they also attracted a crowd who didn't like their vibe and came to disrupt the gigs. One of the U2 haters produced a knife one night, and but for Mannix Flynn having disarmed him, he might have done a serious injury to someone. The incident was reported by someone in the crowd and the police were called, but despite a search the weapon was never found.

Nigel pushed for us to broaden our musical programme, despite the board's worry that we were inviting trouble on ourselves. We invited John Cooper Clarke and Linton Kwesi Johnson to make their Irish débuts at Project. Cooper Clarke was to perform on a Sunday evening at eight, but there was no sign of him for the sound check at seven o'clock. Frantic phone calls to his management in England elicited nothing. Aer Lingus information likewise didn't operate on a Sunday back then so we couldn't tell if he'd travelled or not. We searched the few pubs in Temple Bar that were open – Timmins and the Granary – and we trawled the quays as well. At eight thirty, with the theatre packed to the rafters, I had to go out in front of the audience and tell them that Cooper Clarke was a no show.

I went to the bar of the Clarence Hotel to drown my sorrows and there, sitting in a corner drinking a pint, was John Cooper Clarke. I approached him.

'John, you were due on-stage a half an hour ago in Project,' I said.

'Someone was supposed to come and get me.'

'You were due to do a sound check at seven o'clock.'

'What time is it now?'

'It's nearly a quarter to nine.'

He held up a book.

'I was just going over what poems to do. I've never played Dublin before. I'm excited.'

There were several words to describe how I felt but 'excited' wasn't among them. I ran out of the hotel and down Essex Street shouting at every person I met that the gig was on.

'Cooper Clarke is here, go back to Project.'

I was panting and shouting like a crazed person, waving my hands and proclaiming the mystery that the poet Clarke was alive and about to read his poetry. I wanted to kill him, of course. I wanted to find the knife that Mannix had hidden and murder him on the spot. At nine-fifteen Cooper Clarke took to the stage, drink in hand. The theatre was half full. He hobbled on, and I don't know how he managed to stay erect, because the boots he was wearing had six-inch heels. The points looked like they would slice through steel. They were alligator hide. He made an apology for the late start, said something indecipherable about W.B. Yeats and launched into a poem called *I Married a Monster From Outer Space.* It was electrifying. Poetry at a hundred miles an hour. He had a book in his hand but he didn't once look at it. He spat the lines out with attitude, with venom, with verve and with hate. He crucified the subject of the poem and stuck a spear in her side just to finish her off. It was misogynistic, outrageous and compulsive. I'd never before felt a poem collide with an audience and mow them into the ground.

I looked at this gaunt man, with his long hair and his Roman nose, his skin-tight jeans and his alligator boots and I wondered how he could call anyone a monster from outer space. It was ironic and it was intended. Over the next hour and a half John Cooper Clarke delivered the best solo performance I had ever seen. He turned his audience on, as though he'd injected them with heroin. Each poem felt like a high that surpassed the high of the previous one. The words felt like they were coming at two hundred miles an hour, or more. He finished with *Beasley Street,* a homage and a valediction of the street in Salford, Manchester – hence his title as the Bard of Salford – where he'd been born and reared. For me, it could so easily have been Sheriff Street… *where deadly nightshade is their flower and manslaughter their meat.*

* * *

Aliens weren't exclusive to John Cooper Clarke. Shea was working on a play where aliens were taking over the city of Dublin.

They were living in the sewers under Dame Street, Lord Edward Street, Christchurch and Parliament Street – only a stone's throw from Project itself – from where they were about to emerge and take over the running of our society.

'I'm going to write this play in three days,' Shea told me, 'it's the only way to do it. Get the play down and then improvise it. What do you think?'

I thought he was mad. I didn't think you could put a time on it and force the process. Anytime I tried to do that, it went haywire on me. I had to let the subject dictate its own pace. I had to let it breathe.

'I'm not sure you can write a play in three days,' I said.

'Maybe not, but you can certainly do it in ten. Dario Fo writes them in a few weeks. Shakespeare didn't take long either. If I get the first act done over the weekend, will you type it out for me?'

I loved Shea's optimism, and the fact that he couldn't type. He was always in too much of a hurry for the menial things in life. Fran usually did his typing for him. She was very good and made few mistakes.

'Is Fran not available?' I said.

'She is, yeah. But the typewriter is broken.'

I was working on the first draft of *Down All the Days*. I was writing it by hand as I always did.

'I'll loan you my typewriter. I don't need it at the moment.'

My electric typewriter weighed a ton. Shea put it in Doireann's pram and wheeled it across to his house. Six days later he asked me to read the script. Well, the first two thirds of it. He'd stayed up five nights on the trot to get it done. He'd typed it himself. He'd only used two fingers. It was a difficult read. He'd pressed too hard on the keys, so the letters had punctured the paper, leaving holes everywhere. It was plastered in Tippex too.

As always with Shea, there was brilliance in it and there was banality. I said lots of encouraging things and I told him to get it typed again so that it could be properly read. He got defensive over my comments on his typing.

'Do you really think it looks bad?' he said.

'No, it's just the typos and the spacing.'

'Whats wrong with the spacing?'

'It should be double spaced. It's too cramped. You need to see more white on the page.'

'More white. I never thought of that,' he said.

'You need to leave a space after a full stop. It's hard on the eye otherwise.'

'How many fingers do you type with?' he asked.

'I use all ten,' I said. 'I learned how to type from a manual.'

I was determined to get my own draft of *Down All the Days* finished so I backed off from directing the play, *Inner City/Outer Space,* as it became known. It divided the critics and it divided audiences, too. I think the major mistake was Shea directing it himself. I felt guilty over that. There were so many places where it needed discipline and it got only his indulgence. Mannix was again wonderful and Susie Kennedy, playing a mermaid, stole all of her scenes. Johnny Murphy and Gabriel Byrne were brilliant in the comic scenes. The play infuriated the critics but the person most upset by it was Neil Jordan. He tackled Shea in the Granary on the opening night.

'I told you I was working on a story about aliens, Jim, I told you that,' Neil said.

Neil was normally placid and laid back. This was as angry as I had ever seen him. He had his two hands on the lapels of Shea's jacket and he was shaking with emotion.

'Maybe you did, Neil, I don't remember, honestly.'

'We were sitting in a café on Middle Abbey Street. I told you about aliens taking over Liberty Hall. You had no right to steal that idea.'

'I didn't steal it from you.'

'I can't use it now, yeah? You fucked it up on me, that's what you did, yeah?'

'People come up to me with ideas all the time, Neil. I use what I like, that's the way I work. It's not stealing.'

'Well, I don't want you taking my ideas.'

'Don't discuss them with me then.'

It was an uneasy *détente*. I could see that Neil wanted to kill him. They were alike in so many ways. They were both poor listeners. The idea in their own heads always fascinated them more than the ideas in anyone else's. There were many times in conversation with the pair of them when I realised they hadn't heard a word I'd said. You accepted that with Neil and Shea. It must have come as a shock to Neil to realise that Shea had been listening to him; and it must have been an equal shock for Shea to realise that the idea may not have originated in his own head. They were both brilliant and both self-obsessed and it was this tunnel vision, this blocking out of reality bordering on contempt, that helped them both to succeed so brilliantly later on in the world of film.

* * *

I finished the first draft of *Down All the Days*. It had taken six months to complete. My writing table was in our bedroom in Ardilaun Road. I finished it in the afternoon, checked it for spelling errors and brought it downstairs for Sheila, proofreader and syntactician extraordinaire, to read. I handed it to her.

'That's my new creation,' I said, 'be gentle with it.'

She put the manuscript on the table with attitude and tutted at me. I knew there was something up.

'What's the matter?' I said.

'Nothing's the matter. You were just too busy to notice, that's all,' she said.

She half laughed and put her hand on her tummy. She was pregnant and this was her way of telling me.

'I'm expecting a baby, and I'm so happy I can't tell you,' she said.

After the debacle of Doireann ending in the C section, we had decided to try immediately for another baby. It had been so traumatic that Sheila felt if she waited any longer she might never have the courage to go again. She also thought there was a good possibility she'd have a second girl if she got pregnant quickly.

I knew she was back to her normal, playful self. I had never seen her look more complete or more radiant.

'Are you going for a home birth this time?' I asked, jokingly.

'No. I'm going for a hospital birth and you're going to be there with me.'

I submitted *Down All the Days* to the Abbey, and Joe Dowling came back with very positive comments. He thought it was a show for the main stage because of its scale. He thought that Mr Brown, the father, was the key character, and he had ideas for how he should develop. Mrs Brown was a more success-ful creation, but she was easier to realise. He also felt that the relationship between the Narrator and Young Christy posed problems and he wasn't sure that they could be resolved by clever staging alone. He asked me to work on a second draft and re-submit it. I was disappointed that he wasn't making me an offer. I needed hope. I needed there to be a cheque in the post. I needed something concrete. There was another baby on the way. I needed reassurance.

'Do you want to take an option on it?' I said.

'No, I want to see a second draft.'

'That could take a while,' I said. 'That could take several months.'

'I don't want you to rush it, that's the last thing I want you to do. Take your time.'

I got up to go, disappointed, but I couldn't articulate it.

'There's one more thing,' Joe said.

'What's that?'

'We have a writer-in-residence scheme here at the Abbey.'

'Yeah, I know that.'

'It's worth four thousand pounds. I want to offer it to you for the coming year. Is that something that would interest you?'

I ran out onto Marlborough Street and down into Parnell Street and I headed up Summerhill towards Ballybough because I was so anxious to tell Sheila the news that I never thought of taking a bus or a taxi. All the way home, I thought of Sean O'Casey and Brendan Behan, Tom Murphy and Tom Kilroy, Brian Friel and W.B. Yeats, all the writers who had been produced at the Abbey. I was being invited to follow in their footsteps. My name would appear on their headed paper under 'writer in residence'. The world premiere of my adaptation of *Down All the Days* would take place on the Abbey Stage. As if that was not enough good news for me, word came through from London that the Royal Court Theatre would present *The Liberty Suit* as part of the Sense of Ireland Festival the following March. My star was definitely in the ascendant.

John Stephenson had been headhunted by the Government to spearhead a festival of Irish culture in London. After the disastrous IRA bombing campaign in Britain, it was felt that the arts were central to repairing the damaged relationship between the two countries and generating a positive image of Ireland on the mainland. Substantial funds, by the standards of that time, were made available, and John was chosen to put the programme together. Having resigned twice from Project and come back, John had an indestructible quality about him. He had that great ability to reinvent himself, and quickly. As part of the education and outreach programme of the Sense of Ireland Festival, he convinced the leaders of the UVF and the UDA to share a platform with the leaders of the Provisional IRA. It was the first time since the outbreak of sectarian violence in 1969 that the tribal leaders came together and engaged with one another. Years later it would provide a paradigm for the architects of the peace process.

There were problems, as always. Mannix, for personal reasons, wasn't available for the London run of the show. We cast Gabriel Byrne instead to play Jonnie Curley. Over the four years since he had first appeared on the Project stage, Gabriel had matured into being one of the finest actors in Ireland. As a result of his television appearances in *The Riordans* and *Bracken*, he had become a star. There were television personalities aplenty in Ireland, but Gabriel was different: he had an appeal that made him a real box-office draw. A move to London was the logical next step for him and *The Liberty Suit* seemed the perfect vehicle to introduce and establish himself there.

The plan was to open *The Liberty Suit* in Dublin prior to its London premiere. The Olympia wasn't available, which was a setback. It had been such a great venue first time around and it left us with only the Pavilion in Dun Laoghaire as an alternative. We had played there for two weeks in 1977, but it had no flying facility and we were anxious to improve the show technically for London. I had rewritten it and introduced a female school-teacher, Miss Ryan, who gets involved with one of the prisoners, Peter Murphy. This had been alluded to in the first production of the play but we never saw the teacher. At Shea's suggestion, I brought her on-stage and gave her a couple of scenes, including one where she introduces the prisoners to Oscar Wilde's *Reading Gaol*. I was never convinced that introducing her was a good idea. It always felt to me that the frustration of the prisoners was more believable in her absence; that once she appeared in the flesh, it diminished our sense of their sexual oppression.

I never intended to direct *The Liberty Suit* – I was of that old-fashioned school who believed that an author should not direct his own work – but it was a revival, albeit with rewrites, and we knew that it worked as a piece. Joe Dowling had offered Jim (it was about this time that I gave up and started to refer to him as Jim professionally even if he was always Shea within the family) the world premiere of Tom Murphy's play *The Blue Macushla*. The timing was in direct conflict with *The Liberty Suit*, so I took on my own play. I also took on *The Risen People*, which was going to the Institute of Contemporary Arts (ICA) as part of the Sense of Ireland Festival. In addition to all that, my production of *Waiting for Godot*, which had opened in Project the previous November, was going directly from London to a festival of Irish culture in Charleston, USA, organised by Gerry Davis, the gallery owner from Capel Street and sometime Leopold Bloom.

I was literally running from one rehearsal to another. I was never at home, contrary to all the promises I'd made in the wake of the near collapse of our marriage. Sheila knew how important the work was to me, but she wasn't slow to remind me that things were sliding again.

'The kids miss you, and they miss you because they love you so much.'

'Once I get the Sense of Ireland Festival out of the way,' I said, 'things will get back to normal, I promise.'

'Normal. I don't know what normal is any more,' Sheila said.

'I have a rehearsal tonight, we'll talk about it when I get back.'

There was a knock on the door, persistent and strong. I went out to answer it. Mannix was there with a man I'd never met before. I invited them in. Sheila offered them tea and Mannix said yes. The man with him looked uncomfortable. The tea was poured and we made small talk and then Mannix introduced the man as his solicitor. He handed me a letter and said that it concerned authorship of *The Liberty Suit*. I wanted to open the envelope and read it but not with him standing there. I knew that it was bad news, and even though I didn't know what it said, I felt guilty. Well, I felt like I had done something wrong because otherwise they would not be in my house, they would not be here with a letter for me to read. I had a case to answer and it was inside the envelope, but I didn't want to engage with it until after they had gone.

It seemed like an eternity before I walked them down the hall and out the front door. I came back in and read the letter. It took me a minute or two to realise that 'our client' meant Mannix. In relation to their client I had abused my position. I had not credited him properly even though the play was clearly based on his experiences. His contribution was invaluable and he was entitled to be credited as the co-author of the play. Following on from that, he was entitled to 50 per cent of the author's royalty accruing from exploitation of the play. These were reasonable demands and my failure to comply with them would result in them taking out an injunction to stop the play.

I felt that my integrity was under attack. I had to defend myself against these charges. I couldn't let it be said that I had abused Mannix. I had written the play in an attempt to prove his innocence. There had never been any motive to exploit him. I had, however, taken his name off the front page of the script when I'd submitted it to the Abbey. I had to acknowledge that to myself. I'd written a programme note for the Olympia production outlining our collaboration but he hadn't been formally credited on the poster or the programme. That was a mistake. He should have had his name on the title page from the outset. But I didn't believe, then or now, that he was the co-author of the play. I had written it with his collaboration and I was prepared to agree a wording that reflected that. Regarding the royalty, I had always given him 25 per cent and I was prepared to push that to 33.3 per cent.

I went to see my old friend, solicitor Garret Sheehan, and he referred me to his colleague, John Gaynor. I put my position to him and he translated that into legal speak. We communicated with Mannix's solicitors and awaited their response. They were not for turning. It was co-authorship and 50 per cent, nothing less. I dug my heels in. I didn't really care about the money. I couldn't countenance a notion that we'd shared the writing. Yes, we had talked about every aspect of the story, from his childhood through his incarceration to his release; we included songs he'd written while he was in gaol; but I made all the executive decisions about what was in and what was out. I felt in my heart that I'd written the play.

It was a wonderful collaboration that made the play possible and that was the tragedy of where we had ended up. There was no play without Mannix; there was no play without me. To resolve the issue, one of us had to compromise. If ever there was a case for mediation, this was it. It needed the two of us in a room with a good listener and I have no doubt we would have come to an agreement. But it was not to be. We were young and full of idealism and integrity, but too much of it. We were both right, and if we were both right, then neither one of us could be wrong. There was only one place to which we were headed, and that was the High Court.

* * *

Sheila was progressing nicely to full term. I was looking forward to naming the baby. Sheila had chosen for Doireann and it was my turn now. I had a feeling it would be a girl. Two boys and two girls just seemed like the perfect balance, the yin and the yang. I was looking forward to the birth. Eight years since I'd been at Rossa's and I was too nervous then to take it in and enjoy it. It was my second chance and possibly my last, too. Sheila had said as much. Four and she was done, that was it. I wanted more but it wasn't in my gift. That was Sheila's department.

Rehearsals were very difficult. The actors were torn apart. They didn't want the show to go down, but Mannix was their friend and they felt for him. First time around we had taken on the world with *The Liberty Suit* and now we were taking on each other. The actors were generous and tried to hide their feelings. It was important to keep the head down and get on with the work; but it was impossible not to feel that the play's cutting edge had been blunted by the row. It had been so much more than a play three years earlier. It had been a transformative experience for us and for the audience. It had put rehabilitation back at the heart of the penal debate. It had woken up a generation to the reality of life behind bars.

The High Court action was set for Friday, February 1st. We'd had a preview of the show on the Thursday night and it had gone well. I had a notes session scheduled with the company for the Friday afternoon. It was purely academic, however, if the injunction was granted. With a judgment against us, there would be no show. The run would be over after one performance. The shortest run in the history of Irish theatre; and maybe the shortest in the history of the world. I met with John Gaynor and my Senior Counsel Kevin Feeney, who had prepared the brief. Kevin was a brother of Jim, the doctor who had delivered Rossa in the Coombe. They were both brothers of my friend, John Feeney, who had given me work as a freelance journalist on the *Catholic Standard* newspaper. Kevin was confident we'd win. Across the atrium, not twenty feet from us, stood Mannix and his team. It was a surreal feeling. Mannix and I, two men who loved each other, about to do battle, surrounded by people for whom it was a professional thing. They weren't emotionally involved, it was their job, and ultimately, they didn't care.

We trooped into the courtroom. I was more nervous than the night the play had opened in the Olympia. The barristers made their pitch to the judge, Mr Justice Finlay. I found it hard to hear them. They weren't actors, of course. Their major concern was legal argument and point scoring, not projection. Mr Finlay looked down and caught sight of Mannix. Then he looked across and caught my eye. His face scrunched up. It wasn't heartburn. He was genuinely upset.

'I saw the play in the Olympia,' he said. 'I thought it was very good.'

Then he called the barristers forward and they had what amounted to a private chat. I wanted to restage the confab but I knew it was not my place.

'I understand a lot of money has been spent on this production,' Mr Finlay said. 'I can't make an order that would cause that investment to be lost. I understand, however, that the parties are not far apart on the other matters. I'm glad to hear that. Genuinely. I'll put it on the list again and hope that you can resolve matters in the interim.'

We came outside to the atrium and Kevin Feeney shook my hand. It took John Gaynor to explain to me that their application for an injunction had failed. The show would go ahead as planned. It was just a question of working out a deal on the billing and the royalty split.

'What's your best offer to them?' Kevin Feeney said.

'Offer them 30 per cent and in collaboration with,' John said.

I was glad the whole thing was over. I felt elation, relief and sadness. I had invested so much emotional energy into this, I had rehearsed my speech from the dock but never got to make it.

Kevin Feeney came back after consulting with Mannix's people.

'They'll accept 33.3 per cent and in collaboration with, the billing to appear on everything – posters, programmes, front of house, everything.'

We all shook hands and I went outside onto the quays for a cigarette. I put the fag in my mouth and searched for matches. I had none. I looked around to cadge a light from someone. Mannix was standing along the path from me. He struck a match. He held it between his hands to protect it from the wind. I bent down and my face touched off his fingers. I heard the click of a camera; and then several more clicks. I stood up and saw Frank Miller, the Irish Press photographer, standing beside us. That was the image that would define the day, Mannix helping me out when I needed a light.

* * *

That night, the show went on and everyone was relieved that the court business was over. I went home and Sheila's waters broke at two in the morning. There was no panic. We waited until eight o'clock, got organised and I drove to the Rotunda. I stayed with her while they put her on a drip and into a ward. The contractions were mild. I went out and bought all three morning papers. The court case got extensive coverage. The photo of me getting the light from Mannix apeared in the *Irish Press*, beside it was a profile of Frankie Byrne, the agony aunt who fixed the nation's problems. If only. I left the papers with Sheila and went out to meet Sandy Craig. He was a journalist writing a piece for *Time Out* magazine to coincide with the play's opening at the Royal Court. He was a writer himself and had written for 7:84. His play had been seen at Project in 1978. Later on, he was one of the founders of City Limits.

I met him in the bar of the Clarence Hotel. He was sitting in John Cooper Clarke's seat. He was very engaged by the story of how I met Mannix and the evolution of the play from that. He felt that it was a peculiarly Irish thing; that it couldn't have happened in England. He had read the script and was full of probing questions and revealing insights. The interview went on longer than I had anticipated. I rushed back to the hospital but couldn't find Sheila. She wasn't in the ward and she wasn't in the delivery room. Finally, I located her sitting up in bed with our new arrival, a baby girl, seven pounds and seven ounces. She was raging that I'd missed the birth. That was three in a row. I was in the childbirth doghouse with no chance of remission.

'I suppose you're going to call her Joyce,' Sheila said.

I'd forgotten, it was February 2nd, James Joyce's birthday. He would be ninety-eight if he were alive.

'How did you remember that?' I said.

'I didn't remember. I saw it in the newspaper.'

Joyce. Joyce Sheridan. The name sounded ok, but I didn't want her to grow up under a shadow. I admired James Joyce. His daughter Lucia had grown up with the weight of that name around her neck. She lived in a sanatorium in England somewhere. No, I would not call her Joyce. She would get her own name, she would grow up to make her own mark. I loved the name Nuala, a shortened version of Fionnuala. She looked like a Nuala to me. Sheila loved the name as well. Nuala completed the family, for the time being at least. We brought her home to Ballybough and I headed off to try and make sense of Ireland to an English audience.

11

The Sense of Ireland Festival, rather than representing the beginning of something, signalled an end for me. We had brought two of our best shows there, we'd put Project Arts Centre on the London map as it were, but we had also run out of steam. We'd had five years of non-stop manic activity at the centre in Essex Street and we'd taken it as far as it could go. The court case over *The Liberty Suit* had soured things, and we could never return to where we had been before. The whole enterprise had been built on enthusiasm and innocence: we had no fear of failure, no reputation to protect or guard. We were now at a crossroads, looking for a new direction. Shea had been hurt by the critical reaction to *Inner City/Outer Space* and *The Ha'penny Place*, the latter a musical adaptation of the *Threepenny Opera*, which I had directed in the Dublin Theatre Festival of '79. It had brilliant music from Philip Chevron, of the Radiators and later the Pogues, a great cast headed by Mannix, Agnes Bernelle, Jeananne Crowley, Peter Caffrey, Johnny Murphy, Mary Ryan and Alan Amsby (Mr Pussy); but it was a work in progress as a script, and not quite 'there' when it opened. However, the criticism, when it came, was personal

234

and vindictive. Reviewing it in the *Evening Press*, Con Houlihan wrote:

> *To call the new show at The Project a hotch-potch would be to sug-*
> *gest a semblance of unity. And unity is something it has not got. In*
> *his last work, 'Inner City/Outer Space,' Jim Sheridan proved*
> *beyond all doubt that he has an exceedingly cluttered mind. Why*
> *he should choose to repeat the proof is not easy to understand...*
>
> *Mr Sheridan must take a look at himself — preferably a good*
> *hard long one. I doubt if he has the humility to do so. There was*
> *a time when he was a hungry fighter — he has become a fat cat so*
> *quickly that one doubts the wisdom of subsidies. For the second*
> *time in a few months he has hurled at the public a grotesquely*
> *unedited work.*

Hugh Leonard once said to me that you must never let the critics know that they've hurt you. Shea didn't feel hurt, he felt wounded.

'Fuck this country, I'm getting out of here,' he said to me.

'Come on, it's Con Houlihan. You know what he's like; he probably had a fight with someone in a bar before he wrote that.'

'I think I could sue him. Suggesting I've become a fat cat. That's libel. I'm not going to let him say that about me.'

'They can say what they want. Paper never refused ink. You'll be eating your chips off it tomorrow.'

'I'm going to go down to Mulligan's pub and confront him.'

'That's the last thing you need to do. You'd be better suing him than doing that.'

Shea got a legal opinion indicating that he had a case. For the next three months, he asked everyone he met if he'd been libelled. Everyone agreed that he had. He wasn't a fat cat and he hadn't abused the Project's subsidy. Everyone agreed with that proposition. He was so sensitive around that issue. It was back to the destruction of the toilets again and his fury at their removal. Every dog in the street knew there was no money in what we were doing. Shea and I had split a salary between us for years, and the suggestion that we were making ourselves fat on the spoils of Project was an outrage. The truth is that Con Houlihan loved us and had such high hopes for Project that, in his disappointment at the show, he went over the top and acted more like a father betrayed than a theatre critic. That is not to excuse his excess, which was out of order. Indeed, the next time I met him (outside Mulligan's on Poolbeg Street as it turned out) he threw his arms around me and told me that he loved me and that he loved Jim too.

'I love you boys, I fuckin' love you, you understand me… no bullshit now, I'll have none of that….'

Con went on a rant about some taxi driver who had taken a fiver from him and driven off without giving him his change. He waved his fist at a cab stopped at the lights on Tara Street when the driver waved his fist at him in return. Con ran down the street and started banging his fist on the roof of the car. The driver pulled away but Con ran after him holding on to his side mirror. Cars were blaring their horns and swerving to avoid him. He lost his footing and fell down in the middle of the road. I went to his aid but he couldn't get up. I didn't know if it was the injury or the drink. I waited with him until an ambulance arrived. He refused to go to hospital. I, and some colleagues from the *Irish Press*, got him standing. We started back in the direction of Mulligan's.

'A brandy and port, I need a double brandy and port,' Con said. 'There's fuck all wrong with me.'

By the time we got back to Mulligan's, he was walking unaided. Another taxi passed and he ran after it, waving his fists at it. There was nothing I could do to stop him. He was a wild man, a country man, chasing cars on the streets of Dublin, looking for revenge. He was our best and our worst critic, a demonic creature, a man possessed, beautiful and out of control. Ironically, he was like something straight out of a Jim Sheridan play.

* * *

I was in two minds regarding what to do about being the Abbey Theatre's writer in residence. We had always regarded the Abbey as the enemy, and we saw Project and what we stood for as a kick against it and the arts establishment. We were radical; they were conservative. They had a big grant; we had a small one. They were old hat; we were newfangled. Ronan Wilmot, the Abbey's press officer, suggested the two institutions needed to build bridges. He organised a 'friendly' soccer match. The teams lined out one Sunday afternoon in Terenure, and never was there played in Ireland a more unfriendly game of football. It was a 'stop the man at all costs' affair, with outrageous penalty decisions given against Project by a referee who worked in the accounts department of the Abbey! It was generally agreed that Project had the better players and the Abbey had the better jerseys. The match in reality, however, was all about proving who had the better artistic programme.

I couldn't help feeling I was betraying the side. I was conflicted. Who would I play for in the soccer match? I couldn't play against my old comrades – Paul Bennett, Gabriel Byrne, Peter Caffrey and Johnny Murphy. I went to see Tom Murphy for guidance. He was inseparable from the Abbey even though his first play, *A Whistle in the Dark*, had been rejected by them. He was their major dramatic voice of the seventies and yet he had also worked in Project, delivering a brilliant production of his play *Famine* for us. We met in the Trocadero restaurant, where Tom had treated me after he'd seen *No Entry* at Project four years earlier.

'The Abbey needs a play from you, something wild and irreverent. It's all too safe right now.'

'What are you working on?' I asked him.

'I'm finished. Retired. I'm returning to the land, doing a spot of farming. I've planted some potatoes. I'll need to harvest those.'

I was shocked at Tom's decision. I interrogated him further, but he was determined that playwriting was in the past for him. I didn't know him well enough to realise that he retired after every play he wrote. He turned his back on all of his writing. It was part of how he worked. He had to stop. Each play that he wrote was like a destruction of his personality, an emptying of his psyche. He was spent when it was done, he had nothing left. In many ways, that was what made him so special. No two of his plays were alike. He could move from realism to expressionism and from magic realism to farce, because that's where he was at any given point in his life. He changed and the work changed with him.

I was deeply affected by that meeting with Tom. I felt that it was a signal for me to stop; the five years at Project were over and it was time to reinvent myself. I didn't have a garden big enough to plant potatoes in. I did have a young family. Four children under ten and me not yet thirty. Sheila working as a playgroup leader, the only guaranteed money we had coming in.

We lived in hock to the local shop – Penny's of James Avenue – and would have gone under without them. Ballybough was a tough neighbourhood with lots of social problems, which added to the stress of our lives. In the end, though, it all came down to money, and we didn't have enough of it to get by. I had to do something about our finances.

Sheila's brother, Francis, came up with the solution. He'd been working in an electrical store in Bolton Street and felt that it was time for him to go out on his own. There was money to be made in the trade, and he could source the stuff at wholesale prices. All he needed was a van, insurance, and someone to drive it. I had a clean licence and several years as an insured driver. Francis only had a provisional licence. It was nigh on impossible for him to get insurance; but he could be the named driver on an existing policy. Francis had a friend with a VW Estate for sale. Our only problem was that we had no money. However, there was a baby grand piano sitting out in the O'Donoghue family home in Hollybrook Road, Clontarf. Sheila was always told that her grandmother had intended that she should have it. She took her inheritance early, sold the piano and we bought the VW.

Paul, the youngest of the O'Donoghues, came to work with us, or rather he came to work for Bright Spark Electric, the name Francis had given our commercial enterprise. We got some headed paper printed, but it didn't matter much – it was a cash business really. We bought our produce wholesale – radios, clocks, fuses, batteries, plugs and sockets, tool sets, record players, tape machines, alarm radios – and we sold them in the indoor markets around Dublin, especially the Liberty Market in Meath Street and the Dublin Bazaar in Thomas Street. The Bazaar was owned by Tony Byrne, and I had once made a radio ad for him with actors from Project. We also had a stall in the Phoenix Park racecourse on Sundays and Kildare Town on Wednesdays. It was a cutthroat trade, and we quickly discovered that our competitors were selling the same goods as us for less than we could buy them wholesale. In business terms, we weren't competitive or, to put it in Dublin speak, we were fucked.

Our customers were working-class people, and their survival was on the line every time they purchased something. One of the most successful traders in the Liberty Market was Hassan, a smiling Indian who had come to Ireland in the fifties because he believed that De Valera was one quarter Indian. With his son, Sachan, he sold damaged tins of peas and beans. They looked like they'd been smashed against a wall – battered, bruised and dented. Hassan sold them at half price, and could not get enough to meet demand. Customers fought with one another to buy the damaged goods. On Fridays and Saturdays, he came into the Liberty Market at nine o'clock and he was gone by eleven having sold his entire stock. I asked him to what he attributed his success. He pulled out his green passport with the harp on the front and held it up.

'Mr de Valera, greatest Irishman ever, only for Mr DeValera, Hassan would not be here. I owe it all to Mr De Valera.'

It wasn't the answer I was looking for. I turned to Sachan and asked him the same question.

'People want a bargain. If the tins were perfect, people would not buy. People must think they are getting a bargain.'

Out of curiosity, the next time we were in McCabes Wholesalers of Ballyfermot – the business was owned by Noel McCabe, a brother of my friend and colleague Vinnie – I asked if they had any damaged goods for sale.

'Nothing really, apart from irons. We have some defective irons,' Noel McCabe said.

The irons looked reasonable, loose handles and some wiring faults, discoloration and broken dials. In total, they had one hundred and twenty in stock and Bright Spark Electric bought the lot at fifty pence a unit. We put down our sixty pounds and brought the consignment to the Liberty Market. We put a price of two pounds each on them. We sold them as 'broken irons' that needed fixing. We sold the lot in one hour. The profit margin was 400 per cent. We went back to McCabe's, but they were out of broken irons. We went to other wholesalers but they had nothing in the quantity we required. We went back to competing against traders who had a ready supply of defective goods. We also competed against traders who possessed qualities that were indefinable and brilliant. One such man was Albert.

Albert hung around the Liberty Market, running messages for the traders. His ambition was to have his own stall. He was the lucky charm of the place, always dressed impeccably in a flowery shirt, with a waistcoat, watch and chain, the gilt on it slightly faded. On occasion, people got him to man a table while they went to the pub to use the toilet (or have a drink, truth be told), and the longer they were away, the happier it made Albert. One day he bought a cassette tape machine from me. It had cost Bright Spark Electric eight pounds but I gave it to him for six because he had helped me carry in some boxes that morning. He set the tape recorder up on an orange box and put a hand-written sign in front of it. *One only tape recorder, compleat with mike, £9.95.* Beside the £9.95 there was a figure of £12.95 with a line through it.

In no time, he was inundated with enquiries. It had the unmistakable look of a 'good bargain' about it.

'Is there a guarantee with that tape recorder?' a woman in a red coat asked him.

'Ten years,' Albert said.

'That's a very good guarantee.'

'That's a very good tape recorder.'

'Is £9.95 the best you can do on it?'

'I'll give it to you for £10.95,' Albert said.

'It says £9.95 on your sign there.'

Albert got his felt pen and put a line through the £9.95 and wrote £10.95 beside it.

'You can't do that,' the woman said.

'Yes I can, I'm a trader. This is my stall.'

'It's only a fucking orange box.'

The woman in the red coat turned to me. She came over to my table and picked up an identical tape recorder to the one Albert was selling. She gave it a good inspection.

'Is there a guarantee with this?' she said.

'Yeah, there's a two year guarantee with it,' I said.

'He's giving me a ten year guarantee,' she said.

I looked at Albert and wondered would he be alive in ten years' time. I figured the odds were probably against it.

'How much are you charging?' the woman asked.

'It's £12.95.'

'That's robbery. Highway robbery. That man is selling it for £9.95.'

She looked over at Albert, and he was so proud, standing there behind his orange box, chest stuck out, watch chain dangling from his pocket.

'I can't beat his price,' I said.

She walked back over to Albert.

'I'll give you £9.95 for the tape recorder,' she said.

'Complete with microphone,' he said, admonishing her.

She took out her purse, fished out the money and handed it to Albert. He was beaming. He had made a sale. That was what mattered. He had turned a profit, he'd made 70 per cent on his outlay. He was a trader. A stall holder of the Liberty Market in Meath Street. He didn't have the 5p change for the woman so he borrowed it from me. He went out to the pub to break the tenner so he could pay me back but I told him not to bother. I'd catch him again. He came back an hour later, singing. I had sold nothing in the interim. Albert had spent his profit and was drunk and happy. He bawled out his song:

Old man river, that old man river, he must know something, he don't say nothing, that old man river, he just keeps rolling along....

In my heart, I knew that I wasn't a businessman. I didn't have what it took to make a go of the market. I had resigned from Project, the only business I understood, to be with Bright Spark Electric, a business I knew nothing about. I wasn't an entrepreneur. I understood how it worked, I knew the mechanics, but it was fundamentally of no interest to me. It required an attitude to profit that I didn't have. I was more interested in people, their stories, families, history and songs; reducing them to customers didn't hack it for me.

* * *

Ma and Da decided it was time to leave the family home in Seville Place, number 44. They had moved there from East Wall in 1957 when I was five. Gerard and Paul had been born there, in 1962 and 1964 respectively, bringing our number to nine:

seven children and two parents. We were reduced to eight with Frankie's passing in April, 1967. Shea, Ita, Johnny and I had all left in the seventies and were married, rearing our own families. By the early eighties it was just Ma and Da with the two youngest, Gerard and Paul, who had nearly finished secondary school. The house in Seville Place – two storeys at the front and three at the back – was too big for their needs. The time to downsize had come. Da was looking at retirement and they were both looking at sixty.

The reality was that neither of them wanted to leave Seville Place. They had made their lives there. Da had been active in so many aspects of the parish. He had helped to establish the North Wall Community Association, which led him on to organising the community games. He took charge of the basketball and the swimming teams and coached them throughout the winter for their summer onslaught on medals. In addition to that, he'd had a lifetime involvement in the credit union movement and gave of his time to that voluntarily. Ma wasn't far behind him and helped out with the old folks and the ladies' club, in addition to which she worked part-time in the bar of the North Star Hotel in Amiens Street, five minutes' walk from Seville Place. They were part of the fabric of the North Wall, and never would have disentangled themselves from it except that they were suffering appalling intimidation.

A hard man (in truth he was only a teenager) from the Sheriff Street flats, Davey Smith, started to make Ma and Da's life a misery. Smith was out of control, involved across a whole range of antisocial activities, from joyriding to arson; an early school drop-out, his parents had no influence over him. He was feared in the community and was gaining a reputation for ruthlessness among businesses up the town. One day he was pushing stolen goods down Seville Place in a pram as Da was walking home from work. They knew each other. Smith had participated in the community games as a twelve year old. He'd been part of the swimming team and Da was glad when he gave it up because he was a disruptive presence. Later that same day, the police called to his flat and found the stolen goods.

In the days and weeks that followed, he began to throw stones at the windows of 44 every time he passed. Ma saw him one day (from behind her curtains), but she was afraid to confront him. He had an aura about him that was deeply unsettling. She feared that he would come into the North Star Hotel and do damage to her or the property. Her best hope was that over time he would get tired and move on to other things or end up behind bars. Things, in fact, got worse. The stones he threw got bigger. He broke a window, Da replaced it and he broke it again. I was with Sheila and the kids visiting in Seville Place one Saturday when I saw Da taking out a broken pane of glass. I asked him what had happened and he brushed it off. It was only after I spoke to Ma that I got to the truth.

'You can't let this happen, Ma, you have to do something about Davey Smith,' I said.

'We're moving, son, we'll be gone out of here and then it won't matter any more.'

'You can't let this bastard drive you out of your home. This is not Belfast, Ma. This is Dublin.'

I was so angry I could have killed Davey Smith. When I thought of what my parents had put into this community and what this little upstart was doing to them, I felt like breaking his legs, or worse. I ended up having a row with Da over it. I advised him to go to the Gardaí because things were so bad, they couldn't get any worse. He didn't see it that way.

'We won't be here much longer,' Da said.

'Do you have a buyer for 44?' I asked him.

The question was met by silence.

I went up to Sheriff Street to confront Davey Smith. He lived near my old friend, Tina Molloy, who'd been in the Saint Laurence O' Toole's Musical and Dramatic Society with me. I was walking into Brigid's Gardens and there he was, walking towards me, a flagon of cider in his hand. He smiled at me and said hello. I asked him why he was breaking the windows in my parents' house. He denied it.

'I know it's you and I want it to stop, do you hear me?' I said.

'Your oul' fella ratted on me to the police.'

'You're calling my father a rat?'

'Yeah, I am.'

'My father never did anything like that in his life. The only thing he did for you was to bring you swimming with all the other kids. Am I right?'

'Yeah, he brought me swimming.'

'And now you break his windows?'

He took a long slug from the flagon and offered it to me. I didn't take it up.

'Your Da's a rat.'

It was said without conviction. He walked away from me and I knew he didn't believe it. But that was no guarantee he would stop what he was doing. I was glad I had confronted him none-theless.

I needed to talk to Da about money. I knew that with the proposed move from Seville Place he would be holding on to every penny he had and calling in all monies owed to him. He had paid off a student loan that I had taken out with the branch in Belfield, UCD. I still owed him for that. My problem now was that I needed to raise £2,500 to get *Down All the Days* produced. Chris O'Neill, sometime actor, star of the long-running television series *The Riordans* and owner of the Oscar Theatre in Ballsbridge, thought the play was an outstanding commercial proposition. He was sure it could make money and I fell in love with his enthusiasm. I got it into my head that this show was going to be the makings of me, and of Sheila too, that this was the one that was going to turn our fortunes around. Why should I let the Abbey have it when I could make money on it myself! I went to the bank and they offered me the loan on condition that Da went guarantor. All I needed was his signature.

Da was reluctant to get involved. He'd been stung by the student loan. My failure to discharge it meant they came after him and not alone did he have to honour my commitments, an interest rate of 16 per cent, but they hit him with a guarantor surcharge of 9 per cent. He paid 25 per cent interest on the loan. It made him understandably apoplectic and over time that only mellowed to rage. I was embarrassed that he'd had to pay it off for me, but I was coming to him now with a solution.

'I can't go guarantor, not at the moment. It's immoral what they charge.'

I had to make him change his mind. I suggested to Chris O'Neill that we consider Da for the role of Paddy Brown, the father in *Down All the Days*. He thought it was a bad suggestion because he believed that we needed a television star, someone who would put bums on seats, someone who would help us recoup. I liked the sound of the word recoup, it was a producer's word, a money word. I was determined to make this venture a commercial success. So I forged Da's signature and drew down the money for the show. Chris put in £2,500 because he was a gambler, like me. Together we applied to the Arts Council and got a grant of £5,000, giving us a total production budget of £10,000 for the play that was about to make us rich.

We approached Joe Lynch to play Paddy Brown. He'd been a star of radio, when radio really meant something, before he headed off to England and regular appearances in *Coronation Street*. It made him a household name on both sides of the Irish Sea. We figured he would be a serious box-office draw. Having sent a script to his London address by registered post, I met him in his suite at the Montrose Hotel in Donnybrook, opposite UCD. He was in Ireland recording a television programme for RTÉ. I'd never met anyone in a suite before. It was impressive. There was a large vase of flowers on the sitting-room table, and when Joe sat down I had to move my chair to see him again.

He was complimentary about the script and about Christy Brown. He remembered Christy's first book *My Left Foot*, and he'd read parts of it on radio when it was published in the late fifties. He took my script from his briefcase and put it on the table.

'I'm not going to bullshit you,' he said. 'I think the father in this story is very dark. I don't believe my Irish fans would like to see me take on this role.'

I was shell-shocked. He was turning it down. It was the part of a lifetime, in my opinion, and he was saying no. We went on to talk about all sorts of things – the state of the world, the state of Ireland – and he was very enthusiastic about the work of the Project, but negative, in a sense, too.

'You and your brother will never get any recognition here. Not until you go abroad. They don't recognise talent in Ireland. You only have to look at me.'

I came away from the encounter feeling disturbed and nervous. Joe Lynch wasn't going to help us recoup. Niall Toibin wasn't available. Shea, who was directing the show, thought we could take a good actor and turn him into a star. Make the play bigger than the performers. I was reassured by him. It was the play that would help us recoup. In February we held auditions. Vincent Smith came in and blew us away with his reading of Paddy Brown. He was a regular in *The Riordans* and would get us good publicity. Geraldine Plunkett read for the Ma and was brilliant, even though she was not yet the television star she became. A ten-year-old boy, Tom Murphy, same name as the playwright but not related to him, owned the part of young Christy from the outset. Twenty years later he would win a Tony on Broadway for *The Beauty Queen of Leenane*. Tragically, he died of cancer in 2007 of the age of thirty-nine. Garret Keogh, stalwart of many shows at the Project, was cast as the Narrator.

Rehearsals began in mid-March 1981, just after St Patrick's Day. It was a difficult time in Ireland. Bobby Sands had begun his hunger strike on the first day of March and other prisoners joined in at regular intervals, a tactic designed to keep a rolling pressure on the British and Irish Governments. The situation in the Maze prison dominated many conversations and there was a feeling that hunger strike deaths in Belfast could impact negatively on the show. I was of the view that Thatcher would not allow the men to die, that Haughey, John Hume or Cardinal O' Fiach would force a u-turn on her and bring it to an end; or, failing political intervention, that her own maternal instincts would force a change of heart and allow her to give in with grace. Cardinal Basil Hume caused great controversy when he referred to the actions of the prisoners as suicide, a proposition that bolstered Thatcher's stance and underpinned it with a theological validity. There was a scene in the play where the young Christy contemplates suicide but decides against it because he has too much to live for. It made me think of how awful life must be for

Bobby Sands if a slow suicide was a better alternative than the reality he inhabited.

We had a rehearsal on the Saturday of the Aintree Grand National, April 4th. The date is etched in my memory because it was Shane Connaughton's birthday. He was playing Mick, one of Paddy Brown's pals in the play, as well as doubling as an Undertaker. We brought a portable television into rehearsals to watch the race. Shane wasn't a racing man but he felt sure that, as it was April 4th, and it was his 40th birthday, horse number 4 was sure to triumph. My father had handed down many gambling superstitions to me – never refuse the tip of a drunk man, always back the outsider in a three-horse race – and I'm sure he would have had one for this magical set of circumstances.

The horse carrying number 4 was Aldaniti. The jockey on board was Bob Champion. He had fought testicular cancer to take the ride; and indeed Aldaniti himself had overcome serious tendon injuries to face the starter. Chris O'Neill, my producing partner, felt that the gambling gods were telling us to have a go.

'I think we should take a grand out of the production budget and put it on Aldaniti,' he said to me.

I liked to gamble but that was way out of my league.

'What about fifty each way?' I said. 'Then if it finishes in the first four we'll get a return on our money.'

Chris smiled but it was a smile of disappointment. He was one of those gamblers who only came alive when there was something serious at stake.

'It will either win or be last,' he said.

I dithered, thinking through all the consequences.

'A grand on at ten to one, if it wins doesn't matter how the show does,' Chris said, 'we recoup.'

'But what if it loses?' I said.

I had put the mockers on it by suggesting it might lose. Gambling was a lot about instinct and superstition and once you thought about it, or analysed it, you were done for. It was a gut thing and I was killing it with logic.

'Let's leave it.' Chris said. 'You're right, it's not worth it.'

Aldaniti won the National and we screamed it across the line for Shane. He blew out his candles on a cake provided by Laurie Morton, who was playing Essie, one of the Dublin aul' wans in the play. Afterwards, Shane bought us all a drink in the Horseshow House, Ballsbridge, with his winnings. Chris was magnanimous but I knew I'd caused him to miss a golden opportunity.

* * *

Bobby Sands died on May 5th and Ireland exploded. There was anger that this had been allowed to happen, that the country had once again been plunged into chaos because of the actions of the British Government. Had they learned nothing down all the days, down all the senseless years? The last time we had been engulfed by an event of this magnitude was nine years earlier, Bloody Sunday in Derry, January 1972. On that occasion, the people of Dublin had marched to the British Embassy, myself and Sheila among their number, and we had burned that edifice to the ground. In the wake of that, the Embassy of Her Majesty's Government had moved from the centre of the city. It had become a fortress, situated on Merrion Road, no more than a quarter of a mile from the Oscar Theatre.

The effect of Sands' death on audiences at the Oscar was cataclysmic. We kept the theatre open but our business dropped from over 80 per cent to under 10. People were afraid to go out, fearful, they would get caught up in riots. A second hunger striker,

Francis Hughes, was also nearing the end of his life. Theatres and cinemas closed and the shutters came down all over the city. After three weeks we bowed to the inevitable and dropped the curtain on *Down All the Days.* I went to the bank manager to try and work out a repayment strategy on the £2,500. He offered me a term loan over three years. I negotiated that to five. I asked him if the bank would sponsor me, but he didn't understand.

'If I wrote something, you could put your name over the title,' I said.

'What are you writing at the moment?' he said.

'Cheques that bounce,' I said.

It was ill-judged. I should have stayed serious. My financial situation was so bad that guillotine humour was never far from my mind. He had asked me a relevant question, however. What was I writing? The Abbey was expecting a play from me. I hadn't written a scene of it yet and the money was gone. I thought about Tom Murphy's potatoes. I wondered if he had abandoned them. Had he forsaken the earth and gone back to what he did best? The last play Tom had written before his retirement was an adaptation of Liam O'Flaherty's *The Informer.* It was playing at the Olympia Theatre, the headline event of the 1981 Dublin Theatre Festival, with Liam Neeson in the lead role of Gypo Nolan, the character made famous by Victor McLaglen in the 1935 movie directed by John Ford. Liam was from Ballymena and had first been seen at the Lyric Theatre, Belfast. His Dublin premiere was in a production of *We Do It For Love* produced at the Lyric at The Abbey. This project debut was in a production of *Says I, Says He,* Ron Hutchinson's brilliant play set amongst loyalist paramilitaries. In some ways, Liam appeared almost too tall to succeed as an actor – as though that would limit him in the choice of roles he could take on – but he had a charisma and a stage presence that was evident from the start.

The Informer was disappointing, and it was difficult to tell how much was down to the script and how much down to the production. Tom had directed it himself and maybe that was a mistake, taking on a complex adaptation and a world premiere. I'd brought my neighbour with me, the actress Eileen Colgan – she was the widow of my mentor, Alan Simpson, who had died tragically of a heart attack in 1980 – and we both retired to the bar at the interval where we drowned our disappointment. We didn't take our seats for the second act.

Liam Neeson and Helen Mirren, his then girlfriend, came into the bar after the show and people were polite but the writing was on the wall for *The Informer*. Tom was in a corner talking to friends, and I stuck around because I wanted to ask him about his potatoes. Sheila came into the bar, and I was delighted to see her, but wondered what she was doing there. It was after midnight. She should have been at home with the children. She was upset and crying.

'I didn't expect to see you here,' she said, 'I thought you could be dead.'

The Gardaí had called to our house in Ardilaun Road. Our beloved Morris Traveller had been involved in a serious collision on Gardiner Street. The passenger of a second car was in the Mater Hospital. The Garda who called had asked Sheila for my description, and then said that a man fitting that description was seen running from the scene of the accident. Sheila had responded that it could not have been me because I would never run away from an accident. I couldn't get my head around the details because I had parked the car outside the stage door of the theatre. We went out to see if it was still there. It was gone. Sheila had promised the Gardaí she would take me to Fitzgibbon Street station if she found me. Eileen Colgan insisted on coming with us. On the way there, we detoured to Gardiner Street. The Morris Traveller didn't look too bad to me. I thought it might be towable. It was a drink-induced evaluation because the car was a near write-off. That didn't stop me opening the bonnet and taking a look at the engine. By the time I was finished, I had oil smudges all over my clothes and person.

I reported to the Garda at the front desk in Fitzgibbon Street – I told him that my car had been stolen – and was immediately taken to an interrogation room. After a few minutes, two detectives, one wearing a jacket and one wearing just a shirt, came in and sat opposite me. They were aggressive from the get go.

'You fucking did it,' the jacket said.

I genuinely had no idea what he was talking about.

'Did what?' I said.

'You fucking did it,' he repeated.

'You crashed the car and then you ran away. You ran from the scene of an accident because you were driving on the wrong side of the road,' the shirt said.

'You fucking did it and now you come in here and you report your car as stolen. You're a smart fucker so you are but you're not smart enough,' the jacket said.

It was like a scene from a Dario Fo play. The police are about to frame me. It doesn't matter what I offer in my defence, they are convinced I'm guilty and they are going to pin it on me, whatever it takes. I thought about the Sallins three and Jer O'Leary's speech on their behalf in Project some three years before. I was thinking about miscarriages of justice when I heard Eileen Colgan's voice booming from an adjoining room.

'I want a glass of champagne. I'm saying nothing unless I get champagne,' she roared.

I wasn't sure if her demands were helping me or not.

'You're saying you were in the bar of the Olympia Theatre?' the shirt said.

'That's correct. I was at a show there. *The Informer.*'

'You don't look to me like a man who was at a show,' the jacket said. 'You look like a man who was involved in a traffic accident.'

He stared at my hands. They were covered in oil.

'Are you gonna tell us the truth or not? There's a man fighting for his life in the Mater. I wouldn't want it on my conscience, I can tell you. Why don't you tell us what happened?' the shirt said.

'You crashed the car and you ran from the scene, isn't that the truth?' the jacket said.

'We have a description and it fits you, you were seen running away.'

For a brief second, I wondered if they were telling me the truth. Had I left the theatre and crashed the car? Is that the reason they were so angry with me? It might be easier to agree with them and bring it all to an end, I thought. A part of me knew that this was insane. I'd been in the Olympia all night. I wasn't a liar, I was a truthful person, I had nothing to fear, the person in hospital had nothing to do with me, someone had stolen my car, I was sticking to my guns, whatever that meant and whatever the consequences.

At that moment, a detective came into the room, Frank O'Hara. I knew him because he had been involved in a case on our road in Ballybough. Two elderly sisters, the Fitzroys, had been burgled and over fifteen thousand pounds in cash taken from their home. My mother came upon the scene and alerted me immediately. I found handbags stuffed with notes that the robbers had missed. I calmed the Fitzroys as best I could and waited for the Gardai. Two detectives arrived, one of whom was Frank O'Hara. We got to know one another as a result of the robbery at the Fitzroys'.

He shook my hand and asked me what I was doing in Fitzgibbon Street. Two minutes later, I was out of the interrogation room. Sheila was delighted that the ordeal was over, but Eileen Colgan had taken up residence. It transpired that one of the detectives had taken a shine to her and was insisting on her remaining in the station until a bottle of champagne made its appearance. We headed home to Ardilaun Road under a Garda escort, and cracked open a bottle of Dom Perignon, a fitting end to a turbulent night.

I never did get the opportunity to ask Tom Murphy about his potatoes.

12

Pam Brighton rang Project from London looking for me, unaware that I was no longer working there. At the time, my home phone was cut off for non-payment, a situation that was too familiar. I met Art Ó Briain, the Centre's new Director, on the street, and he passed on the message. I'd had no contact with Pam since the debacle that was *Emigrants* and I still harboured resentment over the way she had behaved towards me. I swore then that I would never have anything to do with her, personally or professionally, until she apologised for her behaviour.

I made a reverse charge call to her from a phone box outside the Fluther Good pub on Ballybough Road. There was no apology, nothing of the past; what she wanted was a play from me on the IRA hunger strike.

'People over here don't get it, they don't understand what's going on in Belfast, we need a play that gets under the skin, know what I mean, Peter?' she said. 'We need something to unsettle the British public.'

I was unsettled. What about me, a member of the Irish public, where was my apology? I wanted to ask her about *Emigrants*, but she was on a roll, and when Pam was on a roll you didn't get a word in.

'I'll pay you five grand, Peter, plus expenses. You'll need to go to Belfast, visit the Maze, talk to the families, I'll pay for everything, just bring me back a fucking good play. No, make that a brilliant fucking play.'

I was in no position to turn down five grand sterling. That was six thousand Irish pounds. I was flattered. Not by the money; I was gobsmacked that she'd asked me. She could have turned to any number of writers, she could have asked someone from Belfast, Martin Lynch, Graham Reid, Ron Hutchinson, but she hadn't asked any of them, she'd asked me. She must have been wary after the *Emigrants* experience but still she had come to me. Maybe this was Pam's way of saying sorry.

Sheila urged extreme caution. She wanted our finances improved as much as I did, but she had lived through the madness of three years earlier when she had almost lost me to alcohol.

'Is she directing the play?' Sheila asked.

'I don't think so.'

'You need to find that out. That's the most important thing.'

'You're right.'

'If she's directing the play, then I think you should turn it down.'

'Five grand is a lot of money.'

'Not if you end up in a mental asylum it's not.'

Sheila's ability to analyse a situation amazed me. There was a natural assertiveness about her. It was alien to me. I came from a long line of procrastinators and people-pleasers. In the tradition of my father, I didn't like to offend anyone. I always wanted people to think well of me, and I would travel any distance and put myself through multiple humiliations to that end.

'Go down to the phone box now and call her,' Sheila said.

'I'll call her tomorrow,' I said.

'You won't call her tomorrow. If you don't do it now you won't do it at all.'

'I have to call her tomorrow. I have to give her a decision on the play, one way or the other.'

'I think you should do it tonight, then she'll know you're really serious. I wouldn't leave it until tomorrow. But that's me.'

Two months before Pam contacted me, an envelope had been delivered to my home from an address in Belfast. Inside the envelope was a cigarette paper, or a 'comm' as it was known in Republican circles. On it was the smallest writing I had ever seen. Tiny block capitals in blue biro. It was signed by a prisoner in the H Blocks. His comm pointed out that the blanket men were political prisoners and not criminals; they were men of conscience who would not be in prison in any normal society. They had started on the blanket protest because they had no other option. It ended with a plea for me to raise my voice because they had been deprived of theirs.

The cigarette paper stayed with me. It was simple and powerful. I realised it was a propaganda tool but it was no less powerful for that. Criminals didn't engage in it because, presumably, they were too busy getting on with crime. Political people did it precisely because they were political.

I rang Pam the next day and accepted the commission. Her big Yorkshire laugh bellowed down the phone like a machine-gun.

'Get your bloody phone reconnected, ya daft sod.'

'Soon as you send me a cheque it will be back on.'

'No serious writer makes his calls from a public phone outside of a pub on a street in Dublin, called after a character from a Sean O'Casey play.'

'I don't have any choice.'

'I want to be able to talk to you about the script. And the actors. And the production. Do ya know what I mean?'

There was a pause, like she'd temporarily run out of things to say. This was my golden opportunity.

'We haven't talked about a director,' I said. 'Have you given any thought as to who will direct the piece?'

'I'm not worried about the director, Peter. Let's get the fucking thing written. That's all I'm worried about, the script.'

I wasn't displeased with that. Sheila asked me what she had said and I told a white lie.

'We're going to decide on the director after it's written,' I said.

'That means she's going to do it.'

'No, it means I have a veto. I'm part of the decision. I have to be happy.'

'Or unhappy.'

Nothing more needed to be said. It was a loose understanding. In my gut I knew I was inviting heartache. We needed the money too much for me to take a stand. I wasn't assertive enough, as a person. I was a people-pleaser, like my Dad.

* * *

My first research trip to Belfast was organised by the Association for Legal Justice, ALJ. They housed me with the Burns family in the St James's area of the Lower Falls. I slept in Daniel's old room at the front of the house. He had died as a result of a stray bullet during a gunfight in 1976. He was eleven years old. It made me think of our Frankie, naturally. It was eerie to lie in Daniel's bed and to look out the window at the night sky, as he must have done hundreds of times. He had died in his bed, the one I was sleeping in, another 'victim of the troubles.' I felt a strange communion with this person I had never met. It was like his soul was floating out there in the atmosphere and he knew Frankie, they were pals. I felt happy that they knew one another. They weren't one bit sad, they just wanted to play together and that reassured me. I felt I was in the right place, doing the right thing.

As a well-known Republican family, the Burns's were kept under close watch. Army patrols in the area stopped outside their house on a regular basis. On occasion, the soldiers gave a raucous rendition of *Danny Boy* at the tops of their voices. The family did their best to ignore the taunts, but even in their telling me this story I could feel the hurt and the impotence. It made me think about how I would feel if that was directed against my family, against my parents, against Frankie, or any of my brothers. It was psychological abuse of the very worst kind.

I had arranged to visit a prisoner in the H Blocks. He was the brother of a journalist I knew in Dublin. Conor (not his real name) was in for his part in the murder of an RUC officer in Derry. I had never met him before, but he knew I was research-ing a play on the hunger strikes – Mickey Devine, the last of the hunger strikers and a friend of Conor's, had died two months previously.

I boarded the minibus outside the Sinn Fein office on the Falls Road and headed for the M1 and Moira. On the way, the passengers, who were mainly women, placed plastic capsules in their mouths beneath their tongues. The bus parked outside the main gates and we were searched and screened before being brought to a holding area. There was a delay there and the kids started to get bored, which made them unruly and made the mothers uptight. Finally, we were escorted to a prison vehicle and driven the short distance to the visiting compound. When the rear doors of the blacked-out vehicle opened, no one moved. Everyone stared at the floor. There was a prison officer counting the heads inside the vehicle. I looked at him as he went about his silent business. He locked eyes with me and didn't budge. Neither did I. A staring contest ensued. I was determined not to break first. I wasn't going to be intimidated by this man. He gave in, finally, but the hatred in his eyes was palpable.

The visit to the H Blocks was invaluable, not because of any new information gleaned but more for what it gave me of the atmosphere and the architecture of the place. Conor confided that as those men refusing food were separated from the main body of the prison, it resulted in the general prison population not knowing what was going on. They had to rely on visits and smuggled-in radios to keep abreast of what was happening in the other blocks. It was information lockdown. The plastic capsules passed from mouth to mouth during visiting time contained newspaper and/or magazine articles that ended up being read from window to window along the line. The same window to window method was used for the teaching of Irish, making the Maze Prison the largest Gaeltacht area in the six counties, second only to Gaoth Dobhair in Donegal.

The ALJ, over the course of a week, introduced me to ex-blanketmen and former hunger strikers. I met the girlfriend of one of the recently deceased men, a woman torn apart and devastated by what she'd been through. I met Sarah Conlon, the wife of Giuseppe and mother of Gerry, part of the group known as the Guildford Four, whose case would become a *cause célèbre* some years later. Everyone in Belfast knew that the Conlons were innocent. Giuseppe was devoutly religious, regarded as someone who wouldn't hurt a fly. He didn't remotely fit the prototype of an IRA activist. He'd gone to London because his son was in trouble. No other construction made any kind of sense. He had no political involvement. In prison, he served at mass and went to the sacraments. The priests who ministered to Giuseppe knew that he was innocent and they passed that information to the authorities. It was an 'appalling vista' for the British establishment, however, to admit that their police and judicial systems had forced confessions from innocent people. They allowed Giuseppe to die in prison, knowing that he had played no part in the Guildford bombing.

I came home and started to write a play about the Conlons. I wrote the first act in three days. It literally poured out onto the page. I sent it to Pam.

'It's a good story, Peter, but it's not the one we want.'

'I think this could have a huge impact, Pam, I really do.'

'The hunger strike is much more important. Bobby Sands is the new Che Guevara. The British public need to know why he did it and how he did it. D'ya know what I mean, Peter?'

I couldn't disagree with her. It was just that Sarah Conlon reminded me of my Ma. A small woman but determined to prove that her husband was not a bomber. Or her son, for that matter. Ten years down the line, when my brother Jim got to make his movie of this story, *In The Name of the Father*, my Ma played Sarah's mother, and my Da played Giuseppe's pal who worked as a marker in the bookie's shop.

I abandoned the Conlon play and went off to write something on the hunger strikes. I took up residence in Annaghmakerrig, Tyrone Guthrie's old house near Newbliss, County Monaghan, now a writer's retreat. It was tough on Sheila with the four kids

– Rossa and Fiachra in primary school and Doireann and Nuala at playgroup with her – meeting all their needs on a daily basis. At least I could talk to her in the evening now that we had the house phone back on.

I had a critical decision to make before I could proceed to write the play. Was it a documentary piece, or was it something 'inspired by real events', with latitude to go beyond them? In other words, was the central character Bobby Sands or not? I hadn't spoken to any of the Sands family and it felt like it would be presumptuous of me to put words in his mouth without some sort of understanding. The other thing was, of course, that I didn't want to be restricted or to feel constrained to take a particular political line. I wasn't writing something to make Sinn Féin or the IRA happy. I was writing something that was independent, objective and free from interference. Most of all, I was writing something human, an emotional story about people caught up in a tragedy that could, and should, have been avoided.

I called the central character Pat O'Connor, and once I decided that, I was away. He was the Officer Commanding the Blocks, the O/C, but he wasn't Bobby Sands. I gave him an independent and separate back story. I made him a good chess player – Kieran Doherty, the eighth of the ten to die, was the prison champion and was never shy in proclaiming it – and I used chess as a metaphor for the conflict between the British Government and the protesting prisoners. The idea for that came from the match between Bobby Fischer and Boris Spassky, which took place in Reykjavik, Iceland in 1972. I watched it on television – Slot players were in Chicago at the invitation of George Murphy at the time – where it was portrayed as an instalment of the cold war between Russia and the United States. I remember particularly that the final move of the day had to be concealed in an envelope until the recommencement of play the following morning. It made it edge-of-the-seat stuff. I had never imagined that chess could be so exciting and so tense. I wanted to infuse the play with a similar tension.

I wrote the first act in ten days, finishing late on a Thursday night. I wasn't due home until the Sunday. I decided to surprise Sheila and left Annaghmakerrig on the Friday morning. I took the bus from Newbliss and walked from Busáras up Gardiner Street into Summerhill. At my local pub, the Sunset House, I dropped off for a rewarding pint of Guinness and a small Jameson whiskey (Jemmy and pep). I left there and came down over Ballybough Bridge, into Croke Villas and around the corner to Ardilaun Road. For some reason I have never understood, Sheila was perched at the window of our upstairs bedroom with Doireann and Nuala, looking out at a cloudy sky. Sheila in the middle with her arms around the two girls. It was a picture of perfect happiness. I felt such pride that this was my family. Sheila saw me and got the girls to wave. I dropped my briefcase, scaled up the plastic downpipe, scrambled in the open window and hugged the three of them. I hugged my three girls until all need for hugging had left me.

I had never done that before. It was a pure adrenaline rush. I sent the first act to Pam and she rang, delighted with it. The Hull Truck Theatre Company, of which she was the new Artistic Director, was going to produce the play at the Edinburgh Festival of 1982. A year after the end of the Sands hunger strike, British audiences were going to get an unmediated glimpse of life inside Long Kesh thanks to my play, now called *Diary of a Hunger Strike*. Pam had little doubt but that it would cause a furore, and – wasn't that what we wanted – controversy, more controversy and lots of media attention. I was thrilled, but I was superstitious too. I had a second act to write. Pat O'Connor, at the end of the first act, had just declared that he was taking on a fast to the death. I had to put my protagonist on that fasting road. I had to gradually strip him of his senses, and take away his bodily functions. I had to put him in a hospital bed and I had to let his family watch him die. That was the task facing me and I wasn't looking forward to it, not one little bit.

* * *

Towards the end of 1981, Ma and Da finally sold the family home in Seville Place. They moved initially to cottage in Portrane, 'Sandy Dell,' which I had helped them buy with the money from the Abbey Theatre. It was a stupid investment on my part because we couldn't afford it, strapped as we were for cash on an ongoing basis. I should, of course, have put the Abbey money towards the losses we were carrying from *Down All the Days*, which was now a term loan, an instalment due every month. In my heart I knew that we would be asking Da for the return of our investment, sooner rather than later. It wasn't the time now, however, not with them moving house.

Sheila and I were seeing a lot more of my parents; and so too were the grandkids. Portrane was quite a bus journey away and Ma still had her part-time job in the North Star Hotel. Da, despite taking early retirement from CIE, was still working at the dog tracks in Shelbourne Park and Harold's Cross. It meant that anytime they were in town, it was easier to come to us for dinner than trekking out to Portrane. Da was great with kids, he'd been brilliant with us growing up, and now I was getting the chance to see him in action all over again. He made stories up on the spot and it was wonderful to see Rossa and Fiachra hanging on his every word, totally engrossed. At the dinner table, his knee was always reserved for the youngest (Doireann and Nuala took it in turns) and he was a genius at getting kids to suck on a bone or to eat what he had on his plate. It was a hoot to see him balancing a bottle of YR sauce on his head – when I was a child his party trick was a bottle of Guinness and I never saw him spill a drop – and he could walk around and take his dinner plate out to the kitchen without the bottle sliding off his head. It beat Coco the Clown hands down.

I never received any formal training as a theatre director but I'm convinced that my ability came from observing life in the kitchen of our home in Seville Place. All human life was there. Da wrestling with one of the lodgers on the floor while Ma stepped across them holding a teapot and a plate of bread, admonishing Da to 'get up and have your supper.' Their now frequent visits to Ardilaun Road brought it all back to me. On top of that, Fiachra bore more than a passing resemblance to Frankie. I'm sure that must have been difficult but life-affirming for them, knowing that their son lived on in their grandson. As a consequence, Fiachra was my mother's favourite; she spoiled him rotten and we had to be very vigilant because she unashamedly tried to give him more than the others. Sheila was brilliant at ensuring, despite Fiachra's protests, that all monies from Granny were pooled and evenly divided!

It really brought home to me the importance of family, having them around. I knew they had worried about us marrying so young in circumstances where Sheila was expecting a baby, but now they got to see the dynamic of our family in action; and it wasn't a million miles from their own, in truth. I told the boys 'Andy Burkers' – stories based on characters from my youth – and organised elaborate games of hide and seek. We ate together as a family, and Ma was delighted that I tried to help Sheila in the kitchen – Da never boiled an egg in his life. Although, like him, I had to have a slice of bread and butter with my tea after dinner, three hundred and sixty-five days a year; that made Ma laugh.

'Jesus, your father will never be dead while you're alive,' she'd say.

Then she'd give out to him that he never washed a dish or cooked a meal.

It was nine months before they moved into their new house at 51 Carleton Road in Marino. In that time, I got close to again. It was sad that he'd given up the acting; I missed being on-stage with him. The Saint Laurence O'Toole's Musical and Dramatic Society was a community thing, based around the parish. That is what the arts essentially were in Ireland: an expression of family and an expression of community. That is why traditional music was so vibrant nationally. The Abbey Theatre had been based around the Fay Brothers and their amateur acting company, many of whom were also members of the Gaelic League. They were language enthusiasts and fervent Home Rulers. I had touched off the same thing in my research trip to Belfast. The struggle there was centred around families. They carried the Republican torch in the H Blocks where the Irish language became an important expression of their political and cultural identity, just as it had been in the literary revival of the late nineteenth and early twentieth centuries.

I was living in Ballybough, a deprived, working-class area of Dublin, and I had given nothing to it in terms of community. I'd been too busy with my professional career, I didn't have the time. Da had asked me once or twice what local clubs the boys were involved in and the answer, of course, was none. They had karate and sea scouts, but those were activities that happened outside the area, Mountjoy Square and Dollymount respectively. Da's question stirred my conscience. I started to think about a project that would take people from the locale and develop stories with them. I wasn't interested in an amateur drama group, however. I was interested in something that would be an expression of their lives, something relevant, with a cutting edge. It also had to be something that celebrated the native wit and capacity of Dublin citizens to overcome adversity. I didn't want depressing social realism, there was enough of that all around us, I wanted something life-affirming and bawdy, irreverent and entertaining.

I approached a local organisation, the North Centre City Community Action Project, NCCCAP, who were based in Summerhill Parade just over the Ballybough Bridge. Their director, Mick Rafferty, was someone I greatly admired. He came from Phil Shanahan House in Sheriff Street and was a year behind me in the Christian Brothers Primary School in Seville Place. My father encouraged him into the North Wall Community Association and he quickly worked his way up the ranks and became its youngest ever chairman. He went on to become an electrician, but he read widely and pursued courses in philosophy, English and other subjects. I met him at a seminar in UCD during my final year and, although not a registered student at the college, he gave the best analysis of the work of Martin Heidegger I'd heard up to then or since.

I pitched my idea to Mick. He loved it and said he'd do his best to get funding for it. As it happened, he was planning a major arts festival to coincide with the demolition of the tenement buildings on Sean McDermott Street, Gardiner Street and the Gloucester Diamond. It was going to be called the Inner-City Looking On Festival.

'It would be great if your drama project could put on something for the festival,' he said.

It was refreshing to deal with Mick's positive energy. We struck up a great working relationship from the get go. We went for a pint together in the Sunset House, just down from the office on Summerhill Parade. We were looking over a proposal I'd written, when news came on the television that the Government had fallen. Jim Kemmy, the socialist TD from Limerick, had withdrawn his support to the Government over the issue of VAT on children's shoes. Before the election campaign started, Mick received a phone call from a junior Fine Gael minister in the outgoing coalition, local TD Michael Keating. He said he had some money if Mick had a suitable 'employment project.' I had two weeks to find ten participants for a temporary six-month youth employment scheme. The objective was to teach them drama skills for the production of a play that might help in their personal development. The money came from the Department of Education, the first time ever that a community arts project was funded in this way. We were helped in no small way by the fact that the civil servant with responsibility for the scheme was Tony Ó Dàlaigh. He'd been active in amateur drama with Strand Players and had also been the administrator for the Irish Theatre Company, ITC, when it was established in 1974.

We put up notices all around the north inner city looking for people who could 'tell a story or sing a song.' We thought the words 'drama' or 'theatre' might put people off. I also felt that the 'youth employment' tag was too restrictive. We needed older people in the group to give it balance. The department came back and said that we could have two men and two women who were over 25. They also said that I could have a second supervisor to help me run it. I asked my old friend Annie Kilmartin, who had acted in *No Entry* and *The Liberty Suit*, but she was busy with her own company, Moving Theatre. She recommended Maggie Byrne, and I knew after I met Maggie that she was perfect for the task.

We conducted the interviews in the offices at Summerhill Parade. They were also the election headquarters of Tony Gregory, chairman of the NCCCAP. Tony had polled well in the previous election and was trying to build from that base. He'd gone to O'Connell's Secondary School and had been in the same year as Shea. He'd come into politics through his admiration for Seamus Costello (assassinated on the North Strand in 1977 as part of the Official IRA feud), and he was associated with the Irish Republican Socialist Party, which Costello had founded. Indeed, he'd been questioned by Gardaí on the night of the Sallins mail train robbery because they believed his car had been used in the getaway. They only backed off from arresting him when they discovered that the engine was stone cold.

A number of women arrived with their daughters, looking for places on the course. One such was Florence (Florrie) Cunningham. She breezed into the room with Rebecca, who looked about fifteen.

'I came down to do a bit of canvassing for Tony,' Florrie said. 'I saw the notice in the window. This is me daughter Rebecca, the nuns tell me she has a lovely singing voice. I've never heard it. Sing for the man there.'

Rebecca looked totally embarrassed. She shook her head and looked away. I asked Florrie about her own singing voice.

'I'll sing something for you if Tony gets elected. True as Jaysus, I once sang a song for Alfie Byrne, do you remember him? He was the Lord Mayor of Dublin about twenty fucking times.'

Mick asked her about her current occupation.

'I look after the old people, down in Sheriffer, the Convent of the Little Flower. I push their wheelchairs and change their nappies.'

I was taken aback and Florrie saw the look on my face.

'I give the old people dogs' abuse but it keeps them alive. I don't actually change their nappies, I just threaten them with it, that's all. We have a great laugh over it.'

She had taken over the room. A natural born storyteller, she was exactly what we were looking for.

'There's a place available on the course and I'd like to offer it to you,' I said.

'Do you hear that, Rebecca, the man wants you.'

'No, no, it's not your daughter, it's you we're offering it to,' Mick said.

'Me?' Florrie said, faking demure, putting her finger to her lips and biting her nail. 'Who's going to abuse the old folks if I take this course?'

The interviews were chaotic and Pauline Kane, the administrator of the NCCCAP, did her best to keep order. Lots of young people came for interview. Two such were Vinnie Murphy and his friend Lou Bergin from Marino. They lived only yards from my mother and father in their 'new' house on Carleton Road. Vinnie brought his guitar and sang me a song he'd written. I made him an offer immediately and he accepted. So did Lou Bergin. Two girls from Da's basketball team in Sheriff Street, Alice Butler and Deirdre Fagan, came in. I couldn't say no. Mick Egan, who'd performed with the Children's T Company in *One Bad Apple*, joined the group. So did Liz Bono, an actress looking for new ways of working. A talented footballer, Fran Moore, who played for local team Belvedere FC, fancied a change of direction. Seamus Kelly, with his wonderful head of curls and bags of enthusiasm, joined our ranks. Then there was Jean Doyle who, like Florrie, brought her daughter Anne to the interview as a cover. When I asked her what she sang as a party piece, she gave me the most beautiful rendition of 'When I Fall in Love' that I have ever heard.

We were twelve: ten participants and two supervisors. A drama project administered by an unknown community organisation in Summerhill, Dublin. That's how it was until Tony Gregory was elected for the constituency of Dublin Central. Not only that, he held the balance of power in the new Dail. Taoiseach-elect Charles Haughey and his advisors came to our offices on Summerhill Parade to hammer out the programme for government. The deal was done in the same room where I'd chosen the participants for the course. It felt like the hand of history was on our shoulder.

We gathered on a cold February morning in the SCAB (Standard Community Amenity Building) in Rutland Street, off Summerhill. I told the group we had three weeks before we would present our first play to the public. They all wanted to know what it was. I told them I hadn't a clue.

'Is it *Cinderella*?' Jean Doyle asked.

'I'm not playing an ugly sister, no fucking way,' Florrie said.

'It's not *Cinderella*,' I said.

'*Jack and the Beanstalk*,' Florrie said. 'I'll play the big fat cow. That's what me husband calls me.'

'It's not a pantomime. We're going to make it up,' I said.

'Make it up? About what?' they chorused.

'Us. Ourselves. We're going to make a play out of our own lives and we're putting it on in three weeks. Now let's get started.'

* * *

We decided to do something on the law. A few of the group had been on the wrong side of it. One of our number had been committed to High Park Reformatory (it was in reality a Magdalen laundry) as a teenager, and another had gotten the probation act for stealing a bra from Dunne's Stores, so there was no lack of personal stories. There was also Nell McCafferty's brilliant column for *The Irish Times*, 'In the Eyes of the Law', and that became an important source of research. That also introduced group members to the National Library and their extensive archive of newspapers. Solicitors Pat McCartan and Garret Sheehan spoke to us about some of the more bizarre aspects of the system they encountered in their work of representation. A very fruitful afternoon was spent in the company of Sue Richardson and the Prisoners Rights Organisation, PRO.

Some of our research was hands on. We sat in Court Number Four and watched Mr Justice Robert O hUadhaigh dispensing justice. It amused some and made others angry; but an eye-opener it was, indisputably. O hUadhaigh was a Jekyll-and-Hyde figure, unpredictable and subjective. There were days he attacked the Gardai (for no good reason) and others that he praised them to the hilt (also for no good reason). One day, a thief was given the probation act and the following day the same crime merited twelve months in Mountjoy. It was pure theatre, and Justice Ó hUadhaigh loved playing to the gallery. It was great fun unless you were at the receiving end of his sentencing. In his honour, we called our play *Who's On In Number Four?* but it was only ever known as 'the court sketch'.

The play opened on a cold Friday evening in March, 1982, at the Jetfoil Lounge on the North Wall. A well-known heroin den, its owner, Niall Mulvihill, was originally from the East Wall and had known my parents when they lived in Abercorn Road. His family ran an off-licence on Church Avenue, near Johnny Cullen's Hill, before they branched out into the pub business proper – they were one of Da's main sponsors for the community games.

Niall was always game for a laugh and welcomed the drama with open arms.

We had a very simple set, which comprised a bench and dais for the Judge, a small dock for the witnesses, and a table and chairs for the legal representatives. I hadn't intended to be in the play but no one else owned a suit so, by default, I was cast in the role of the solicitor, based on Garret Sheehan. Standing by the side of the makeshift stage I was nervous, not for myself, but for the others, most of whom had never experienced a first night before. It was approaching nine o'clock and the audience were well oiled and noisy, eager for us to kick the play into action. Lou Bergin, who was playing Ó hUadhaigh, had his gavel in his hand, waiting for the lights to come up that would mark his entrance. Fran Moore, the operator, was looking at me waiting for the nod.

At that moment, the doors of the Jetfoil flung open and the Gardai poured into the pub. It was a raid. The uniformed men took up positions behind the audience and the plainclothes detectives surveyed the situation from what was the front of the stage. In some respects, it looked like part of the play, as if we'd planned it. The Jetfoil resembled a real courtroom. The thought entered my head that this was a perfect atmosphere for the play. A once in a lifetime opportunity to present our drama in the presence of live Gardai. I nodded at Fran Moore who brought the lights up. Lou Bergin entered and started to berate the audience.

'Do you know where you are?' he asked them. 'You are in a court of law. You are in my court, court number four. Silence in court.'

The Jetfoil went from noisy to silent. Lou Bergin took up position on the bench and introduced the first case. Mick

Egan, dressed as a Garda but wearing a clown's red nose, took up position to deliver his evidence against the accused, Florrie Cunningham. She was being charged with stealing a bra, the property of Dunne's Stores of Henry Street in the jurisdiction of Dublin. The audience erupted. The two detectives approached me and asked me was I in charge.

'Yeah, I'm the director. I also play a solicitor in the play.'

'You'll have to stop this, we're here to do a search,' one of them said.

'We have information there may be drugs on the premises,' the other one chipped in.

'I thought I asked for silence in this courtroom!' Lou Bergin barked over at us. 'Did I ask for silence or did I not?'

It was a brilliant piece of improvisation. I couldn't have been more proud. Someone in the audience shouted:

'Police out.'

Others took it up and it became a chant. They banged their fists off the tables at the same time.

'Police out, police out, police out....'

It gained momentum and the room sang it out in unison.

'Police out, police out, police out....'

It became very uncomfortable for the Gardaí and they started to withdraw.

'There'll be trouble over this,' one of the detectives said to me as they headed for the exits.

I was too nervous to care. The play got started and there weren't too many gaffes, most people remembered their lines. The audience loved the Garda with the red nose and they loved Florrie's story of robbing the bra because she had a new boy-friend and didn't want him to see the one that was held together with safety pins. I gave it my all as the solicitor and the audience cheered when I made fun of the prosecution and exposed their evidence as blatant and wilful lies. The play ended with an ensemble rendition of *The Lunatics Have Taken Over the Asylum*, with three-part harmonies scored by Vinnie Murphy and wonderfully insane choreography by Maggie Byrne, featuring Lou Bergin as a demented Ó hUadhaigh that owed a little to John Cleese and the Minister for Funny Walks.

There are many kinds of robbers
But as far as I can see
The ones who steal most from the people
Are the ones who are walking free
The lunatics have taken over the asylum.

We got a standing ovation from the Jetfoil audience. I was relieved, albeit temporarily. I knew the detectives from Store Street station would be back; it was only a question of when. I was at home on the Monday following the performance – a day off after the effort to get the show on – when there was a loud knock on the door of Ardilaun Road. I turned to Sheila.

'That will be them,' I said.

'You'd better go out and talk to them,' she said.

'What am I going to say?'

'Tell them the truth. It is only a play after all.'

There was a second knock, louder than the first. I walked down the hall and opened the door. Standing there were two young fellas, one tall and skinny, one small and fat, and they looked about fifteen or sixteen. They wore serious, worried expressions on their faces.

'We were at the play on Friday night,' the small one said.

'Yeah.'

'We're up in court next week,' the tall one said.

'And we want you to represent us,' the small one said.

I started to laugh.

'What's so bleedin' funny?' the tall one said.

'I'm not a solicitor.'

'You're better than any poxy solicitor we ever had,' the small one said.

'You were bleedin' brilliant telling that Judge where to get off, the poxbottle liar,' the tall one said.

I tried to explain that I was acting, putting on a performance, that I wasn't the real thing, I didn't have a law degree, but they were unconvinced. I wrote out Garret Sheehan's details on a piece of paper and told them to mention my name. As they were leaving, the tall skinny one offered me 'a bit of blow.' I declined, telling them that I stuck to the alcohol and didn't mix my drugs. They smirked in disbelief, but it was the truth. I had always enjoyed a smoke, but then I found that in conjunction with alcohol it tipped me over the edge and made me paranoid. In addition, Sheila thought that the boys, now ten and eight, were starting to notice the 'herbal smell.' Fiachra, in particular, hated cigarette smoke and complained about it all the time. I decided to give up dope on the pretext that it might set a bad example for the boys when, in reality, it was starting to interfere with my drinking, and I needed to preserve my relationship with alcohol at all costs.

Niall Mulvihill was delighted with the court sketch and wanted us to stage a second performance in the Jetfoil. I think the play brought a 'respectability' to a venue that was very dodgy, to say the least.

'You should write a play about me,' Niall said. 'I'd give you a story about what's going on in this town, a story about the real Dublin, bent coppers and bent politicians too.'

'I might take you up on that sometime,' I said.

I was very cautious because I felt that heroin was a mean and addictive drug. I had never tried it and didn't ever want to get hooked on something that was so patently destructive. It had already impacted on Sheila's family, and I had seen the devastation it wrought. It was a subject that interested me and I wanted to write about it, but I didn't know how far I could trust Niall Mulvihill. His pub, after all, was at the epicentre of the heroin trade in Dublin. At the time of my conversation with Niall, one of, Sheila's brothers was on his way to Istanbul, hoping to bring home with him something stronger than Turkish Delight.

I promised Niall Mulvihill that I would bring our second sketch to the Jetfoil. The court sketch proved immensely popular and we toured it around community centres north and south of the Liffey. We presented it for other youth training schemes, old folks groups, football clubs, political groups, trade union seminars and get-togethers – indeed, we presented it at the seventy-fifth anniversary of the Marine Port and General Workers Union in their hall on Gardiner Place, a performance that was filmed (amateurishly, unfortunately) for posterity. We were much in demand, and figured we needed a name for the group. So, after a fierce internal debate, we settled on 'City Workshop', a name I loved then and now.

For our second offering, the members of the City Workshop decided to take on the issue of supplementary welfare. For the uninitiated, this is the system, Dickensian in concept, whereby the poorest of our society are means-tested to ascertain if they qualify for a State handout. It is totally arbitrary, all down to the investigating officer, and they can award you the maximum (believing that you have no means), the minimum (believing that you have money from somewhere else), or nothing at all (implying that you are a criminal trying to defraud them). In addition to money, you can be entitled to butter vouchers and a fuel allowance, if you know to ask for them, and there is even provision for grants to send children to pre-school. It is a total hornets' nest, a monument to form-filling, and designed to strip away what remains of your dignity and self-esteem. The members of the City Workshop had all been through it and we had the greatest fun making a play that exacted our revenge for what we had been made to suffer.

In an improvisation during the making of the piece, Jean Doyle, playing a character based on a woman she knew from Capel Street, kept asking the welfare officer, played by Lou Bergin, for 'mrickets.' No one had a clue what she was talking about.

'I want mrickets, mrickets.'

'I don't know what you're saying, Missus, I don't know what mrickets are.'

This went on for a few minutes, everyone intrigued at how the improv was going. I could see that Jean was totally enjoying the fact that no one understood her, that she was playing true to the character and true to the situation.

'I want me mrickets, I'm entitled to mrickets.'

'Tell me what they are, what are they used for?' Lou said.

'They're for the fire, you put them on the fire.'

'You burn them, do you?'

'No, you stand there looking at them.'

By this stage some members of the group had twigged what Jean was talking about. There were sniggers all around the room.

'Of course you burn them, they're mrickets, mrickets for the fire,' Jean said.

The meaning of it finally dawned on Lou.

'You're talking about briquettes, peat briquettes for the fire.'

'That's what I said, mrickets.'

I stood up and grabbed Jean in a bear hug. In six weeks at the acting game, she had come such a long, long way. A mother of five, she had lived her life always wanting to be on a stage. She had left school at twelve without any qualifications whatsoever, but she was as bright a person as you could hope to meet. She had wonderful native intelligence. Improvisation was like a second nature to her. She would come in to work on a Monday morning and say:

'I have an idea, let's try an improv on it.'

Six weeks earlier, she hadn't known what the word improv meant. She personified my belief that Dublin working-class women had extraordinary buried talent. They'd survived and raised families against mighty odds and all they needed was opportunity. That golden word, denied to so many. It brought me back to my father and the dream he had repressed for so long, that of being an actor, on a stage telling a story. The City Workshop became the embodiment of a dream for me because it wasn't just any story but OUR story we were telling. We were giving value and meaning to our struggle – the courts, the social welfare system – and we were doing it in a way that pricked the conscience of the audience and entertained them at the same time. It was a dictum I had picked up from John McGrath – the first priority is to give your audience a great night out – because no worthwhile process takes place when an audience are bored.

The welfare sketch followed a similar structure to the court sketch, combining drama and song in equal measure. The improv that Jean had woven with Lou went in unaltered and proved one of the show's high points. Indeed, many people in the north inner city referred to the show as 'mrickets', and Jean couldn't walk down Parnell Street or Summerhill without someone shouting the word after her. We toured the show widely and built relationships with other communities in Dublin, principally Donore Avenue and Fatima Mansions, East Wall, Killinarden in Tallaght and Finglas. We played the Jetfoil, and again Niall Mulvihill invited me to write something based on his knowledge of the Dublin crime scene. I didn't know at the time that he was involved with 'The General', Martin Cahill, and that this association would lead, twenty years later (January 2003), to his murder. He was sitting in his taxi (he'd moved on from being a publican) at the bridge on Sheriff Street when a masked man shot him through the window of the car. He somehow managed to drive the car, and got as far as the entrance to the Mater Hospital Accident and Emergency Department before he crashed into a line of parked cars and slumped across the steering wheel, dead. No one was ever charged with his murder and it remains an ongoing investigation to this day.

13

Chris O'Neill and I met regularly. We'd become close and Eleanor, his wife, is godmother to my daughter Doireann. Aisling, their daughter (now a star of RTÉ's *Fair City* – a series I wrote the pilot episode for in 1988) played with our kids growing up. Aisling made her stage début, aged nine, as the boy in a production of *Waiting for Godot,* which I directed at the Focus Theatre. Chris and I stayed close, even after he and Eleanor separated. We met on the pretext that we had the fallout from *Down All the Days* to deal with. The truth is we were drinking companions. His intake didn't bring unwarranted attention to mine and vice versa. Chris had a house in Camden Terrace, a laneway off Camden Street, which doubled as his office. It was next door to The Sword public house and Chris could order his drinks through a hatch in the wall.

I loved those late-afternoon and early-evening meetings, getting slowly drunk as we fixed what needed to be fixed. It was at the tail end of one of these encounters that I accepted a commission from him to write a play about a struggling garage band trying to make it in the rock 'n roll world of 1960s Dublin. He gave me one thousand pounds in cash from money he'd won on the horses and there was only one stipulation – the show must contain the song *Runaround Sue* by Dion. Nothing else, just that song. I figured there was a first love connection to *Runaround Sue*, but he wouldn't tell me. He cackled when I asked him for a reason, one of the few people I knew who could really cackle.

At the same time as I committed myself to Chris, I accepted a commission from Paddy O'Dwyer of the Dublin Youth Theatre. He wanted something contemporary, edgy, with a large cast, lots of female roles if possible, and he wanted it for their autumn slot. It became the play Bust and featured Aiden Gillan in one of his first stage roles. I wasn't drunk when I accepted the gig, which makes my action all the more alarming. I now had two commissions to fulfil, I was the joint artistic director of the City Workshop, I was on the steering committee of the Inner City Looking On Festival, and rehearsals for *Diary of a Hunger Strike* were due to commence in London in August. As if that wasn't enough, I called a meeting of all the community arts groups in the Dublin area with a view to forming a representative organisation that would lobby the Arts Council and others on our behalf. I was on a major high, artistically, and I the adrenaline of it was keeping me alive.

My priority was the City Workshop because that was where my heart lay. I should have concentrated fully on that but I didn't know how to say 'no.' The funding for the City Workshop was guaranteed for six months, but there was an understanding that, if things went well, we would get an extension for a second six months. A plan was formulating in my head for a series of plays that would chart the history of the north inner city in the twentieth century. The first of these, covering the years 1900 to 1925, would form the first part, and I thought we might have it ready for the Inner City Looking On Festival in July.

I presented the idea to the group and opened it out for discussion. What was going on in the neighbourhood in those years, I asked? Well, there was the Lockout, the collapse of houses in Church Street in 1913 that led to a public inquiry, the 1916 Rising, the War of Independence, emigration, the founding of the Abbey Theatre, the Magdalen Laundry in Sean McDermott Street. The area was steeped in history, national and local. There were the tenements, too, of course, once teeming with life but now depopulated and about to be torn down. Indeed, there had been a plan to turn Gardiner Street into a giant car park, a proposition that might have gone ahead had it not been for the deal that our chairman, Tony Gregory, had negotiated with Haughey and the Fianna Fáil government. Tony had secured a commitment that decent houses would be built to replace the tenements. We were living through history with the Gregory Deal, and it felt important that, whatever we chose to say about the 1900 to 1925 period, it should parallel the momentous times we were living through in the present.

I don't recall who first mentioned Monto – a red light district named after Montgomery Street – and a place celebrated in song, in poetry and in prose. It once occupied an area of a square mile behind what is now the Department of Education in Marlborough Street. That had been a British Army garrison before independence and the Monto, of course, catered for the sexual needs of the soldiers billeted there. I knew the song of the Monto:

If you've got a wing-o, take her up to Ring-o,
Where the waxies sing-o all the day;
If you've had your fill of porter, and you can't go any further,
Give your man the order: 'Back to the quay!'

And take her up to Monto, Monto, Monto
Take her up to Monto, lan-ge-roo,
To you!

That song, ironically, was not of the period but had been written for a revue show in the Gaslight Theatre in Dun Laoghaire in the 1950s. It had been penned by sometime *Irish Times* contributor George D. Hodnett (known to all as 'Hoddie') and it was taken up and made popular by Luke Kelly and The Dubliners. Luke was married to actress and singer Deirdre O'Connell and, with her, he built the Focus Theatre in Pembroke Lane, home to the famous Stanislavski studio where so many actors, including Tom Hickey and Johnny Murphy, started their careers.

I'd read the Nighttown sequence in *Ulysses* where Stephen Dedalus visits Bella Cohen's brothel in the Monto and is rescued by Bloom. I was aware that Oliver St John Gogarty (Buck Mulligan in *Ulysses*) had written a poem, and that if you took the first letter of each line it read 'The Whores Will Be Busy'. I knew nothing of the real history of the Monto, however, and I was particularly interested to find out when and why it had foundered. I wondered was there a historical parallel to the destruction of the tenements that was happening in front of our eyes?

I sent the group out on a mission to investigate. I gave them a week to crack the story. They came back from the National Library, the National Archive and other locations armed with information. The Monto had disappeared as a result of the efforts of the Legion of Mary and its evangelical founder, Frank Duff. He had been appalled by the prostitution and the wrecked lives of the women who plied the trade – on a field trip there Duff had found hovels where the girls and their pimps drank methylated spirits and smoked opium. The drug was widely available at the time – indeed, shop window advertisements offering opium for sale can be seen in photographs of the period. Frank Duff had been friendly with the Taoiseach of the time, William T. Cosgrave. The existence of this 'place of sin' was an affront to their Catholic morality. The Taoiseach had the situation of the Monto discussed at the first cabinet meeting of the fledgling Free State in 1922.

On March 12th, 1925, a series of police raids took place on the brothels of the Monto. That evening, a votive mass was celebrated in the Pro-Cathedral on Marlborough Street. At the conclusion of the mass, a procession was formed and it headed down Sean McDermott Street. Crucifixes were nailed onto the doors of the brothels. The girls were moved to convents around the city. Some went to the Liberties, others to High Park and some more to Seán McDermott Street, just down the road. One night, that was all it took. One night, and the Monto was gone forever. Church and State, hand in glove, the most powerful alliance in the land, magisterial, pervasive and unstoppable.

As it happened, there were still some of the 'girls,' now old women, living and working in the Magdalen Laundry in Seán McDermott Street in 1982. Through her contacts with the nuns in Sheriff Street, Florrie Cunningham got access to them. She interviewed them and they had such sad stories. They had become institutionalised after the breakup of the Monto and had spent their lives in repentance, literally washing their sins away. One of the women Florrie interviewed had known Dicey Reilly, who had worked for Becky Cooper, a madam who ran a brothel in Tyrone Street, afterwards called Railway Street, and recently renamed James Joyce Street after the author of *Ulysses*. I knew the song of Dicey Reilly, a great ballad (sung as an up-tempo 'come all ye') that was a favourite in the pubs of the inner city where I drank. I hadn't known she was a prostitute, however. I dug out an old book of Dublin street songs and found a version of it by Dominic Behan.

> *Long years ago when men were men and fancied May Oblong*
> *Or lovely Becky Cooper or Maggie Mary Wong*
> *One woman put them all to shame, just one was worthy of the name*
> *And the name of that dame was Dicey Reilly.*
> *Oh but time went catching up on her like many pretty whores*
> *Sure it's after you along the street before you're out the door*
> *The balance weighed their looks all fade, but out of all this great brigade*
> *Still the heart of the rowl is Dicey Reilly.*

The song is a dirge and the viewpoint of the singer is of one looking back, remembering the past, recalling someone of great beauty who has fallen on hard times because of her addiction to alcohol. Indeed, Annie Apple, who sat under the bridge in Seville Place and abused all passers by, was a modern-day version of Dicey Reilly. There were so many aspects of the song that intrigued me. The uniqueness of her name, Dicey, for starters. Where did that come from? It sounded like a Dublin nickname but it wasn't one heard nowadays. The references to the other women, including a Chinese prostitute, Maggie Mary Wong, gave the Monto a surprising international dimension. The mention of May Oblong – I knew that a play existed called *The End of Mrs Oblong* – and, of course, oblong is the shape of a coffin. Becky Cooper, a madam referred to by Joyce, was the sister of John 'Shankers' Ryan, an informer who was reportedly court-martialled and executed in Phil Shanahan's public house on the corner of Railway Street/ Foley Street, in 1921.

Dicey is called the 'heart of the rowl' in the last line of each verse. It is a reference to the sweet spot of the tobacco, the heart, much sought after by the connoisseur. In the pattern of the song, 'door' is made to rhyme with 'whore,' which makes it 'dure.' That was how my mother, a countrywoman from outside Dundalk, pronounced that word. Here it was cropping up in a quintessential Dublin context. Could the author of the song have been from outside the Pale? The use of the word 'brigade' (and the brilliant internal rhyme with 'fade') is also apposite, because so many of the Monto customers were soldiers. Dicey, it seems, stood out amongst all the competition. The song that celebrated her was a remembrance touched with genius.

The City Workshop members unearthed reams of material. We had found the story of Honor Bright, a young prostitute from Wexford, the mother of a young boy who herself was found murdered at Ticknock, outside Dublin, just before the Monto was closed down. A police superintendent and a doctor were charged in connection with her murder, but they were acquitted. There were no songs about Honor Bright, but Brendan Behan had put her into his play *Richard's Cork Leg* and called her 'Crystal Clear'. We might have done something similar, but we didn't have a story, not as yet. We had songs, we had anecdotes, we had poems, we had Nighttown, we had the Magdalen Laundry, we had the Legion of Mary, but we didn't have a structure on which to hang our material.

We were sitting in a circle throwing ideas about, getting frustrated. We had been days at it. We were under pressure to find a story and start rehearsals.

'I don't know if this is any good,' Jean Doyle said, 'but my grandparents lived in the Monto.'

'That's a good start,' I said.

'They lived in Railway Street. I used to sleep in between them when I was a child.'

People were curious as to why Jean slept in between them.

'My grandfather Christy used to wake up and imagine that he was still in the trenches. He'd try to beat up my Granny, Sadie. It was my job to stop him.'

It turned out that Jean's grandfather, Christy Costello, had enlisted in the Dublin Fusiliers at the start of the First World War. He'd served at the Front and had an eye blown out in the Battle of the Somme. He came home to Dublin traumatised, and waited for the British authorities to send him a glass eye replacement. In the meantime, he attacked Sadie. She was known in the locality as 'the jelly woman' because of her ability to absorb his blows.

'He was very vain, my grandfather, he wouldn't leave the house in Railway Street without his glass eye.'

'How long did it take him to get it?' I asked.

'Six years.'

'Six years?' we all blurted out, a mixture of incredulity and laughter.

It seemed unbelievable. A man holed up in a house in Dublin waiting six years for a glass eye to be delivered. We all wanted to know what caused the delay.

'It was the colour,' she said. 'They kept getting the colour wrong. It took them six years to match the colour with his good eye.'

It turned out that the authorities in Britain had sent him five glass eyes over six years before Christy was convinced he had a match. Then he put the glass eye in, polished his boots and put on his army uniform. He went out into the streets of

Dublin, where people cursed at him and threw stones at him. He didn't understand that Ireland had changed. Men in British Army uniform were no longer welcome on the streets of the capital. Indeed, they were despised. While Christy was holed up, we'd had the 1916 Rising, the War of Independence, the Treaty and the Civil War. The world that Christy Costello had inhabited was gone. It had crumbled and vanished as surely as his eye had been blown out in the green fields of France.

I was stunned by Jean's revelations.

'Is that story any good to you, Peter?' Jean said.

I didn't know what to say. I had just listened to a story that was a perfect metaphor for the collapse of imperialism in Ireland.

Jean opened her handbag and started to pull the contents around.

'I'm sure I have one of them here,' she said. 'I always carry one with me.'

Seconds later, Jean pulled out a small, cardboard box. She opened it. Inside was a glass eye, sitting on a piece of faded red silk.

'This was one of my granddad's,' she said, taking the glass eye and putting it into her own socket so that she looked ghoulish and obscene. She took it out and passed it around the circle. Some people were afraid of it and shied away. Others took it and caressed it. It felt like a way into history. It explained family and it explained country. It connected the First World War, the Rising and the Monto. She had carried this story inside her and now she was releasing it into the world, she was presenting the City Workshop with pure, theatrical gold.

'Jean, that is one of the best stories I have ever heard in my life,' I said. 'We need to put Christy Costello on the stage and bring him to life again.'

We went at our Monto play with all guns blazing. The group improvised scenes and Mick Egan and I went away and wrote the play. Vinnie Murphy worked his magic on the songs – and he wrote original material for the show also. Two local residents from the North Strand, Catriona Crowe (who worked at the National Archive) and Padraig O'Faoláin (the painter), came in and taught us an English anti-war song song, *The White Cockade*, which we adapted for our purposes and made it a 'shamrock green.' While Mick and I were busy with the writing, Maggie staged and choreographed much of the show. It was collaboration in the best sense – Jean's family story layered with songs and anecdotes from our reading, research and interviews.

We sat down to discuss a title for the show, and couldn't decide between the various names that the area was known as – Monto, the Kips, Nighttown, the Digs, Dublin's red light, the Village. Someone suggested we combine the names and we did. In the end we chose three, *The Kips, The Digs, The Village,* and that became its title, my favourite of any play I've been involved in. We made other changes and called the family at the centre of it the Kirwans, though we kept the names Christy and Sadie, with Jean taking the role based on her grandmother. We created a character based on Dicey Reilly, but we called her Dolly Partridge, a decision I regret. We should have left it alone because when we sang the song in the show, 'Dolly Partridge' didn't have the same resonance as Dicey Reilly and felt slightly forced. Florrie Cunningham played this part and managed to get laughs where she had no right to. Honor Bright transmuted into Rosie Kirwan and Liz Bono brought an ethereal quality to the character that was as unsettling as it was appropriate. As well as organising the music, Vinnie played the mad Christy and revealed himself as an actor of the highest order.

I was so nervous on opening night, I could barely watch. I felt like I was exposing my family to potential ridicule. I had two large whiskies in the Granary bar next door to Project Arts Centre before curtain-up, and then proceeded to feel sick. I was in the toilet of the Project, splashing my face, when I heard the audience burst into laughter. It was the opening scene between Florrie as Dolly Partridge and Seamus Kelly as Charlie, the IRA man.

> DOLLY: Ah, you're the same as all the rest of them, when it's put up to you, you run away… that's why there's shopkeepers and tradesmen, and then the poor.
> CHARLIE: Yeah, like you.
> DOLLY: Me? I'm not poor. No, I'm a whore. It's you that's poor.

The audience warmed to Florrie, and every time she opened her mouth they laughed. Florrie has one of those malleable faces: she can make it scrunch up and contort, and she is not self-conscious about it in any way. It makes for great comedy, and she rose to the occasion magnificently on opening night, as did all the cast.

The day after it opened, the show sold out for its two-week run in the Project. This was helped by a glowing review from David Nowlan in *The Irish Times*, who was bowled over by the authenticity of it all. *The Kips, The Digs, The Village* became the hottest ticket in town. The Inner City Looking On Festival struck a chord with Dubliners and made the summer of 1982 an unforgettable time in the capital. The Italians won the World Cup, but nothing compared with U2 playing open air in the boys' playground in Sheriff Street, blasting out from the roof of the small pavilion, with people dancing past midnight to Bono, the Edge, Larry and Adam, the citizens marking the passing of tenement Dublin by celebrating all that was best in ourselves, by celebrating all that was best in our culture.

* * *

Life in Ardilaun Road carried on as before, with Sheila managing the house and the kids so that I could indulge my passion for the theatre. My salary running the City Workshop wasn't great – I was paid as an AnCo supervisor – but Mick Rafferty was able to dig into NCCCAP funds and top it up by twenty pounds a week, a godsend. The main thing was that it was regular money, and we could depend on it every week, a welcome change from living on the dole and trying to get my plays produced where I could. More than all of that, however, I was happy. I loved the community dimension of the work with City Workshop. I loved taking these people with little or no experience and putting them on the map, artistically. It fed into everything I believed about the arts breaking down barriers and allowing working-class people the opportunity to express themselves. City Workshop was at the forefront of a movement that was challenging perceptions of 'good art,' and, in the process, it was shining a light on arts funding and how that was distributed largely for the benefit of the middle classes.

The umbrella group that had formed continued to meet and spread its wings. We hadn't put a name on ourselves yet, but we didn't want it to sound academic or aloof. We were looking for something funky and accessible. Annie Kilmartin of Moving Theatre came up with the name CAFÉ – Creative Activity For Everyone. There was no space more communal than a café, and the acronym nailed our colours clearly to the mast. We wanted participation for all. We wanted to end exclusivity of all kinds. To borrow from Paris in 1968, it was '*L'Odéon est Ouvert.*' We organised regional meetings in Cork, Galway and Belfast. The response on the ground was really heartening. People were clamouring for change. It felt like, as a society, we were at a turning point. Everyone was talking about computers and how they were going to shape the future, for good or ill. Indeed, 7:84 Theatre Company in Scotland had produced a play on the subject that had been seen at Project. It was written by Sandy Craig and called *The Future*. I will never forget his thesis that in a few years all of Shakespeare's plays could be stored on something no bigger than the head of a pin.

Everyone was talking work and society. We were moving inexorably in the direction of becoming a leisure society. This had enormous implications for culture. In a society where people no longer worked, we had to look at how we would spend our free time. As well as the impact of computers, there was the emergence of the free market under Reagan and Thatcher. The Iron Lady was dismantling traditional British industry; she had set out to smash the coalmining communities of Yorkshire and Lancashire, Labour's traditional strongholds. She had taken on the unions and polarised Britain. Sandy Fitzgerald of the Grapevine Arts Centre (then situated in North Frederick Street, it would later move to Moss Street and become City Arts) sent me an article from the *Guardian* newspaper. It concerned a town in Yorkshire called Consett, whose coal industry had shut down. The headline read: '*The Future is Consett and it's Not Working.*' For Consett, read Britain; for Britain, read Ireland.

At a CAFÉ regional meeting hosted by Martin Lynch in Belfast, Sandy Fitzgerald used the *Guardian* article as a stimulus to our discussions. The meeting took place in a club in Turf Lodge, a working-class estate in the west of the city – Martin's brother Seamus was at that time the Belfast leader of Sinn Féin The Workers Party, political wing of the Official IRA. We'd had to clear the club of its regular clientele in advance of the meeting, and they weren't best pleased because it was a Saturday, with all the attendant sport on television. One man refused to leave and he was at the bar counter, asleep. We were sitting in a circle (*de rigueur* for all community arts groups) discussing the crisis in employment and its implications for us. Martin Lynch put forward the thesis that work was central to the human condition, that we needed to work because it gave structure to our lives. Without work, he suggested, life was meaningless.

It was an extremely animated discussion. From where I was sitting, I could see that the man at the bar had woken up. He started listening intently to our deliberations. He then put his hand in the air, looking for permission to get in. He just sat there with his hand in the air. Slowly but surely, everyone became aware of him. Annie Kilmartin turned around and asked him if he would he like to make a contribution.

'I know I'm not a part of your group, I don't want to take liberties,' the man said.

'That's all right,' Annie assured him. 'You can say something if you want to.'

'You're talking about work there, am I right?'

'We're talking about the future, Paddy, we're talking about the twenty-first century,' Martin Lynch said.

He clearly knew this man.

'You think work is good for you, is that what you think, Martin?' the man said.

'I do,' Martin replied. 'I think it gives you dignity.'

'Is that what you all think?' the man asked us.

A variety of answers made their way across the room towards him. He got down from his stool and headed for the gent's toilet in the corner. As he went in the door, he turned to us, looking very serious.

'I'll tell you this,' he said, 'if work was good for you, the rich would be doing it.'

There was a truth in his statement that was hard to contradict. We lived with a nineteenth-century view of work: that of labour, of manufacture, of digging coal out of the earth, of heavy industry. The industrial revolution had transformed society and we were about to reinvent ourselves all over again. The steam train had driven the earlier change; now it was almost obsolete. The pursuit of wealth was powering the new revolution. Bob Dylan had put it rather succinctly when he wrote 'money doesn't talk, it screams.' We were creating a world, where manufacturing was not at the heart of wealth creation.

How would the arts community respond to this, and what could CAFÉ do to fashion a policy that took account of it?

* * *

I should have withdrawn *Diary of a Hunger Strike* the day Pam told me that she was going to direct it. I didn't have the courage to make the hard decision. I convinced myself that things with her would be different this time around, that the experience of *Emigrants* could not repeat itself. I headed off to London for the start of rehearsals, leaving Maggie in charge of City Workshop. Pam had assembled a top class cast. The two prisoners, Pat O'Connor and Sean Crawford, were being played by John Keegan and Charlie Lawson, both from Belfast. John came from the nationalist tradition and Charlie from the loyalist tradition so there was a great deal of talk about hands across the divide and the ability of the arts to transcend division. Charlie Lawson complimented me on the 'fairness and balance' of the play, but he left me in no doubt that his sympathies lay not with the IRA, but with the UDA (the Ulster Defence Association, the leading loyalist paramilitary group).

'As an actor, I have to put my politics to one side,' Charlie said, 'I have to see this as my job, and that's what it is: a job.'

I appreciated his honesty, but I felt that sparks would fly, at some point, in the process. Pam, as usual, did little to conceal her politics.

'Charlie's in crisis, he wants to be British but over here he's just a Paddy, it must be an awful pain in the arse.'

'I am British, Pam, it says so on my passport.'

'You're not British, you don't even talk like us,' Pam said.

It was all good banter but it barely hid the divisions simmering underneath. I told my story about trying to change a Northern Ireland banknote in London and being refused because they said it wasn't legal tender.

'It is legal tender,' Charlie said, 'the Bank of England must honour any note with Her Majesty on it.'

'Is that the Queen you're talking about?' John Keegan said.

'Yes, her Majesty the Queen, my monarch.'

'Queen of Great Britain and Northern Ireland,' John said.

'Exactly.'

'So if Northern Ireland is such an integral part of Great Britain, why do they have to tag it on at the end like that?'

'Because we're Northern Irish as well as being British.'

'You're a Paddy, now grow up,' Pam said, bringing the conversation to a halt; but I could see that Charlie was not happy. It must have been difficult for him, isolated in a group with strong nationalist and republican sympathies. His way of dealing with it was largely to play the clown.

There is a pivotal scene in the first act of the play where Sean Crawford, the prisoner played by Charlie, asks his cell mate, Pat O'Connor, the reasons why he joined the IRA. Pat tells him that Bloody Sunday in Derry was the turning point, that there was no sitting on the fence after that. Sean Crawford reveals that he was only ten years old when the events in Derry took place.

'Can I make a suggestion here, Peter?' Charlie said.

'Of course you can,' I replied.

'In the interests of balance, can I refer to it as Londonderry?'

I figured he was trying to be funny.

'Bloody Sunday in Londonderry,' I said. 'I've never heard anyone refer to it as that. It even sounds weird.'

'My character is quite socialist,' Charlie said, 'I think he might.'

'You're an IRA volunteer, you would never refer to it as anything other than Derry. Bloody Sunday in Derry. Now stop taking the piss,' John Keegan said.

'I'm not taking the piss, I'm exploring character possibility.'

But he was taking the piss and it was his way of dealing with the compromise he had to make to play this character. It was a playful reminder that conflict was at the heart of everything in Northern Ireland. The two sides couldn't even agree on the name of their second city. Nationalists called it Derry because that reflected its ancient name of Doire Colmcille, the abbey of Colmcille. Loyalists called it Londonderry because that erased its historic past and made it a new place that reflected their victory at Derry and the Boyne. The row over the name was the conflict in microcosm. In the rehearsal room it was all good fun, but I knew that we were stepping around landmines and that eventually one would explode. I was busy with rewrites and that kept me out of rehearsals and occupied.

Sheila and the children arrived, giving me further reason to stay away from rehearsals. I brought Rossa, Fiachra, and Pam's son Ned to see Sylvester Stallone in *Rocky 3,* which had just opened in London. They loved the trip into Leicester Square on the tube, eating slices of pizza while we queued to get into the cinema. The boys were blown away by the movie with its simple narrative, a boxing story that is a love story, a man putting himself through enormous pain and sacrifice to redeem himself, to become whole, to be a champion.

'I hope your play is as good as *Rocky*,' Fiachra said to me.

'Do you have any music in it?' Rossa said. 'The music in *Rocky* was great.'

Eye of the Tiger, with its driving heartbeat rhythm, was a perfect complement to the film. The boys imitated it as they shadow-boxed one another in the tube all the way home.

'I'm Rocky Balboa,' Ned said.

'No, I'm Rocky Balboa,' Fiachra said.

'You're both wrong, I'm Rocky Balboa,' Rossa said.

They all wanted to be Rocky. I wondered if they would want to be Pat O'Connor.

* * *

The production moved to Hull for the final ten days of rehearsal. Di Seymour had come up with a brilliant stage design and Pam had it built in a space in the centre of Hull. It meant that we had over a week on the real thing before we moved to Edinburgh for the opening at the Assembly Rooms. As the rehearsal process entered into its final week, it all started to unravel. I met John Keegan in the pub after a run-through on the Monday of the last week.

'She's going to destroy your play, Peter,' John said, 'she's going to fuck it all up.'

Pam had decided that the second act didn't work. It was too static. The scenes involving Pat O'Connor and his girlfriend, Bernie Maguire, were too full of exposition at a point where the story demanded action. To borrow the boxing metaphor, we were in the dressing-room when we needed to be in the ring. The hunger strike by definition, however, was an act of passive aggression and didn't allow itself a slugfest conclusion. It was fought by a man who got weaker, not stronger; the drama was in his dying and the action had to be carried by those around him. Frances Quinn, who played Bernie, felt that Pam's loss of faith could do irreparable damage to the show.

'I think you have to defend your play, Peter,' she confided in me. 'I know my scenes work, I really do, and I can't let Pam undermine me at this stage.'

In fairness to Pam, I knew that the second act was inherently flawed. I tried everything I knew to improve it. I rewrote and rewrote to a point where I didn't know why I was rewriting any more. I looked at the characters' names on a page and thought they were in a play by someone else, I felt I had no real relationship with them. I worked through the night and came in with scenes that got one read-through before they were dumped. I felt like I was on the floor creatively. I ended up cutting and pasting four versions of the same scene. I didn't know what was good or bad in the end. I only wanted to hear the words:

'That's great, no need for any more rewrites.'

The play opened in a blaze of publicity at the Assembly Rooms. A lot of talk centred on the male nudity and the fact that one of the characters, Sean Crawford, took a piss on-stage before throwing it out the cell window. Was that real urine or pretend urine? The same question applied to the shit, was it real shit or pretend shit on the walls? Audiences were appalled by the conditions. The reality that men ate food in this environment seemed unbelievable. Was that a dramatic licence too far? The prison conditions seemed such a profound, self-inflicted denial of human dignity. The reaction of the authorities only worsened the plight of the prisoners. It didn't seem possible that this was taking place in contemporary society because it felt, visually and thematically, that this was an Old Testament story, that it came from a time before the word 'humane' had been invented or prisoners were deemed to have rights.

Inevitably, audiences wanted to know how it had come down to this scenario. When and how did the dirty protest begin? How did the IRA justify volunteers living in these abominable conditions? The history of the troubles was, of course, a complex thing. I didn't feel that it was possible, or that it was my responsibility, to answer all these questions in my play. It always boiled down to this: how far back do you go to provide the right context? I tried to make the issues understandable to someone coming to it for the first time. I was well aware, for example, that the demand of the prisoners to wear their own clothes was hugely complicated by the fact that some of them already did. Those convicted prior to March 1st, 1976, wore their own clothes as of right. So, when the hunger strike was in full swing, there were men in the prison (they inhabited the cells as opposed to the blocks) who enjoyed that privilege. I did not want to take up valuable stage time getting into, and explaining, these nuances. For me, the prison was the endgame, the battlefield between the IRA and the British Government, and I wanted to keep the lines clean and uncomplicated. I didn't want it to be theatre as a history lesson.

We were all affected by the response to the play. The second act didn't feel as problematic in front of a live audience as it had in the rehearsal room. That is one of the great mysteries of the theatre: the audience don't always share your concerns, they see things differently. They want to be challenged and sometimes that provocation is enough, you're not required to fill in all the blanks. Pam, however, was not of that opinion.

'We need to tell them why the men are in the gaol,' she said, 'do you know what I mean, Peter?'

I wasn't sure I shared her concern.

'It's such a fucked-up place the north, we need to show that the prisoners were discriminated against before they ever got to gaol,' she said.

I was waiting for the one word I didn't want to hear and then it came.

'We need more rewrites,' she said.

'I can't give you more rewrites,' I said, 'I'm spent.'

I knew that if I told Sheila I had more work to do on the play, she would shoot me, and she'd be right. She'd been looking after four kids in London, Hull and Edinburgh while I worked through the night trying to fix the unfixable. The play was not the problem; the problem was Pam and my relationship with her. I should have set down parameters but I didn't. I should have spoken up when I had the chance. I shouldn't have bitten my tongue in the public phone box outside the Fluther Good pub on the Ballybough Road. I should have made my demands clear, so that when conflict arose my position was stated and unambiguous.

'I can't go back to the well any more, Pam,' I said, 'there's nothing there.'

We had a hit show and a divided team. I came home to Dublin to see if I could find a venue that would offer a guarantee to take it in. We had approached the Dublin Theatre Festival but they had no interest in such politically charged work. They didn't want barbed wire on an Irish stage. Or rather they didn't want Irish barbed wire. Had it been Polish or Russian it would have been fine. I felt it was a cop out, and told Michael Colgan (the Festival Director) as much. I told him I would go to the papers with the story.

I wasn't going to be intimidated. I went to the *Irish Independent* and the *Irish Press*. My grievance was that this was censorship. Both papers carried the story, but they were not favourable to the production, or to me.

My next best hope was the Oscar Theatre, but Chris O'Neill, who wanted to take it in, didn't have the money. The irony wasn't lost on either of us that Bobby Sands' death had scuppered *Down All the Days* eighteen months before. The only producer who showed any real bottle was Brid Dukes at the Belltable in Limerick. She thought it important that the play be seen on home soil, despite the fact that local TD, Jim Kemmy, (himself a great supporter of the arts), had spoken out vociferously against the Provisionals and the hunger strike.

The success of the play in Edinburgh ensured that we got a transfer to the Roundhouse in London. I had never anticipated a commercial success for it, so this came as a huge surprise. Pam felt that the play needed work before its London opening. As I wasn't available, she was going to workshop it with the actors and see what came out of that. I didn't want to stand in her way, but I didn't like the omens. There was little I could do about it from Dublin, so I adopted a hands-off approach.

I headed over for the opening night, but the flight was delayed and I missed the play. I got there literally as the lights came down on the final scene. The applause was good and sustained and I hung around the front of house, earwigging. The comments were mostly favourable. I made for the backstage area and straight into a row. Lord Gowrie, a liberal Conservative in Thatcher's government who had tried to negotiate a settlement with the prisoners – I had based my character of Lord Rothleigh in the play on him – had come backstage to congratulate the actors. Chatting away, he confessed that the Republicans were easy to deal with and that he thought Loyalist intransigence was at the heart of the problems in Northern Ireland. Charlie Lawson had to be restrained from punching him. Thank God John Keegan and Walter McMonagle (prison officer McClay) were quick off the mark and intervened. Lord Gowrie did his best to retract, but it was too late. The truth was that neither of the two major political parties in Britain had much empathy with the loyalist cause, and Gowrie was simply articulating what was widely known.

The following night, I watched the play. My heart sank as I noted all the changes made by Pam. In the opening scene,

Charlie Lawson (as Crawford) fishes out a small capsule from his potty. He has swallowed and defecated it. It is a letter from home and he proceeds to read it. It bemoans the fact that no one in the house has a job and the prospect of work feels as far off as ever. Discrimination still rules, alienation is all pervasive. It is pure agit-prop, of course, everything comes down to blaming the social conditions for all that is wrong with the body politic. Once that is addressed, then the causes of conflict will disappear.

I was angry because I had argued this with Pam many times before. Her analysis was Marxist and one that found much favour among the left in Britain. But it didn't get to the heart of the matter for me. You could end discrimination in the economic sense but nationalists would continue to feel alienated. The core problem was one of identity. One section of the population identified with the British State and the other section with the Republic. Until that was addressed, nationalists would feel disenfranchised and some would resort to violence to express that alienation.

My anger towards Pam was nothing to my own self-recrimination. This had all happened before, during *Emigrants*. I had repeated the experience with *Diary of a Hunger Strike* and expected different results. I could blame Pam, but I was the real culprit. For things to change, I had to change. Pam was always going to be Pam. A part of me loved her. I loved her Yorkshire doggedness and I loved her passion for the theatre, but I knew that our relationship was over. She had shown me no respect, she had steamrolled my play and allowed it to say something that I hadn't intended. I was so ashamed, I couldn't even talk to her about it. I needed to get my play back. I wanted this run of it to be over so that I could reclaim it and restore its dignity. I came home to Dublin and I wrote Pam a very long letter, a letter with many questions. I wrote it as much for me as for her. I asked her to come back to me as soon as possible. I'm still waiting for a response.

The play did come to Limerick, the only place it was seen in Ireland. Jim Kemmy attended, and on radio the following day he complimented me on the play but castigated the IRA leadership for their part in prolonging the strike. I tried to tell him that the impetus and direction for the strike came from within the prison, that a solution was in place but that Thatcher wanted revenge for the death of Airey Neave, who'd been assassinated by the INLA in the car park of the House of Commons. We had a good political argument, the pair of us, and I was glad because that meant we weren't discussing the play. I was glad that it finished up its run in the Belltable. I got home from Limerick and found a woman in my sitting-room, having tea with Sheila. Her name was Carolyn Chriss, an agent from Los Angeles. She had seen the play at the Assembly Rooms and had come to Dublin to meet me. Not being able to reach me by phone, which was cut off again, she'd hopped on a plane, turned up at the Abbey Theatre and there got an address for me. A taxi ride later and she was having tea with the family.

'I want to get *Diary of a Hunger Strike* produced in Los Angeles,' she said. 'I want to introduce your work to America.'

Carolyn fell in love with Dublin and with our family. I brought her to my local, The Sunset House pub, and her visit coincided with the opening of the ladies' toilet – the place was decked out in streams of toilet roll and a local woman, Betty Cashin, dressed for the occasion in leotard and fish-net stockings, performed the official 'cutting of the loo roll' ceremony. Carolyn couldn't believe that the pub had been allowed to serve women and not provide a toilet. I explained that the pub had been for years a 'men only' bar until the women stormed the place and insisted on being served alongside their husbands. That, in turn, led to the women using the men's toilet and, finally, the installation of their own designated WC.

It was a far cry from Los Angeles, and Carolyn thought it primitive but appealing. She came to our house for dinner and couldn't believe the energy and madness surrounding the presence of four children in a house so small.

'Where do you escape to write?' she asked me. 'Do you have somewhere in the country?'

'No, I write upstairs, mostly during the night when the kids are asleep.'

'I never thought about having kids before,' she said, 'but seeing yours, I'm having second thoughts.'

Carolyn went back to America to make a baby while Sheila and I discussed long-term solutions to contraception. For the greater part, we'd used the contraceptive pill and after Nuala's birth, Sheila was back on it again. We worried about the long-term side effects of it, however. Sheila was only thirty-two. Another fifteen years of chemical ingestion to manipulate the cycle wasn't an appealing prospect. As things stood, Sheila had an ongoing problem with blurred vision and we weren't sure what the cause of it was. We needed a permanent solution. We loved children, but a precarious life in the theatre wasn't an economic base from which to expand the family any further. The options seemed to be sterilisation for one or the other of us. I didn't like the idea of it for me. I was a writer, a creative person, I didn't like interfering with that part of my psyche. What if I lost the gift, or the desire to write? Or worse still, what if my libido was damaged or disappeared altogether? I was a sexual being and I could not contemplate being otherwise.

I talked about it amongst my male friends. Most of them were horrified. The idea of letting a doctor within six inches of their penis was anathema to them. On the other hand, one or two thought it was a good solution for sleeping around.

'You'll be made. No danger of getting some young one up the pole.'

The truth is, the opposite was the case. Contemplating sterilisation was like re-committing myself to the marriage. It meant that I would never make babies with another woman. I had to be sure that I was in the marriage I wanted. I had to decide that Sheila and I would be together forever. I was making a permanent commitment again. We would never separate.

I broached the subject one day with Gerry Davis, the painter and gallery owner from Capel Street. As well as his interest in fine art, Gerry was a Jewish man who played Leopold Bloom when the occasion demanded. He was always someone I could open up to and maybe I was Stephen to his Bloom; I always found him trustworthy and fatherly.

'You know that Yeats had the snip, he had it done in his fifties,' Gerry said.

'I didn't know that,' I said, 'didn't know they could do it in those days.'

'He always said that he wrote his best poetry after his vasectomy.'

It was the reassurance I was looking for. If my plays could improve with the snip, I wanted immediate sterilisation. I went to see a doctor at the Irish Family Planning Association and he talked me through the procedure. I was delighted and reassured when he told me that my ejaculation would feel the same as before.

'Your orgasm will be no different, except that it will contain no semen.'

'Where will the semen go?' I asked.

'It goes into your body and gets reabsorbed,' he said.

I felt sorry for the semen, chasing down a one-way system into oblivion.

'Are you a Catholic?' he asked me.

I thought about that for a moment.

'Yes, I am. Of sorts. I pick and choose, I suppose.'

'I'm obliged to tell you that it goes against the teachings of the Church.'

'Does that mean I'll be excommunicated?' I said.

'Probably. You might want to talk to a priest,' he said.

I was glad there was a consequence to having the vasectomy. Excommunication. I'd have something in common with one of my heros, Brendan Behan. He'd been put out of the Church for refusing to condemn the IRA after he'd been caught carrying a bomb in England. In *Diary of a Hunger Strike* I had also refused to condemn the IRA, but the Church were going to get me for the vasectomy. I was having the snip out of love for Sheila, but the Church didn't care much about love. They were more concerned with the letter of the law. I didn't need to discuss it with any priest. My excommunication convinced me I was doing the right thing.

I went into the clinic for the half-day procedure, and the nurse looking after me seemed delighted to meet me.

'I wish there were more men like you,' she said. 'You're so brave.'

I didn't feel brave. The doctor had assured me it was pain free, so what need was there for bravery? I'd have a local anaesthetic, he'd snip the vas and stop semen getting into my penis. I wouldn't feel a thing. I could go back to work immediately, it was that innocuous.

I stripped down to my hospital gown. The nurse put me up onto the gurney and then she gently slapped my scrotum.

'Come on, testes, let's have you, testes, another brave man, testes.'

I'd had them referred to as balls, bollix, testicles, nuts, chestnuts, manhood, scrotum, undercarriage, but never testes. I didn't like it, not in combination with the word brave. Testes felt like a word you might use to distract a child before you stuck a needle up his arse.

'That's good testes, lovely, lovely testes.'

I took the needle like a man, and the procedure was over in minutes. Sheila collected me and we went home to Ballybough.

'I might do some writing later,' I said.

'I think you should take it easy,' Sheila said, 'you might not feel so good when the anaesthetic wears off.'

How do women know these things? How do they know what's coming? I had forgotten that my balls were still numb. When the anaesthetic wore off, less than an hour later, I felt like somebody was holding and a blowtorch to my balls. I had never experienced a pain like it in my life. Anyone who has ever played football knows what it is like to get hit with a ball in the nuts – well this was a hundred times worse, and it didn't feel like it was ever going to end. I wanted to die, and my only decision was how to end it. I was going to get into my car and drive off the pier in Howth. On the way to Howth, I was going to go via the Irish Family Planning Association and I was going to choke

Nurse Testes to death because other brave men were going to suffer my fate, other brave men were going to be fooled, it was no way for a brave man to lose his semen. It was no wonder Yeats had written good poetry having survived this massacre. He knew how lucky he was to be alive.

14

The Incomplete History of Rock 'n Roll, featuring Dion's *Runaround Sue*, opened at Project as part of the 1982 Dublin Theatre Festival. I'd been so busy with *Hunger Strike* that I had taken a hands-off approach and let the director, Michael Sheridan, get on with what he had to do. He had cut and reshaped it quite drastically and I was in no position to be critical. I wasn't sure that it delivered the message I'd hoped for, but I was too depressed to care. It was a popular success, and that made Chris O'Neill happy. He'd recouped, to use his own favourite word. He'd gambled and won.

Bono and Phil Lynott came to see the show. Rossa and Fiachra didn't care much for the theatre – they associated it with a lot of hard work and no money at the end of it all – but my stock rose mightily when I introduced them to the stars of Irish rock.

'What do you think of your Da's play?' Phil Lynott said.

'I think it's good,' Fiachra said.

'But not as good as *Whiskey in the Jar*', Rossa said.

I had begun to teach Rossa basic chords on the guitar, and already he was developing his own musical taste. I had started him off on The Beatles, but he'd graduated to Dire Straits and David Bowie and he was still only ten. He loved guitar riffs, and *Whiskey in the Jar* was among his favourites. Phil Lynott was happy to take Rossa's compliment and mature enough to bring the conversation back to the play.

'Your Da is a great storyteller, you should be proud of him,' Phil said.

'We are,' Fiachra said. 'We're dead proud.'

'All the best storytellers come from the northside,' Bono said.

'Hold on there, I'm from Drimnagh,' Phil said, 'I'm from the southside.'

Phil Lynott grabbed Bono in a headlock and they started messing about. Rossa and Fiachra thought it was the funniest thing they had ever seen. Two rock stars wrestling over where they came from. A black man and a white man, two Dubliners, standing in the foyer of the Project Arts Centre, talking about my play like it was something important.

I first met Phil Lynott in 1968. I was on the dance committee of our school, O'Connell's CBS, in North Richmond Street. We held a dance in the school hall once a month and it drew enormous crowds, in excess of a thousand, regularly. Skid Row, Brush Shields' band loved playing the school; it paid well and ended early. On the day of a gig, they'd set up the gear, do a sound check and then it was the serious business – a five-a-side football match between the band and the dance committee – played with the intensity of an FA Cup Final. Phil Lynott always wanted their team to be Manchester United and we had to settle for being Liverpool, Spurs or Arsenal. Phil fancied himself as a version of George Best, but Brush Shiels, in truth, was their best player. He came from a family of decent soccer players and had played League of Ireland with Bohemians. Phil was all style, but he was too leggy, selfish on the ball and easily dispossessed. He lacked technique, but had a great goal celebration, waddling around and doing a version of ballet arse just like he'd been to a Slot Players workshop. It made everyone in the hall laugh when he scored. Sometimes we let the ball go in just to see his celebration.

I reminded him of those encounters, standing in the foyer of the Project.

'I haven't given up the dream of playing for Manchester United, not just yet,' he said.

'What about you, Bono,' I said, 'who do you dream of playing for?'

'I don't follow anyone. I don't understand football. I don't like it, I guess.'

'You should follow Liverpool,' Fiachra said, 'they're my team, they're the best.'

'Kenny Dalglish is a bag of shit,' Phil said, 'go on, admit it, he's a bag of shit.'

'No, he's not,' Fiachra said.

'A bag of shit, a bag of shit,' Phil repeated and he chased Fiachra through the gallery until he caught him and put him in a headlock.

Phil Lynott had such charisma, and yet there was something ordinary about him. He did nothing to hide his wonderful Drimnagh accent. I would never have known from that encounter in Project that he had a serious drug problem. But then, people close to me weren't aware that I had a serious alcohol problem. I was adept at covering up, especially in the public arena. It was less than four years later that Phil succumbed to his heroin addiction. I know that Bono and others did everything to help him fight his demon, but without success. I remember watching the Live Aid concert on television – the gig that propelled U2 onto the world stage – and wondering where Phil was. It would have been so appropriate, as a black Irish man, for him to have taken centre stage at that event. We had suffered our own famine and it was still imbedded deep within us as a people. Phil's presence at Live Aid would have represented our history and the plight of Africa in a very special way. It wasn't to be. Six months later he was dead.

The impact of Phil's death on Rossa and Fiachra was enormous. For the first time in their lives, they knew someone who had died as a result of a drug overdose. They asked me to put on the news. They hated the news, normally. Now they wanted to hear and see every bulletin. They hated that drugs the had killed Phil. They hated the pushers who had supplied him. They wanted to know if the police would catch the culprits and put them in gaol. What they didn't know was that heroin was being sold in the streets less than a hundred yards from our home. The Ballybough area, like the north inner city generally, was becoming awash with heroin. Rossa and Fiachra were impressionable young teenagers. They hated drugs but hadn't yet come under any peer pressure to try them. In the wake of Phil Lynott's death, we had big decisions to make as a family.

* * *

The Kips, The Digs, The Village really put the City Workshop on the map. We got our extension – Tony Ó Dàlaigh as ever a tremendous advocate and supporter – so that we were secure for at least another six months. After the success of the Monto play, we turned our attention to the Dublin docks and started researching for our second full-length offering.

I had played along the north quays as a child, and it was the best playground in the city. There were the ships, first and foremost, and sneaking on and off them was the best 'pirate' adventure this side of the Caribbean. There was the ferry that crossed the river, and if he was in good humour, the ferryman might let you on without paying the tariff. There was the cargo discharged from ships, and I especially loved climbing timber mountains to become king of the castle. I loved the smell of the timber as much as I did scaling it. There was a singer-out who stood over the hold and sang out his instructions so that the winchman on the quayside could operate his crane with safety. It was pure opera. Grain was ever present on the cobblestones, and I loved biting into it and sucking out the sweet centre. We collected pocketfuls to snare pigeons with and, if I was lucky and made a catch, I had to release it back into the air because my Ma hated pigeons and wouldn't let them near our house. My favourite person was the rat catcher, and watching him at work with his cage and his poisons and listening to the death squeals of the rodents was frightening and exhilarating in equal measure.

Then the dockers disappeared. Their cranes went rusty. No more ships docked on the Liffey. The sounds and the smells of my childhood went with them. I asked my neighbour, a button man called Tommy Hogan, what had happened.

'Cargo used to come in ships,' he said, 'now it comes in metal boxes.'

Containerisation killed the Dublin docks. It removed the need for labour. A shipload of timber, say, had needed twenty men to discharge it. Now it was down to two: a crane operator and a driver. Up until the late sixties, the docks employed two and a half thousand men on a daily basis. Some of them were regulars or 'button men,' who were called first – thus the 'read,' where the men stood and a stevedore shouted out

the names of the men and gangs who would work that day
– before the casual labourers, who were called last. It was
archaic and open to obvious abuse of power. It was expected
of men picked for work that they would stand the stevedores
a drink in the pub. This custom persisted until Jim Larkin
arrived on the scene and tried to stamp it out. He got the
publicans to shut their doors at lunchtime – from half past
two until half past three – in order to get the men out of
the pubs and back to work. It became known as the 'holy
hour' and was part of our culture, baffling all and sundry as
to why the pubs in Dublin closed at lunchtime. The custom
was finally abolished in 1988 due to pressure from the tourist
industry.

An agreement signed in 1973 between the employers and
the Marine Port and General Workers Union reduced the number of permanent dockers in Dublin port to fifty-seven. It was
a decision that had catastrophic consequences for the river and
the communities around it. The Sheriff Street flats, built in the
early fifties to house those workers who serviced the docks, suffered a terminal blow. Unemployment became the norm, and
many of the older families moved out of the area. Inevitably,
the social fabric of the place began to crumble, and as it did,
drugs appeared and took centre stage. By the time my parents
left there in 1981, the writing was on the wall. To borrow that
phrase from Consett – the future was Sheriff Street and it wasn't
working.

It felt to me that there were two plays in this disintegration
– one that centred on the docks and its demise, and another that
looked at the arrival and impact of heroin. I took on the writing duties for the docks play, which became *Pledges and Promises*,
and Mick Egan took on the drugs piece, which became *A Hape*

A Junk. Together with *The Kips, The Digs, The Village*, the plays became known as the City Workshop Trilogy.

The second play proved much more difficult than the first. Everything about *The Kips, The Digs, The Village* was new. We were a new company, doing a new play. We had no expectations, we had the wind of the Inner City Looking On Festival behind us, we had the Monto and Jean Doyle's extraordinary story of her grandparents, we had songs of war and songs of rebellion and so much local history to draw on. Now we had an audience that wanted us to surpass the experience of the first one, in reality an impossible thing to do.

Pledges and Promises explored a world dominated by the pawn-shop and the docks, one world the preserve of the women and the other the preserve of the men. We discovered that the folk-lore department of University College Dublin had done a study of work and life customs among the citizens of the North Wall in the 1950s. The research included a wonderful chapter on the nicknames of the area – among them the weird and wonderful attribution of the name Git to any male child baptised Christy – and this inspired Vinnie Murphy to write the 'nicknames song.'

Swift Reilly, Starry Clarke, Runner Lacy and The Lark
Ball Alley Gaffney, Fishy Brian, Lie Low Murphy, Nettle Doyle
Broc Boland, Fly Welsh, Nugget Bar, The Rambler Dent
Dodger Reilly, Bass Byrne, Tasher Gordon, Bubbly Pint,
Lax Butler, The Ranter Kirwan, Cock Lawless, Peppery Kiernan
Muddler McDonald, Boots Lacy, Punch Connolly and Abba Daly

My own favourite name was Wagger Nugent, a one-legged docker who'd been left disabled as a result of a crane accident, and called Wagger because the word 'described how he ambled.' I made

Wagger one of the central characters of the play. On the opening night in Project Arts Centre, an elderly woman approached me.

'My name is Anne Nugent,' she said, 'and Wagger Nugent was my brother.'

She seemed very emotional, and I figured there was trouble on the way.

'We were very close and he only died less than a year ago.'

'I'm very sorry to hear that,' I said.

'I wasn't expecting to see him in the play, it brought him right back to me.'

She opened her bag and undid an internal zip. From the pouch, she withdrew an envelope. She opened the envelope and took out a photograph. It was of a one-legged man leaning on a crutch, with the loose trouser-leg folded up and held in position with a large, silver, safety pin. The man in the photograph bore an uncanny resemblance to Mick Egan, who portrayed him in the play.

'He lived with me up until the day he died,' she said. 'He never married, you see.'

There was no trouble, and Anne Nugent was delighted that we had brought her brother back to life for her. As much as she lamented his passing, she was bereft by what had happened to the old neighbourhood, the North Wall, and the way it had been allowed to atrophy while the authorities blamed the residents.

'They destroyed the docks,' she said 'and then they blamed the people. Wagger would have loved your play, son.'

My father worked for many years in the CIE Midlands Depot (now the site of the National Convention Centre). He also worked in the train station at Amiens Street (now Connolly station) and the Point Depot (the O2) when cargo trains terminated there. Among his visitors at the Midlands was a bag lady called Mary Ann McGilligan who came in to use the bathroom and have a wash. Her song was *Mick McGilligan's Daughter, Mary Ann*, hence the nickname. She sang it to the bus queues and the cinema queues on Eden Quay. She was tragically killed when she ran out in front of a bus in pursuit of a little gurrier who'd helped himself to some of her takings. I based a character in the play on her (Jean Doyle perfectly capturing her eccentricity) and made her a sort of soothsayer, a mad aul' wan who predicted the future. This was a speech she had in the wake scene at the end of the play:

I was standing down the Point, I was. And I looked into the Liffey. And there rising out of the water was a monster. A gigantic monster. A gigantic steel monster. With clawlike hands. And the monster unfurled his fingers, and from his hand in a never-ending stream flowed a tarlike black mass. When the dust had settled, the river was no more. And where water once bobbed and ducked, flowed and eddied, was a still sea of green grass. Three dockers looked down upon this scene, held their breaths in disbelief, their heads shook from side to side and they muttered in unison 'a dream, a dream, all a dream.' But it was not so, for my eyes beheld the monster. And the monster devoured all. And from his entrails when he burst, swung the three unbelievers, snottered to the beast by their dockers' hooks. This is the truth, for I perceived it so.

It was my apocalyptic vision of the river in the wake of its demise as a source of employment. It was a paean to my lost childhood, too.

The play ended with a union meeting where the cast sat among the audience and encouraged them to ask questions of the union officials seated on-stage at a table. At the end of the proceedings, a vote was taken on whether the dockers present should take the redundancy lump sum or fight to hold on to their jobs. A show of hands was called for and a tally was taken. Every member of the audience got to vote. It was agit-prop, in the best sense, where the audience was empowered to decide the play's ending. In making that decision, they were deciding the future of the docks and the city.

Mick Rafferty made his acting début as the Union Official. He was brilliant, because the role required a great deal of improvising, a skill he had acquired in abundance as the Director of the NCCCAP. He had been pivotal in the negotiations with Haughey and his advisors and he now brought that same skill-set to his role in the play. It was good for the City Workshop because it meant that the Director of the NCCCAP, the sponsoring body, was integrated into its flagship arts project.

At the opening night party for *Pledges and Promises* in Mick's house, the strangest thing happened. It was well past midnight, long after most people had gone home to their beds. We had consumed a great deal of alcohol and smoked a few joints. The marijuana was particularly strong, and I remember my mouth was feeling dry, like I had no spittle left. A joint came my way and I passed it on because I just felt too out of it. I decided to smoke a cigarette instead. I got the Major into my mouth but couldn't find my matches. The fire nearby was blazing. I picked up the tongs, fished a burning coal from the fire and lit my cigarette. Then I dropped the coal on the rug. I heard and smelled the singe of burning wool.

'Fuck... fuck....' I said as I tried to pick up the burning coal.

I was too stoned to scoop it up. The coal kept on breaking, burning the rug more. I didn't know what to do, whether to laugh or cry. Someone came to my aid and got a shovel under the coal and scooped it back into the fire.

'You did that on purpose,' Mick said.

I looked at him.

'You did that on purpose,' he repeated.

'No, it was an accident... it was the cigarette....'

'I don't believe that,' Mick said.

'Come on, we're not welcome here, Peter, let's go home,' Sheila said.

Sheila wasn't stoned. She never smoked, not even a cigarette. If it was time to go, Sheila would know. They were the sort of things she knew intuitively. I would outstay my welcome, anytime, anywhere, but I had a bad feeling about the coal, and maybe it really was time to go.

'It was an accident,' Anne Rafferty, Mick's wife, said, 'please don't go.'

'All the men are stoned. Stoned and paranoid,' Sheila said. 'I'm taking Peter home.'

That was the word. Paranoid. I'd been trying to find it but it wouldn't come. It was lost, lost somewhere in my subconscious. I was paranoid. Paranoid over the word. Paranoid over paranoid. I knew the word, knew it as well as I knew my own name. If I lost paranoid I could lose myself. That frightened me. Made me more paranoid. I couldn't stop thinking about these things. I knew it was the dope. There was something in the dope. It wasn't nice. There was nothing nice about losing your mind. It was supposed to make you relax and take all your cares away, but it was having the opposite effect. I was concerned and worried. I was paranoid. All the way home in the car with Sheila driving, I couldn't stop my mind falling into this black hole. Sheila didn't have these thoughts because she was sober. Why couldn't I be sober and not have these thoughts too? What if the feeling of paranoia didn't go away, what if it stayed with me for the rest of my life, what would I say to the kids?

It felt like we were two hours getting home, but it was less than five minutes. I'd lost all sense of time. Sheila got me up the stairs and into bed. I wanted to sleep and forget. I wanted to start a new life when I woke up. I wanted to live in a paranoia-free world. I never wanted to smoke dope again as long as I lived. I wanted to sleep, sleep, sleep. Not to dream, pure sleep. Obliterate the past and wake up fresh. I woke up thinking of the rug. How big was the hole I'd made? I'd have to make amends. I'd buy a rug and replace the damaged one. I was paranoid. Was that the dope or was it guilt?

We went into town and bought the rug. Sheila picked it out, she was better at that stuff than me. I brought it around to Mick's house. He was embarrassed.

'There's no need for that,' he said.

'You accused me of doing it on purpose.'

'That was the dope talking. That wasn't me.'

'I was shocked by that. That you'd think that. Do you think I could do something like that on purpose?'

'I'm sorry, that dope had me very paranoid.'

There was that word again. Only this time it was good.

We replaced the old rug with the new one and went for a pint. We sat in the snug of the Sunset House and lowered a lovely, creamy, full-bodied pint of Guinness apiece. Two arms raised in unison, it went down beautifully, two buddies together, friendship restored.

'I'm finished with the dope,' I said.

'Why is that?' Mick said.

'It spoils the alcohol for me. I love my pint and the dope gets in the way. It tips me over into paranoia.'

'It's a bad thing when the drugs get in the way of the drugs,' Mick said.

It was the truth. I had to rescue my drinking from the jaws of marijuana. I had to leave the dope behind. And I did. I cut out joints and I banned dope smoking in my house. We still played poker occasionally and a game called Mastermind, but we never let dope be smoked in the house again. Some of my former partners in crime were appalled, and felt that I was turning my back on the cultural revolution of the sixties.

'Rossa and Fiachra are at an age now where they pick up everything, I can't have them smelling dope in the house,' I proclaimed.

'That's a bit reactionary… surely you wouldn't want to stop them having a blow if they wanted to…? Thought they were children of the revolution… what's wrong with them growing up to smoke a bit of dope…?' the chorus of disapproval barked at me.

I couldn't make decisions for them about their future drug use. All I could do was offer an example. After the incident in Mick's house, I wanted my home in Ardilaun Road to be a dope-free zone. I owed that to my children as a father.

* * *

Mick Egan had really developed as a writer during his time with City Workshop. He copped on early to the principle of taking characters and situations to extreme places, of pushing people to their limits and seeing how they act and react under pressure. He was also very knowledgeable about drugs and honest as to their positive and negative effects on his life. He was the obvious choice to write the third part of the trilogy, *A Hape A Junk*.

However, group dynamics being what they are, not everyone agreed. Over the course of its first year, City Workshop had seen some changes of personnel. Alice Butler, Deirdre Fagan, Fran Moore and Liz Bono went on to other things. Marie Metcalfe, Mil Fleming, Fiona Nolan, Paul Conway, Trisha Doyle, and Robbie Byrne came in. This alone made for some tension between the old guard and the new. There was a school of thought that the new play should come mainly from improvisation and that Mick should be spending more time in the rehearsal room and less time alone writing. I did my best to protect Mick because, difficult as it was to write a play, it was next to impossible if the company of actors were not with you 100 per cent.

We took the increasing heroin problem as the central focus of the play, and set it against the backdrop of the Pope's visit to Ireland. John Paul II had come amongst us in September 1979 and stolen our hearts and our souls. The country fell in love with him en masse. Over a million people turned out for the Papal Mass in the Phoenix Park. Sheila was five months pregnant and we had eight-month-old Doireann and the boys to look after too, so we stayed at home, making us very exceptional by not being there. In truth, Sheila wouldn't have gone under any circumstances.

The big buzz in the inner city was that the Pope was going to visit the shrine to Matt Talbot at the church in Seán McDermott Street. In preparation, every building on the approach to the church was dressed in the Papal yellow and white. There were welcoming signs everywhere – *We Love You John Paul* – we were Papal junkies waiting for our fix. Matt Talbot had been declared 'venerable' in 1975 and it was felt that Pope John Paul's visit would push him over the line to sainthood.

The Pope didn't make it. There were security concerns and issues with his schedule, but the excuses couldn't hide the disappointment. The inner city had been let down. The Church had missed a golden opportunity to reach out and touch the poor and the needy. John Paul had the whole world in his hands, but not the Monto, or the Gloucester Diamond, or Seán McDermott Street, or the Five Lamps. Having already been abandoned by the temporal powers, the area had now been snubbed by the spiritual powers too. Matt Talbot had fought a personal battle against his addiction to alcohol. Heroin had become the new battleground but, at this critical juncture, the Church and its ministers had chosen to turn their backs on the people and retreat into their holy bunkers.

The other major issue exercising the citizens of the inner city was the plight of the street traders. There had always been a tradition of women selling from prams in and around Parnell Street. Indeed, Moore Street was the mecca of such selling and that tradition, going back generations, was now being threatened by the creation of the 'shopping mall,' most notably the ILAC Centre, which had recently opened and wowed everyone with its glass elevators. There were powerful business interests who wanted Moore Street closed down and the traders dispersed. They wanted customers spending money in their shops and stores. They also had aesthetic problems. They didn't like the look of the prams. There was no quality control on the goods sold, the customer had no rights in the transaction, and so on. Out of this, a campaign by the Gardai to harass the street sellers began. They moved them on, demanded to see trading licences, had them brought to court and generally made life impossible for them.

The fight on behalf of the street traders was carried out by Tony Gregory, our chairman, and Christy Burke, Sinn Féin councillor and community activist. They stood with the women, refused to let them be moved on, were arrested, brought to court and gaoled. A campaign for their release was organised and, as part of that, City Workshop performed extracts from the court sketch outside Mountjoy. The irony was that the general public liked the street traders and weren't interested in the arguments as to why they shouldn't be allowed sell their wares. They brought colour and craic to the streets and it was self-evidently a good thing to have them there. It wasn't lost on people that the most loved Dublin song of all time concerned a street trader named Molly Malone. They did not want to see her modern day counterpart banished for plying her trade. The question remained as to why so many resources and man-hours were being spent on frightening away the street traders when the heroin pushers plied their deadly trade unhindered.

A Hape A Junk opens in a cell in Mountjoy gaol with the central character, John Doran, having an argument with his cell mate, who turns out to be his nemesis, the Monkey, the parasite that hangs on to him and won't let him go. It was one of the best and most inventive aspects of the play, this personification of the protagonist's struggle with his inner demons. It allowed John Doran to reveal to us the nature of his addiction, his vulnerability around it, and his struggle to try and get this monkey off his back. I believe, in retrospect, that the play would have benefited from concentrating more on this relationship and developing it to its full potential. We could have learned something from Brian Friel's *Philadelphia Here I Come,* where the duologue between Gar Public and Gar Private comprises much of the drama. In this way, Friel allows us to explore the thought processes of his character and reveals to us how Gar ends up making the decisions he does. In short, we become co-conspirators with the author.

John Doran and the Monkey just didn't have enough stage time together, with the result that the arc of their story felt incomplete and unsatisfying.

The street traders doing their best to make a few bob out of the Pope's visit provided much of the play's comic relief – Florrie Cunningham again irrepressible as the quintessential Dub. She had sold her body in the *The Kips, The Digs, The Village* and on these very same streets, sixty years later, she's selling holy medals (well, they will be holy after she's had them blessed down in Seán McDermott Street Church) at a healthy profit.

'We'll be millionaires by the time this Pope goes home,' she declares. 'Our troubles are over.'

The audience responded to her, as usual, with laughter. It was nice to see somebody turning a profit, even if the Pope hadn't taken the time to stop off and say hello. The irony wasn't lost on our audience. They understood that they had been treated as second-class citizens.

At the end of the play, John Doran decides that he has only one option left and that is to take an overdose. There is only one way for him to shift the Monkey off his back and that is by his dying. It will be quick, clean and pleasurable. So he puts together his fix and gets ready to inject himself. The Monkey becomes agitated and pleads with him to pull back, but John is not for turning. He sees no future for himself. His father Jack is a docker who sold his button; his sister Pauline is in prison for trading on the street without a licence; he has nowhere to live and no job. He has a criminal record, which puts America out of range. His death is intended as a wake-up call for the audience. They either take action, or they die. They stand together or their community falls apart. The centre cannot hold because there is no centre left. *A Hape A Junk* is their legacy if they don't do something now. The play offered no easy redemption. We understood the reality and we presented it, warts and all.

* * *

The evolution of the City Workshop trilogy was an incredible process. Everyone who was part of it was changed by it. It felt like something genuinely new in the theatre had been created. We were invited by the Dublin Theatre Festival to present the trilogy as part of their 1983 programme of events. We presented the plays in repertory at the Damer Hall, the same venue where Behan's *The Hostage* (or rather *An Giall* as it was in the original production) had premiered twenty-five years earlier. The performances sold out, and on two successive Saturdays we presented all three plays back to back. The response was overwhelming.

We got an invitation from the Royal Court Theatre in London to present the trilogy at their theatre upstairs. It felt like something we couldn't turn down. I said yes and then went about trying to raise the money. I wrote to the cultural relations committee at the Department of Foreign Affairs, asking them to cover our travel. As luck would have it, Tony Ó Dàlaigh was a member and supported our application. I rang U2's manager, Paul McGuinness, not expecting to get through to him. Paul took the call straight off. I explained about the London invitation and asked him for a donation to cover our travel costs.

'How much do you need, Peter?' he said.

To my shame, I didn't have a figure in my head. I thought it might be a thousand. That sounded too much to ask for. I didn't want him to think I was cheeky.

'I think five hundred might cover it,' I said.

'You have it.'

I immediately regretted not asking for a thousand. It was a gambler's regret, knowing I had let money slip through my fingers.

The Company met, all excited about the London trip. We looked at the financial aspect of it. The only way we could make it work was for everyone to stay with family or friends in London. We couldn't afford hotel accommodation. Some people had made enquiries about staying in the Irish Club on Eaton Square, not far from the Royal Court. The Club had offered a special rate for a stay of seven days or more. Our engagement at the theatre was for ten days. Most people plumped for staying with cousins, even though, in some cases, they hadn't seen them for years.

We dispatched Seanie Lambe, who was seconded from his work in the office on Summerhill Parade, with the set in the NCCCAP van. It broke down on the M1 outside London, delaying the get-in by twenty-four hours. I was staying out in Kentish Town with my friend Shane Connaughton, and I had provided the cast and crew with his telephone number. It never stopped ringing. The van turned out to be the least of our problems. Six of the cast arrived at the Royal Court and announced that they had nowhere to stay. The cousins either didn't exist or had turned them away. I had a big call to make. I told anyone without accommodation to book themselves into the Irish Club. In the end, almost the entire company stayed there. I'd opened the floodgates and I didn't know how I was going to pay for it. We were in London representing our country and representing our city. It wasn't every week that a prestigious London venue played host to a community arts group from Dublin. We were spilling sweat and performing our hearts out less than four hundred yards from the Irish Embassy in London. The actors deserved a decent place to stay.

I now had to find the money in retrospect. I rang Tony Ó Dàlaigh in Dublin and he told me to write immediately to Foreign Affairs and to cc the letter to the Minister for Labour, the Department that was now responsible for City Workshop. It had been Education when we began, but we were switched to Labour after the fall of the Haughey government – an event that brought an end to the infamous Gregory deal. It turned out to be brilliant advice. I had no money to pay the Irish Club, and, when they came after me, I referred them on to the Minister. A correspondence started that went around in circles for the next two and a half years until finally, at the intervention of Ruairi Quinn, the Irish Club was sent a cheque for the outstanding £967.00.

The theatre upstairs at the Court is small, and we played to capacity houses for our engagement there, January 5-14, 1984. While in London, I met with the Gulbenkian Foundation to suss out the possibility of funding for the City Workshop. I had to come back to Dublin in the middle of the second week to meet with the Arts Council. I was doing everything I could to secure our future. We were two years in existence and the funds from the Department of Labour (under the temporary youth employment schemes) was about to come to an end. A group of people interested in the arts had come together and formed an advisory body to guide us to the next stage of our development. We put together a thirty-four page document charting the way forward and we submitted it to all the relevant funding agencies.

Lar Cassidy was the Arts Council officer in charge of community arts. I came out of a meeting with him at his office in Merrion Square to find a message waiting for me. I rang the NCCCAP office on Summerhill Parade. Ann Byrne, our administrator, informed me that Danny Boyle at the Royal Court needed to speak to me as a matter of urgency. Danny was a young, dynamic artistic director who would go on to great things in the world of film, but he came from a background that hugely supported the type of work we were doing.

'We have a problem, Peter. Some of your actors are losing the run of themselves, I'm afraid,' he said.

My heart sank at the news.

'What's going on?' I said.

'Two of your actors approached one of our ushers last night and demanded the programme money from him. They suggested they felt they were entitled to it.'

I asked him for the names.

'I will make sure that money is returned immediately,' I said.

'It is only a small amount, Peter, I'm not worried about the money, it shouldn't happen, that's all.'

'It won't happen again, Danny, be assured,' I said.

I called Maggie in London and the situation was dealt with, of course. It was depressing to think that the actors were so badly off that they had to resort to this. I was furious with the individuals involved, but I sympathised with them too, sympathy I could never let them see. It made me think about the future and the enormous effort required to keep a company together. We were suffering in London to create a good impression back home. Success at the Royal Court meant we would be taken seriously in Dublin. Joe Lynch had drilled that into me.

'You will never be a success until you are a success abroad.'

The Arts Council turned down our application for revenue funding. They did so on the basis that we were not professional. We were amateur. We were community arts. They only funded arts that were exemplary. Community drama was important, but its social function was on a par with its artistic remit. For those reasons the Council would not be providing funding, but they wished us well and hoped that we could stay together. I almost lost my reason with Lar Cassidy. I couldn't understand that my work was regarded as amateur. He assured me that he was a great supporter of mine, and of the community arts movement, but that the Council weren't ready to make this leap into the unknown. He felt that if they said yes to the City Workshop, they would be inundated with applications from every amateur outfit in Ireland.

'Don't put my name and the word amateur in the same sentence please, Lar,' I said. 'I am the furthest thing from amateur it is possible to get.'

'You're right and I am going to give myself a slap on the head,' Lar said.

And he gave himself a slap on the head.

It wasn't possible to be angry with Lar for very long. You knew that he was on your side and that he would never say a bad thing about you behind your back. He was totally loveable, but he was lightweight in policy terms. I knew that at the table where the hard decisions were made, he didn't have the strength or force of will to get his way. He saw the two sides of the argument when he needed to fight blindly for one.

'Come on, I'll buy you a pint,' he said, and we headed off to Mulligans of Poolbeg Street.

He shouldn't have been drinking with a client, or a prospective client, but that was Lar. He wanted to be friends at all costs. I'd been angry earlier on but now I was depressed. The drink only deepened the black hole inside my head. Lar headed off after the second pint and I hooked up with Jer O'Leary, alias Jim Larkin, in the back lounge. I got him to do some of the speeches from *The Risen People*. Not even Larkin's words could shake me from my inertia. I headed off to see what was happening in Summerhill Parade. I met Ann Byrne, who didn't look happy.

'We got a rejection from the Gulbenkian Foundation. They're reviewing their funding in relation to the Republic of Ireland.'

She showed me the letter. It was more of the same. The tide of community arts was coming and they were all retreating at its advance. It was all high art versus low art arguments. The funders didn't know what to do; they were all looking for ways to avoid the tsunami. I went with Ann for a drink to the Sunset House. The ladies' toilet was in full swing and Ann delighted in using it. The Sunset was changing with the times, but not the Arts Council.

'I'm going to write an opera and set it in this pub,' I said to Ann.

She thought it was a great idea.

'As long as you have a song by Joni Mitchell in it, I don't mind,' she said.

Ann was a Joni Mitchell fanatic.

'It's going to be the first real working-class opera. I'm going to give the two fingers to all this high art rubbish,' I said. 'They wouldn't know art if it stood up and knocked them over the head.'

I drank a pint followed by a large Jameson and peppermint. I just wanted to forget the whole fucking thing. All the work was for nought. Shea was in America. He had gotten out, and maybe he was right. I needed to get my play on in Los Angeles. I needed Carolyn Chriss to work her magic and create an opportunity for me in America. Shea had gone to Canada but he was in New York now. He'd taken the family across the border near Buffalo and got done for speeding. It would make a good scene in a film, I thought. He was running the Irish Arts Centre in Manhattan.

I had no idea what play he had on. I was too busy making City Workshop happen in London to find out. I made a decision to call him. But first I had to get drunk. I stayed in the Sunset until closing time. I got home and my dinner was burnt to a crisp. I didn't care. I told Sheila the news about the City Workshop but she was more annoyed that I hadn't seen the kids before their bedtime.

'I don't think that you'll ever get the support here that you need,' she said. 'But sitting in the Sunset House won't solve anything.'

'I think we should go to America,' I said.

'Maybe.'

I went upstairs and told the boys, who weren't yet asleep. They were delighted and thrilled. They wanted to get up and come down, and I knew I should say no, because they had school the next day, but I said yes. So they came down and wanted to know what suitcases they should pack. Sheila said there would be no possibility of a move to America if they weren't back in bed and asleep in five minutes.

We stayed up half the night talking, and I felt more and more that the time was right. I needed a new adventure. I needed a challenge. Things were coming to an end in Dublin. The only decision I had to make was whether to head for Los Angeles or New York.